# CHRISTENDOM AWAKE

# CHRISTENDOM AWAKE

## ON RE-ENERGISING THE CHURCH IN CULTURE

Aidan Nichols OP

William B. Eerdmans Publishing Company
Grand Rapids, Michigan

Published in Great Britain by T&T Clark Ltd,
59 George Street, Edinburgh EH2 2LQ, Scotland

This edition published 1999 in the U.S.A.
under license from T&T Clark Ltd by
Wm. B. Eerdmans Publishing Co.
255 Jefferson Ave. S.E.
Grand Rapids
Michigan 49503

First published 1999

Library of Congress Cataloging-in-Publication Data

Nichols, Aidan.
    Christendom awake : on re-energising the church in culture /
written by Aidan Nichols.
        p.     cm.
    Includes bibliographical references.
    ISBN 0–8028–4690–4 (pbk. : alk. paper)
    1. Christianity and culture.   2. Catholic Church—Doctrines.
I. Title.
BR115.C8N488   1999
230'.2—dc21                                        99–25714
                                                        CIP

Typeset by Waverley Typesetters, Galashiels
Printed and bound in Great Britain by Page Bros, Norwich

*To England's Holy Patrons,*
*our Blessed Lady and St Edward,*
*and to the Protector of the Realm,*
*St George, this book is dedicated*
*in hope of their powerful protection.*

*Religion, M. Poirot, can be a great help and sustenance – but by that I mean orthodox religion.*

AGATHA CHRISTIE
*The Flock of Geryon*

*Christendom is simply the society which has been informed by the Church.*

CHRISTINA SCOTT
'The Vision and Legacy of Christopher Dawson'

*Jesu, Jesu, converte Angliam.*

Prayer of the English martyrs

# Contents

Acknowledgements     ix

Preface     xi

     I    Introduction: Reawakening Christendom     1

    II    Rerelating Faith and Culture     9

   III    Re-enchanting the Liturgy     21

   IV    Reviving Doctrinal Consciousness     41

    V    Relaunching Christian Philosophy     53

   VI    Reimagining the Christendom State     71

  VII    Reconstituting a Society of Households     91

 VIII    Resacralising Material Culture     103

   IX    Rethinking Feminism     117

    X    Remaking Religious Life     131

   XI    Rescuing the Holy Innocents     145

  XII    Reclaiming the Bible     163

 XIII    Reconceiving Ecumenism     175

 XIV    Resituating Modern Spirituality     203

   XV    Recentring on the End     219

 XVI    Epilogue: Renewing Priestly Mission     233

Index of Names     251

# Acknowledgements

The author and publisher are grateful for the following permissions to reprint:

*The Allen Review* for an earlier version of material used in the Preface, and in Chapter VI ('Reimagining the Christendom State'), in Vol. 11 (1994), pp. 17–20.

*The Downside Review* for an earlier version of material used in Chapter III ('Re-enchanting the Liturgy') and Chapter VIII ('Resacralising Material Culture'), in Vol. CXV 398 (1997), pp. 53–73.

*The Homiletic and Pastoral Review* for an earlier version of material used in Chapter XII ('Reclaiming the Bible'), in Vol. XCVII.2 (1997), pp. 16–23.

*The Month* for an earlier version of material used in Chapter XIII ('Reconceiving Ecumenism'), in Vol. CCLIII, 1496 (1992), pp. 306–10.

*New Blackfriars* for an earlier version of material used in Chapter XIII ('Reconceiving Ecumenism'), in Vol. LXX, 905 (1996), pp. 264–75.

The Catholic Church in Iceland Press for an earlier version of material used in Chapter XV ('Recentring on the End') in *The Third Millennium and the Catholic Church in Iceland: Conference held on the island of Videy, 20 September 1997* (Reykjavík, 1999), pp. 7–23.

A. P. Watt Ltd on behalf of The Royal Literary Fund for permission to quote C. K. Chesterton's 'The Holy of Holies' and 'The Ballad of the White Horse'.

The Harvill Press for permission to quote P. Pakenham's translations of poems by Charles Péguy from *The Mystery of the Holy Innocents, and other Poems* (1956).

The English Province of the Society of Jesus for permission to quote from 'The Wreck of the Deutschland' by G. M. Hopkins.

# *Preface*

CONTEMPORARY Catholicism, so significantly shaped by Pope
John Paul II (though his 'shaping' is frequently of energies
deriving from a variety of sources within the *Catholica* – which is how
it should be, if Rome is the conductor of an orchestra each of whom
has its part), is as ambitious in its world-historical spiritual ambition
as at any time in its history. However, in the countries of the North
Atlantic civilisation (if not only there) its performance falls lamentably
short of its aspirations. In Great Britain, for instance, it would seem
that the Catholic Church is, demographically speaking, the fastest
declining of the historic Christian communities. In my view, directions
taken, emphases laid, trends fostered or at any rate allowed to develop,
have, over the past thirty years, left something to be desired in terms
of a Christian judgement. (Though to be sure, some of the cultural
trends challenged in this book are more like three centuries old.) In a
period of accommodation to civil society, its culture and *mores*, that
crucial activity of 'testing the spirits' laid upon the churches by the
apostle John has not always – by any means – been carried out. The
force of secularism has been underestimated, and the latent power of
a Christian imagination left untapped at a time when strategies for
secularism's subversion should have been conceived. Christianity
will never be wrong to rely in significant part on furnishing simple
icons of goodness to the world. Yet benevolence all round will not by
itself suffice.

At a time when the Catholic Church has supposedly entered the
sphere of the 'Establishment' in Britain, the débâcle of the celebrations
here of the bi-millennium of Christianity are a case in point. As one
correspondent of a national weekly put it:

Rather than the Churches of the United Kingdom welcoming the favour of a place in Peter Mandelson's Millennium Dome they should abjure any such offer. For the Dome (more properly a tent), and the state-funded events of which it is a part, are precisely conceived as a denial of the only reason why anyone in the United Kingdom might seek to celebrate the ending of one and the beginning of another Christian millennium, namely the birth of Christ.

In order to defeat what would otherwise be the absurdity and offence of inviting people of other faith traditions and of none to celebrate the birth of the Messiah, the secular State must relativise Christianity by placing it within the profane project of the Dome. It then becomes but a part of a larger, more significant reality (though exactly what is unstatable), which replaces and thereby counters the venture and hope of the Christian Church. The matter is precisely figured in the proposal to place a large statue of the human form at the centre of the Dome's exhibits, celebrating human self-knowledge and mastery. How could the Churches be party to such an 'entertainment', when the only event that can properly figure the meaning of the millennium is the celebration of the Eucharist, in which the body of Christ is gathered.[1]

The extent to which contemporary humanism feeds off contemporary atheism (and vice versa) has not been reckoned with. The former crowds out God, and the latter's denial of God encourages a kind of living in which the very question of God comes to seem without meaning. Yet the truth remains, as one of the fathers of the Second Vatican Council put it, that 'no one has a doctrine so sublime and consonant with human nature as does the Church'.[2]

I am grateful to Emile Perreau-Saussine for allowing me to see his unpublished study of Alasdair MacIntyre in French perspective, to Christine Fletcher and Amanda Hatfield for their helpful comments, and – not least – to Stratford Caldecott of the Oxford Centre for Faith and Culture for suggesting that I write this book so as to explain my 'vision' and for so generously making available the library resources of the Centre. At the beginning of the decade a courageous and encouragingly influential study was dedicated by its author, Dr John Milbank of Peterhouse, Cambridge, to 'the remnants of Christendom'.[3] In the spirit of Ezekiel I wish to see those *disiecta membra* come together, and 'Christendom awake'.

*Blackfriars, Cambridge*
*Solemnity of the Annunciation, 1998*

## NOTES

1. Dr Gerard Loughlin, of the Department of Religious Studies at the University of Newcastle on Tyne, writing to the London *Tablet* for 7 March 1998.

2. *Nemo habet doctrina tam sublimem et humanae naturae consonam sicut Ecclesia*: Bishop Petar Cule of Mostar, in *Acta Synodalia sacrosancti Concilii Oecumenici* (Vatican City, 1970–8), III/V, p. 545.

3. J. Milbank, *Theology and Social Theory. Beyond Secular Reason* (Oxford, 1990). For some caveats, however, see my essay, '*Non tali auxilio*: John Milbank's Suasion to Orthodoxy', *New Blackfriars* 73. 861 (1992), pp. 326–32; reprinted as 'An Ecclesial Critique of Milbank', in R. Gill (ed.), *Theology and Sociology. A Reader* (London, 1996²), pp. 444–50.

# I

# Introduction:
# Reawakening Christendom

IS it desirable to re-create Christendom – understanding this as a society where the historic Christian faith provides the cultural framework for social living, as well as the official religious form of the State? The answer to this question will depend, firstly, on the reader's own religious convictions – an animist or atheist is unlikely to reply in the affirmative. In the present context it may be assumed that any likely reader of this study is a Catholic Christian, whether in fact or in sympathetic potentiality. There is also, however, a second factor relevant to the answering of my opening question, and here Catholics – as well as Orthodox, Lutherans, Anglicans and others – may find themselves divided *across*, rather than *along*, confessional lines. To what degree are we legitimately satisfied with the current basic condition of our culture? This is not a matter of disquiet over *specific* social problems, which may be common to many who do not find themselves in any fundamental way estranged from the essential character of modern society as such. What I am concerned with is, rather, the *basic nature* of that contemporary society in the West, which we can sum up as progressive, secular and pluralistic.

Those Catholics who assume as a matter of course that derision is the only possible response to the famous anathematisation of 'liberalism, progress and modern civilisation' in Pope Pius IX's *Syllabus Errorum* may not be aware of the case constructed in recent years on different presuppositions from those of the Pope, but with much the same features of the post-revolutionary scene in mind. By the word 'revolutionary' I refer *en bloc* to both the Great (political) Revolution of the West, 1789–1815, and the combined effects of the Agrarian and Industrial Revolutions which in their fountain-head, Britain, happened to coincide with that European cataclysm.

1

According to the thesis worked out by the late American social philosopher Christopher Lasch in a number of studies, modern progress, far from liberating people from a repressive past, has generated a culture where human beings suffer from a reduced sense of self, and search endlessly for an elusive fulfilment, either by accumulating consumer goods, or through the subordination of self to some putatively therapeutic milieu (hence the proliferation of sects, movements, 'isms'). Individuals have become detached from those moral codes and institutions – family, church, local community, artisanal workplace – which once empowered them. The celebration of reason alone, the liberation of the individual, the repudiation of traditional duties as repressive, have engendered a decay in the substance of the self. Just as the modern interventionist State has undermined the fabric of local communities by taking over services formerly provided by families, neighbourhoods and mutual aid societies, so the modern world's consumerist obsessions and its veneration for science and technology have become substitutes for spiritual fulfilment and social justice. An established 'new class' which has lost all sense of community and public morality is marked by impatience with anything that limits the one supreme value – unlimited freedom of choice, and notably with the constraints involved in marital and familial ties.[1]

No doubt there are here certain exaggerations: in the composition of the indictment has space been made for such largely unambiguous goods as the advance of medical knowledge and the wide diffusion, in the Welfare State, of medical aid? There is, however, a formidable *prima facie* case to be answered. Its deepest foundation can be investigated by looking at the interrelation of pluralism and justice.

If we direct on the situation the light provided by the classic theologian of the Western Church, St Thomas Aquinas, we will soon discover, disconcertingly for a modern sensibility, that he regards a radical pluralism in public culture as simply incompatible with the proper exercise of the virtue of justice.[2] How so?

For Thomas, every human being is both goalseeking and made for community. For this reason, a human being will naturally desire the goal he seeks to be a shared or community goal. There can be no right pursuit by the individual of his own development which is not at the same time the development of society as a whole. Our self-fulfilment includes as constituent elements both other-relatedness and co-orientation with other people.

Justice is that virtue whereby we are disposed to uncover and activate relationships which are well adapted to the searching out of our goal, together with others, and in fairness to all. Because all men and women naturally seek goals with others, many such exchanges can be left to their spontaneous activity as individuals. The role of rulers in civil society for Thomas is to ensure the co-ordination of such relationships in so far as individuals do not or cannot realise this on their own account. But the fact that Thomas regards religion as in some way an aspect of justice – since it is an attempt to render what is due to God our Creator, at least in symbolic form – encourages us to take the analysis further.

When Thomas speaks of the common good of society as enabling human beings to reach their goal, at any rate on the level of nature, he presupposes not only that human beings are goalseeking, but also that there is an *objectively right goal preset for them*. It is not merely that man has an inner dynamic (a 'project'), but that this dynamic has an inbuilt direction or trajectory (he is a 'projectile'). Thomas sees this objectively given goal of human society in theistic terms – in terms of a life centred ultimately, even at the natural level, on the one true God. For him the acts of the moral virtues are incomplete until they are unified in religion – in the service of God, and by recognition of his dominion over all creation. Not only those acts which expressly offer religious worship, but all other human activity as well, should be offered in God's honour so that in all things he may be glorified.

Aquinas, then, would regard the malaise and anomie of modern liberal society as deriving from a failure to acknowledge two related truths. First, man's rational goalseeking consists in finding where the divinely given goal lies, rather than in fixing what it is to be. Second, we cannot pursue any particular goal which is not also, implicitly, the pursuit of a wider goal – in the last analysis, that of the whole society. If the goals that individuals or groups set themselves, and the accounts of what society should be which these goals imply, are mutually reconcilable, then society is not radically pluralist, but homogeneous – if also, and rightly, diversified. If, however, those goals and accounts are in conflict, then the human environment in which we live is not one society at all, but an uneasy collection of potentially alternative societies (secularist, Christian, Islamic, and so forth).

The discovery that radical pluralism, so far from being a desirable precondition for human flourishing, is actually a recipe for the disintegration of society as such, must not be regarded as licensing, or in any way favouring, the abrogation of due toleration for all human beings. There is a non-negotiable obligation to respect the human rights of, say, secularists and Muslims, which include, as the Declaration on Religious Liberty of Vatican II insisted, the right not to be coerced in one's religious beliefs (or lack of them). A generous spirit of active toleration in the integrated society which Thomas envisages, but whose concrete character he could not, owing to the historical and ethical limitations of his perspective, fully depict, will certainly encourage creative contributions of many kinds from such believers/ unbelievers. What is ruled out is only their enjoyment of full parity in the constituting of such a 'Christendom' society's overall goals – a definitional truth, I must add to forfend misunderstanding, not a proposal for constitutional reform, as if only the baptised could vote.

In his *Religion as a Cultural System*, the anthropologist Clifford Geertz defined culture as 'an historically transmitted pattern of meanings embodied in symbols, a system of inherited conceptions expressed in symbolic forms by means of which men communicate, perpetuate and develop their knowledge about and attitudes to life'.[3] Within this totality, sacred symbols, according to Geertz, synthesise the 'ethos' of a people – which he describes as the 'tone, character and quality of their life, its moral and aesthetic style and mood', as well as their 'world-view', or what he calls 'the picture they have of the way that things in sheer actuality are, their most comprehensive ideas of order'. In this sense, it is hard to deny that culture comprises a necessary reference to religion. As Christopher Dawson put it in *Religion and Culture*:

> It is clear that a common way of life involves a common view of life, common standards of behaviour and common standards of value, and consequently a culture is a spiritual community which owes its unity to common beliefs and common ways of thought far more than to any uniformity of physical type.[4]

T. S. Eliot in his *Notes Towards the Definition of Culture*, published in the same year, concurred: 'There is an aspect in which we can see a religion as the whole way of life of a people, from birth to the grave, from morning to night, and even in sleep, and that way of life is also its culture.'[5] Though warning against the undifferentiated identification of religion with culture – which would mean, he said, in actual societies an inferior culture and an inferior religion – Eliot asserted that, in the sustaining and developing of European culture, the role of Judaeo-Christianity, as of the Greco-Roman inheritance, is irreplaceable. Whereas Dawson would have done fuller justice to such elements as the Germanic, Byzantine-Slav, Celtic and Judaeo-Arabic contributions to the mediaeval world, he would surely have underwritten Eliot's conclusion offered in his Presidential Address to the Classical Association in 1946:

> If the present chaos is ever to be reduced to the order of something more than an administrative or an economic unification . . . [there

is] need of a cultural unification in diversity of Europe . . . A new unity can only grow on the old roots: the Christian faith and the classical languages which Europeans inherit in common.[6]

And if these words are as relevant in the aftermath of the collapse of the Soviet Union, and the making of the Maastricht agreement, as they were after the Second World War, then Eliot's subsequent comments are particularly pertinent to such post-Cold War imbroglios as the Yugoslav conflict. He spoke of two conditions as prerequisite for the health of European culture: first, that the culture of each country should be recognised as unique, and second, that the different cultures should recognise their relationship to each other, so that each should be open to receiving influence from the others. This is in principle possible, for Eliot, because an interrelated history of thought, feeling and behaviour characterises Europe as 'a spiritual organism'.

The French historian of philosophy Rémi Brague speaks in this connection of a 'Romanity' in European culture whose chief bearer is the Catholic Church. The Church is, for Brague, 'Roman' because she repeats in relation to Israel that operation which the historic Romans performed vis-à-vis the Greeks: she recapitulates the 'ancient' (Israel) on the basis of what she confesses to be her own principle – the 'novelty' who is Jesus Christ. 'Romanity' means renewal by transmission of a heritage and so far from being a claim to intrinsic superiority and thus prestige it is a continuous act of dispossession whereby a culture recognises its 'secondariness' (Brague's term, again) in relation to sources of truth, goodness, beauty, and asks rather to *serve* in their communication.[7] Not for nothing, Brague thinks, did the martyrdoms of Peter and Paul take place in Rome, and not, say, at Antioch or any other great metropolis of the Hellenistic world.

But if Europe is not simply 'the faith', the faith (*pace* Hilaire Belloc) is not simply 'Europe' either. Societies with Western Christian roots are to be found, after all, not only in Europe and the Americas but in countries not counted in the geographical West at all – sub-Saharan Africa, Australasia, the Philippines. Again, societies of an Eastern Christian type have developed in Africa (Ethiopia) and Asia (Armenia). Of course the Church's purview is not restricted to those nations where she has once been a formative presence (or is still today). It accommodates – thanks to the great mission command which ends St Matthew's Gospel – every tribe and tongue and nation. It is difficult to think of any political circumscription on the earth's surface where the Catholic Church is today without representatives or organisation. But representatives and organisation do not necessarily mean efficacy in the social domain.

In the world of the third millennium will the Church have to act as, merely, a counter-culture, where a fuller concept of 'general justice', in the light of God's plan, can be kept alive? Or will she succeed, despite the odds, in pressing her claim to be the bearer of that revealed religion intended for all the nations, and all subsequent history, and so impress on the civil community those principles which alone enable its members to encompass the ends for which man was made?

It is because society cannot recognise such ends until it has been (re-)converted to the saving truth of the Judaeo-Christian revelation that the creation of Christendom must itself await the revivification of ecclesial faith.

Where that faith is concerned, this book issues from three interrelated convictions. First, the primary responsibility of the Church – without whose execution all else falls to the ground – is the doctrinal and spiritual formation of her own members, whether lay or ordained. Secondly, she is committed by her Master's mandate to the diffusion of the reign of Christ the King in all aspects of human living. Hence the continuing importance to her of the notion of Christendom which – as one of the epigraphs chosen for the book makes clear – is society as informed by the mind of Christ's Church. Thirdly, the renewal of Christendom requires the furtherance of all those values – both supernatural, belonging to the order of salvation, and human and humane, belonging to the order of creation – that Christian civilisation attests.

Without a consistently theocentric direction, and one followed through in that concrete fashion, and with those helps and supports that Tradition indicates, ecclesial energies are frittered away. It is not when the Church aims at a purely consensus social good that she inspires heroic dedication to others by such practical means as education, nursing, and all that makes for a better life. The results of a non-dogmatic Catholicism, horizontalist in mentality and concerned chiefly to participate with others in the building of the human city, have been, in the last thirty years, not only disastrous for the missionary, catechetical and liturgical enterprises which fall under the first commandment, love of God. They have also – by a merely seeming paradox – undone much of what previous generation has built up in terms of Catholic institutions, often though not always staffed by Religious women, devoted to those basic but no less essential tasks that belong with the second commandment 'like to the first', the love of neighbour.

It is because, however, the Catholic Church cannot be a sect, simply enjoying the integrity of its worship, doctrine and behaviour within the walls of a fortified city, but ever seeks to mediate in a universal way the Christ who would 'make all things new', that she cannot be content with the life of even flourishing parishes, monasteries, Church societies, but has to strive to permeate and re-form culture, and the circumambient world of thought and institutions in which men and women live.

The question which, for the Catholic Church in Britain (and other Western countries), is today the absolutely paramount make-or-break question must be: Does this community have the *resources* (of symbols in the Liturgy, the material environment, devotion in the home), the *language* (in philosophy and literature) and the *conviction* (in doctrine and morals) to restore a broadly based public faith to the society in which it lives? No other issue in the Church is worthy of consideration with the same seriousness as this. The task the question sets is the vast one of depotentiating the effects of individualism and overcoming the dislocation of both religion and culture in our time.

To clear the decks here, some definition of terms – and indication of the right (and duty) of a Catholic theologian to comment on these issues – seems desirable. The next chapter aims to furnish these.

## NOTES

1. C. Lasch, *The Culture of Narcissism: American Life in an Age of Diminishing Expectations* (London, 1980); *The Minimal Self: Psychic Survival in Troubled Times* (London, 1985); *The True and Only Heaven: Progress and its Critics* (New York, 1991); *Haven in a Heartless World: the Family Besieged* (New York and London, 1995).

2. I followed here M. Lefébure, O.P., 'Introduction', *St. Thomas Aquinas, Summa Theologiae*, Vol. 38, *Injustice* (London, 1975), pp. xv–xxiv.

3. C. Geertz, *Religion as a Cultural System* (London, 1966), p. 3.

4. C. Dawson, *Religion and Culture* (London, 1948), pp. 48–9.

5. T. S. Eliot, *Notes Towards the Definition of Culture* (London, 1948), p. 31.

6. T. S. Eliot, *To Criticize the Critic* (London, 1965), p. 160.

7. R. Brague, *Europe, la voie romaine* (Paris, 1992), pp. 57–8.

# II

# *Rerelating Faith and Culture*

MAN is, ineluctably, a cultural animal, and theology, therefore, as the continuing intellectual mediation of revelation and its presuppositions to human beings, and thus the expression of faith's intelligibility, must take this highly salient fact into account. What follows will necessarily seem abstract, since we cannot avoid some definition of the terms that will crop up time and again, in more concrete contexts, in this study.

## The nature of culture

Before outlining the 'nature of culture' it will be proper to say something on nature *and* culture, culture's relation to (biological) nature. Vis-à-vis nature, we can describe culture as a *new kind of replication*. Human animals, in grouping together to form cultures, manage to overturn that primary law of genetic science which states that no acquired characteristic can be inherited. By means of culture, those born from nature succeed in passing on acquired characteristics in a cumulative way, communicating learned information and acquired habits from one generation to another.[1] Along with such information and habits which constitute (respectively) the intellectual and moral dimensions of culture are also transmitted a vast array of artefacts which make up its material aspect, and of institutional arrangements (large or small) which compose what we can term culture's practical aspect. All of these, evidently, must enter into any adequate definition of what culture is. So must the fact that, as both recipients and transmitters of acquired characteristics – but in no biological, deterministic sense – human beings show themselves to be at once reactive and active, creatures that do not only receive and absorb but initiate and change.

9

'Culture' must embrace the four dimensions – intellectual, moral, material and practical – together with the dual character of man the culture-bearing animal: that 'character', namely, whereby we recognise that the human person is always situated, together with others, in some form of communication where tradition (even an anti-traditional tradition!) is prior, and yet also regard that person as being, within limits, free to respond as they wish to a cultural inheritance on whose content they may innovate if they choose. A culture is, therefore, a system of inherited conceptions (intellectual), a set of common standards of behaviour (moral), a pattern of meanings embodied in symbols (material), and a series of conventions governing human interaction (institutional), by which human beings communicate and perpetuate, but also modify and develop, their knowledge about and attitudes to life.

We can note three features of culture at large which may constitute, depending on circumstances, either a problem or a fortunate chance for theology. First, culture is diverse. Second, any given culture is permeable – to a larger or smaller degree – by influence from other cultures. Third, culture undergoes change. Let us look at each of these features in turn.

As to, first, the diversity of culture: no species is so fertile in producing distinct forms of common life as is *Homo sapiens*. Just as the human mouth can produce a continuum of sounds with a quasi-infinity of possible variations, of which any actual language only selects some, so any given culture chooses only a sub-set of the possible arrangements of common life and thought. Michael Carrithers, professor of anthropology at the University of Durham, emphasises the freedom of persons, however, to vary the tunes cultures play.

> We are, all of us, quite as effective at producing cultural diversity
> as we are at preserving continuity . . . Even when we do something
> that seems traditional, we do so in new conditions, and so are in
> fact recreating tradition rather than simply copying it.[2]

It follows that cultures are heterogeneous – but also that the selections they make from the human continuum are not by any means totally decisive.

Second, on the inter-communication of cultures, whereas an older ethnography treated an individual culture as a unitary, bounded whole, it is now more common to speak of cultures as interrelated in a web of connection which is ultimately global in extent. Some cultures are, it is true, more closed than others; but even the relatively 'open' cultures receive influence from their neighbours in distinctive ways, so that here identity and otherness are, as in the Holy Trinity, not simple contraries. And third, then, cultures do not stand still: indeed, studying cultures in today's world has been compared to studying snowflakes in a blizzard. While an older cultural anthropology was content to describe alien cultures statically, freezing them in an ethnographer's time-warp, the accelerating pace of change in Western culture and perception of its effects globally have alerted students to the need to write about culture more historically. Whether at a snail's pace or with the swiftness of a hare, cultures are always in metamorphosis, they are in perpetual transformation – and yet such transformations possess subjects of which change can be predicated, so we are dealing also with a certain continuity, which finds its explanation in the moral identity of a culture over time. (So, at any rate, our vocabulary *prima facie* suggests.)

Such plasticity of the culture-bearing creature, man, expressed in a diversity of cultures not unconnected to the capacity of the latter for receiving in distinctive ways the influence of their neighbours, as well as for historic change, should not be taken, however, to call into question the unity of the human species – itself both a truth of natural philosophy and a presupposition of supernatural revelation. The very perception of diversity depends on the latter's being a diversity *of some thing*.[3]

The significance for culture of religion lies in the fact that, within the totality of a culture in its intellectual, moral, material and practical aspects, symbols of the sacred operate to unify the 'ethos' of a people. It is with such 'sacred symbols', clearly, that theology has to do.

If now we ask after the implications for interpreting religious symbols of the diversity yet unity, boundedness yet fluidity, and historicity yet continuity, of culture, we find that, first, diversity is a challenge to theology in its *kerygmatic* aspect: theology, in the service of the Church's proclamation, must recast those symbols – which may be non-Christian in a pagan society, sub-Christian in a nominally Christian society, or post-Christian in a society that has abandoned the faith – in an authentically evangelical fashion. Second, the web-like character of cultural relations is a challenge to theology in its *pastoral* aspect: theology, in the service of the Church's care for her people, must undertake to discern what is negative and what is positive in either accepting or resisting some influence from elsewhere. Third, the metamorphic quality of culture is a challenge to theology in its *historical* and *systematic* aspects; for in these regards, theology, in the service of the Church's memory and intelligence, must endure that the whole of the *depositum fidei* remains a living possession of the people of God in that time-transcending way which only a true ontology, both of being and of grace, can ensure.

We can say that all the great theologies of the Church in the patristic and mediaeval epochs have carried out these tasks *in practice* by a tacit awareness of their necessity. But once the issue of culture became consciously disengaged, a process which should probably be dated to the eighteenth century (it is noticeable, for instance, that while modern Greek has a word for the high culture of the fine arts, *kalliergeia*, it must take a Latin loan-word, *koultoura*, for culture at large), it is desirable, as various documents of the Second Vatican Council and two post-Conciliar popes, Paul VI and John Paul II, have urged, that the Church address in principle and explicitly this stratum of co-existence in which, to adapt with apologies the words of St Paul to the Athenians on the Areopagus, 'we live and move and have our being' (Acts 17.28).

## Culture's dangers for theology today

But of course, since those words in the Acts of the Apostles refer in fact to God, and culture is certainly not God, my affirmation of the pervasive importance of the cultural medium raises the spectre of the fearful harm which culture can inflict on Christian theology when the functioning of culture goes awry. From our present situation in the North Atlantic civilisation, we can see three ways in which this may happen.

First of all, a culture may be insufficiently open to transcendence, and thus inhibit the expression of theology's ultimate Reference as well as Source. In his 1995 essay 'Beyond Inculturation', Cardinal Joseph Ratzinger commented:

> The question of man and the world always contains the prior and actually foundational question of God. One can neither understand the world nor live uprightly if the question of the divine goes unanswered. Indeed, it gets to the root of the great cultures to say that they interpret the world so as to order it to the divine . . . Culture at its core means an opening to the divine.[4]

In a secularised culture where agnosticism is intellectually *de rigueur*, those ultimate symbols, drawn from the vocabulary of the sacred, which alone can unify culture by synthesising its most fundamental intuitions of order, goodness and beauty, are suppressed or margin-alised, and the temptation thus arises for a theology which would take its cue from such a culture to conceive of its task in purely 'horizontal' – generally speaking, sociological – categories. Such a theology fails in its kerygmatic function of furnishing authentically evangelical sacred symbols of the ultimate, and at the same time fails culture by acquiescing in culture's suppression of what should be its own most fundamental question.

Secondly, a culture, even if in its dominant conceptuality, its standards of behaviour, its artistic images, and the institutions in which its public life unfolds it accepts, at any rate nominally, the reference-point of God, may at the same time be ontologically non-perspicacious and lacking in internal integration of an organic or architectonic kind. Two chief influences which have the effect of obscuring the real in culture today are, at the popular level, scientism, a continuing vulgarised positivism, and, at the sophisticated level, postmodernism, for both of these are antithetical to the *logos* which is found in common being and therefore to that intelligibility which should animate culture. Until recently, the fault of scientism has lain not so much with science itself as with the collapse of a metaphysics which looked upwards through knowledge of all sorts towards wisdom. The philosopher was someone who confirmed, by the authority of reason, the instinct of the mind to rejoice at created forms at every level of the hierarchy of being. As the cultural critic Harman Grisewood has described a lost sapiential frame-work for cultural experience in the West: 'This reality of forms was guaranteed and upheld by the source of all being, and our joy in these realities, together with our responsibilities towards them, arose from their divine authorship.'[5] Today, in the Anglo-Saxon world especially, a 'new materialism' among a group of militantly atheistic scientific writers – Richard Dawkins, Stephen Hawking, Peter Atkins – offers on the basis of, respectively, biology, theoretical physics and chemistry, a reductionist account of beings, which reinforces this forgetfulness of being among those whose ability to manipulate technology outstrips their wider education. That same ontological oblivion can also result from the spread within the academy of hostility to the *logos* among that loose family of *savants* called 'postmodernists'. As one clear-sighted Catholic commentator on postmodernism has written, for the members of this – admittedly far from unitary – school:

> [P]hilosophy can give us no final answers, nor can it outline ultimate structures, metaphysical, transcendental or empirical . . . The fostering of civilized speech serves as the legitimate replacement for philosophy's former goal: determining the deepest structures of reality and the transcendental conditions allowing for knowledge of them. . . . Given this fresh understanding, it is logical that postmodern thinkers subject to particular invective ontological mainstays such as a common human nature or a universal notion of rationality. Such ideas seek to establish and embed a solid rock, an immovable object within the river of historicity . . .

But, as the same writer concludes:

> [W]ithout a foundationalist ontology of some sort, there is no possibility for logically sustaining the stability of textual meaning or a referential notion of truth, which appear to be essential principles for traditional understandings of doctrine.[6]

The lack of internal integration of a culture will certainly be reinforced by such defective philosophies, but it manifests itself most fundamentally in an inability to say anything coherent or continuous about experience. Speaking of the ritually articulated unity of a sacramental culture in pre-Reformation England, Grisewood, while acknowledging its limitations, draws attention to the evidence of the human records left by that society: 'There was no complaint at the unreality of the environment, there was no sense of disintegration, no sense of *perché vivere*, no sense of eschatological bewilderment, no "alienation".'[7] And he continues; drawing the contrast with our current discontents:

> It is in the nature of our culture, as it has now developed, to fragment the human activities which compose it, and to stratify the perceptions which nourish those activities; so that very different and contradictory centres of attraction command correspondingly disassociated energies. Social equality is one focus; but acquisition of property is another. The millionaire is one attractive image and so is the egalitarian revolutionary leader. Brotherhood and brutality are equally characteristic of our times; technological advance, and the breaking down of ideals of quality . . . Care for life, and carelessness of it are both strongly marked and growing tendencies. We are strained by opposites while we long for unity.[8]

A theology which is cowed by the threat of scientific reductionism or, alternatively, persuaded by the charms of postmodernism to abandon a classical ontology, and which regards it as a merit to reflect the fragmented character of much contemporary cultural experience, will soon lose the power to represent in any authoritative way the truth-claims of the Catholic tradition in their time-transcending character – something which it is the inalienable task (jointly) of historical and systematic theology to assure.

Grisewood's remarks about the gaping holes in the moral texture of culture bring me to the third danger which contemporary culture can pose to theology – that deriving not, this time, from a weakness in pure rationality, but one in practical rationality, namely, shoddy building-work in the moral construction of culture. Though, as I mentioned, ancient Greek lacks any obvious synonym for 'culture', Father Joseph Owens has felt able to write of Aristotle:

In his ethical works he insists repeatedly on the fundamental importance of cultural habituation for shaping one's practical philosophy. Through this habituation, in fact, one originally acquires the starting-points or first principles of moral philosophy. The rest of one's moral thinking proceeds from these culturally instilled first principles.[9]

In contrast to fifth-century Athens, or, for that matter, thirteenth-century Christendom, morality today is characteristically considered to be generated by personal conscience, with little if any reference to law and virtue. Personal will and feelings become morality's main provenance, in an ethics where the meaning of moral judgement, as the Neo-Aristotelian philosopher Alasdair MacIntyre has pointed out, rests finally – this at any rate is the conclusion vulgarly drawn – with the emotional quality of individual response.[10] The full range of the classical and Judaeo-Christian virtues has been sharply retrenched by a simultaneous subjectification, intimisation and politicisation of culture.[11] By 'subjectification', and its handmaid psychologisation, not only is moral objectivity undermined: the whole realm of the social and cultural is abandoned to consumerism and the therapeutic and entertainment ethos of its advertising strategies. Through 'intimisation', only close personal relationships are felt to be of value, for the public world – what the American Lutheran convert to Catholicism, Richard John Neuhaus, calls 'the naked public square' – is swept clean of all religious and moral values. Finally, and by an only seeming paradox, the many processes and codes of culture are now absorbed by 'politicisation' into a realm where power-relations become all-important – at the price of severing the concept of justice from what Mgr Francis Mannion has called 'the integral elements of transformation embodied in the arts, education, family life, and in codes of personal and civic virtue . . .'[12] thus rendering that concept 'abstract and ideological'.

These tendencies cannot fail to have a deleterious effect on theological life, which, if it allows itself to be affected by them, is trivialised by subjectification, reduced to a form of psycho-spirituality by intimisation, and tied to partisan agendas by politicisation. The impact of these phenomena on modern Western Catholicism is especially clear in the manner in which the Roman Liturgy is now celebrated in many settings – parishes, chaplaincies, Religious houses – at the expense of the transcendent and inspiring power of the Church's worship, thus subverting the cultic practice of Catholicism, vital matrix of theology as this is, as well as diminishing the Liturgy's capacity to work a cultural, and even social, transformation of its own. A theology which falls victim to the moral – and, by derivation, liturgical – distortions of contemporary culture has already failed in that activity of Christian discernment which ought to be pastoral theology's guiding principle.

## Theology and culture

In the case of the three 'dangers' I have identified, a theology which is content to reflect a circumambient culture will pay the price exacted. But Catholic theology does not need to be so supine. For theology has some power to modify its own cultural setting, and thus to mitigate these disadvantages. Outside of a Christendom society, theology can be expected to have only a limited impact on the wider culture – one reason why the abandonment of the spirit and forms of such a society ought to be reluctant. Even in a secular or multi-religious context, however, it will always be possible to disengage certain rational elements of *sacra doctrina* as a whole (thus in fundamental theology a substantial *preambula fidei*; in dogmatic theology, significant elements of a philo-sophical doctrine of God; in moral theology a major component from natural ethics), in the hope of correcting the myopia of a secular culture or resolving the conflicting perspectives of a multi-religious one.

Within the specifically ecclesial society, theology, as the attunement of reasoned reflection to divine revelation, should be able to exercise a much more thorough purifying force. Even in a situation where ecclesial society is exposed to profound influence from a non-Christian culture, the *sensus fidei* will at any rate *delay* the invasion of Church culture by any baleful influences from culture at large. Often enough, then, this cathartic action of theology will normally be exercised against tardily arrived ideologies and their related sensibilities. Of these the two most potent 'delayed' extra-ecclesial cultural influences operating within the Church today are an Enlightenment and a Romantic mind-set – the first bringing in its train rationalism and an autonomistic view of selfhood, the second leading to the apotheosis of the local and particular at the expense of the global and universal.

In the light of these considerations, I offer a Trinitarian paradigm for authentic culture. First, a culture should be conscious of transcendence as its true origin and goal, and this we can call culture's tacit 'paterological' dimension, its implicit reference to the Father. Second, the forms which a culture employs should manifest *integrity* – wholeness and interconnectedness; *clarity* – transparency to meaning; and *harmony* – a due proportion in the ways that its constituent elements relate to the culture as a whole. And since these qualities – integrity, clarity, harmony – are appropriated in classical theology to the divine Son, the 'Art' of God and Splendour of the Father, we can call such qualities of beautiful form the specifically Christological aspects of culture. We should remember, however, that the very word 'Christological', as a way of referring to the second divine Person, has always in mind the saving Incarnation as the concrete manner in which the eternal Word relates to us here and now on earth – something which has implications, then, for the 'earthedness' of those forms. (They must reach into our physical *Sitz im Leben*, for how shall a eucharistic theologian proceed, for example, in a culture where 'fast food' has supplanted hospitality?) And thirdly, then, in the Trinitarian *taxis*, the spiritually vital and health-giving character of the moral ethos of our culture yields up culture's pneumatological dimension, its relation to the Holy Spirit, of whom we sing in the *Veni Sancte Spiritus*: *Sine tuo numine, nihil est in homine, nihil est innoxium*. It is not by chance that the Liturgy too is celebrated 'in the unity of the Holy Spirit', for those attitudes which we bring to the adoration of the Father through the mediator Jesus Christ are fully taught only by the Spirit, who alone 'searches the depths of God' (1 Cor. 2.10). And if in these ways a culture that is truly auspicious for theology bears a reference to Father, Son and Spirit, we can add that, when we think of those Persons as constituting the triune God, the divine Triunity, we can find in the Holy Trinity a key to the wider need of humanity's global culture to marry the universal and the particular, the unilateral insights of the Enlightenment into encyclo-paedic universality, and of Romanticism into differentiated multiplicity, the One and the Many.[13]

What we may expect for theology in a culturally inauspicious age cannot be determined, however, from sheer consideration of the inherent possibilities of the culture of some time and place. It must also be decided – and more fundamentally so – by the possibilities that are found within that abiding source of newness of life which is the resurrection of the crucified Saviour.

We should not be looking primarily for 'inculturation', where the faith so easily disappears into cultural dialogue, nor for 'acculturation', where the Church remains basically external to the cultures in which she acts. Instead of these, we ought to be looking, as H. Richard Niebuhr proposed a decade and more before the Second Vatican Council opened, at Christ the saving transformer of culture.[14] Holy Church, as a supra- or trans-cultural reality, is endowed by the triune God, through his incarnate economy, 'with enormous internal dynamism that renders [her] capable of entering into the very heart and soul of cultural existence, salvifically engaging the integral dynamics of that culture, yet remaining true to [herself]'.[15] It is only when theology is written from the heart of the Church, from the fullness of Catholic communion, that it can do justice to the cultural medium which Christ entered by his Incarnation, and which, through his death and resurrection, he constantly judges by his own sacrificial and victorious truth.

> As absolute transcendence and totally free gift is in no way antithetical to, but indeed grounds, the absolute immanence of God's gifted presence; and as the eternal procession of the Word from the Father is in no way antithetical to, but actually brings about, the Incarnation of the Word in the womb of the Virgin Mary; so the transcultural dimension of the gospel is no way antithetical to, but makes really possible, the inculturation of the gospel in myriad cultures. *Because* the gospel is absolutely supernatural and totally the free gift of an all-loving triune God, the gospel must be proclaimed and inculturated among all nations and cultures.[16]

It is by reference to just these convictions that the rest of this study will proceed.

## NOTES

1. K. Ward, *God, Chance and Necessity* (Oxford, 1996), p. 167.
2. M. Carrithers, *Why Humans Have Cultures. Explaining Anthropology and Social Diversity* (Oxford, 1992), pp. 7, 9.
3. Ibid., p. 3.
4. J. Ratzinger, 'Beyond Inculturation', *Briefing*, 18 May 1995, p. 35.
5. H. Grisewood, *The Painted Kipper. A Study of the Spurious in the Contemporary Scene* (London, 1970), p. 19.
6. T. Guarino, 'Postmodernity and Five Fundamental Theological Issues', *Theological Studies* 57 (1996), pp. 656–7, 660.
7. Grisewood, *The Painted Kipper*, p. 63.
8. Ibid., p. 65.
9. J. Owens, C.Ss.R., 'Aristotle and Aquinas', in N. Kretzmann and E. Stump (eds.), *The Cambridge Companion to Aquinas* (Cambridge, 1993; 1995), p. 41.
10. A. MacIntyre, *After Virtue. A Study in Moral Theory* (Notre Dame, Ind., 1984²), p. 31.
11. I take these terms from M. F. Mannion, 'Liturgy and the Present Crisis of Culture', *Worship* 62.2 (1988), pp. 98–122.
12. Ibid., p. 117.
13. C. E. Gunton, *The One, the Three and the Many. God, Creation and the Culture of Modernity* (Cambridge, 1993).
14. H. R. Niebuhr, *Christ and Culture* (New York, 1951).

15. M. F. Mannion, 'Evangelization and American Ethnicity', in A. J. Mastroeni (ed.), *Catholicity and the New Evangelization* (Corpus Christi, Texas, 1991), p. 163.

16. M. W. Lamb, 'Inculturation and Western Culture. The Dialogical Experience between Gospel and Culture', *Communio XXI* 1 (1994), p. 130.

# III

# *Re-enchanting the Liturgy*

THE 're-enchantment' of the Catholic Liturgy is the single most urgent ecclesial need of our time. In a justly famous passage from the *Russian Primary Chronicle*, when the envoys of Vladimir, prince of Kiev, returned from the divine liturgy they had attended in the great church of the Holy Wisdom at Constantinople they reported:

> We knew not whether we were in heaven or on earth, for surely there is no such splendour or beauty anywhere on earth. We cannot describe it to you: only this we know, that God dwells there among men, and that their service surpasses the worship of all other places. For we cannot forget that beauty.[1]

This is not aestheticism, it is religious ontology. It is what we should expect if the Liturgy is itself the glorification of the God of glory, the God whose absolute holiness (and so, from our side, awe), love (and so, from our side, devotion) and beauty (and so, from our side, wonder or admiration) coincide.

Rendering the Liturgy 'enchanted' and (thus) 'enchanting' (I borrow these terms from the English Orthodox liturgiologist W. Jardine Grisebrook), has as its precondition the eschewing of other uses to which – abusively – divine worship can be put.[2] The American Benedictine theologian of the Liturgy, Aidan Kavanaugh, has drawn attention to a worrying tendency in the present vernacular worship of the Latin church to initiate the Liturgy by

> an act of gathering and hospitality . . . so as to produce the approved sort of community which celebrates middle-class values of joining, meeting and 'speaking out'; . . . to move away from the art of ceremony and symbol towards verbalisation as the assembly's main medium of communication within itself.

'Iconography', writes Kavanaugh, 'is disappearing in our new church buildings, giving way to potted plants and shopping-mall-like spaces.' Such tendencies can only

> obscure a sense of sacramentality and of the divine presence as something distinct from and transcending the community at worship ... The Liturgy becomes perceived by many as less an obedient standing in the alarming presence of the living God in Christ than a tiresome dialectical effort at raising the consciousness of middle-class groups concerning ideologically approved ends and means.[3]

These harsh but by no means unmerited words come all the harder from a liturgist much of whose work has consisted in pointing out the normative significance, for the Church's faith, of the 'rule of prayer'. In a majorisation of liturgical life perhaps more Benedictine than Dominican, Kavanaugh has hailed the Liturgy as *theologia prima*, 'prime' or 'first' theology, the principal or primordial source of all theology worthy of the name.[4] Certainly one can regard the Liturgy as being, after Scripture, the most important single monument of that sacred Tradition in which the revelation of the gospel is transmitted over time. One can also regard the Holy Eucharist as the chief action whereby the Church becomes most deeply present to her own being and, in that moment, remembers the divine action in history for what it is: the outpouring to all the world, through her, of the Trinitarian love in Christ. And for both of these reasons, all deformation of the liturgical life of the Church is, as Kavanaugh rightly says, heavy with consequence.

## Liturgy and the Christian aesthetic

One symptom of a healthy American reaction to present malpractice, the *Snowbird Statement on Catholic Liturgical Music*, in calling for more intense and sustained engagement with theological and philosophical aesthetics,[5] encourages, in a way pertinent to all liturgical arts (and not just music alone), the reconnecting of a separated liturgics to the Christian totality as a doctrinal and metaphysical whole. The Liturgy and its beauty is inseparable from our apprehension of revelation itself, and its glory. As the Liturgy is the litmus test of our reaction to our religion at large, so the fate of the Liturgy cannot be separated from the malaise which afflicts much contemporary Christian sensibility not only in worship but in theology, spirituality and pastoral practice as well. In 1967, two years after the Second Vatican Council ended, and while the post-Conciliar *Consilium ad exsequendam Constitutionem de sacra Liturgia* was running at full throttle, an American commentator wrote:

> A psychologist must ask his clerical colleagues: Why are you prey
> to simple solutions; why do you blur the hierarchies of trans-
> cendence and ultimacy, neglecting the worlds of difference,
> represented traditionally by planes of being and classes of angels,
> between the levels and kinds of love; . . . why do you confuse the
> voices of autonomous complexes with the Pentecostal gift of
> tongues; how can you equate falling-in-love with coming home to
> the Godhead?[6]

Those questions have evident relevance to the reconstruction of the
Roman rite, not least in the English-speaking world. One thinks, for
instance, of the elision of the classes of angels from the culminating
section of the Preface of the Mass, and the translators' insistence, in the
collects and other prayers of the Sacramentary, on rendering a whole
variety of differentiated terms with the one word ('love') whose very
centrality to the gospel entails that its use should be sparing and thus
the more potent. Accordingly, they underline the point that the problem
of the integrity of the Liturgy, its true and native beauty, cannot be
divorced from the wider problem of the presentation of Christianity in
its proper identity in the world of today.

In the year following the publication of Pope Pius XII's great liturgical
encyclical, *Mediator Dei*, the Anglican philosopher H. A. Hodges opined:

> Our problem is . . . , in the first instance, that of making Christianity
> visible again, of making people see it as a really possible way of
> looking at things. Secondly, we have to try and make it intelligible,
> so that anyone who sees it as a vision may be able to assure himself
> that it is not a mirage. The first is a poet's business and the second
> is a philosopher's. Both are concerned in the third task which faces
> us, viz.: to make it appear desirable; to discover and to draw out
> those impulses in humanity which it is meant to satisfy, so that the
> relevance and excellence of it may be felt.

And Hodges asked his readers rhetorically: 'Are we sure that it is
now as visible, intelligible and obviously desirable, even to ourselves,
as it ought to be?'[7] What Hodges was seeking, in the service of the
Church's gospel, was, evidently, threefold. He looked for an imaginative
commending of Christian faith which would show that faith to be an
architectonic symbolic structure fit for human beings to dwell in. But
he also wanted a form of argumentative suasion that would indicate
how the knowledge (or putative knowledge) conveyed by these symbols
is compatible with human reason. And finally he hoped to see an

anthropological investigation that could suggest how the symbolic structure which yields a content that the philosopher can find worthy of acceptance also answers to the needs of human nature itself.

Notice how in this the symbolic or imaginative structure is placed first; there then follows philosophical investigation into the resources of meaning thus made available; and only thirdly do poetic reason and philosophic reason explore the fittingness of what is then presented to human needs. That order of priorities *does* suggest the giving of a certain primacy in theological culture to liturgical life, for the Liturgy is poetic reason seeking to lay out the shape of Christian revelation not in theory form but in practice. The strong attraction of Hodges to Eastern Orthodoxy confirms this interpretation, for Orthodoxy is a liturgical Christianity *par excellence*.

In the same year, 1949, a Swiss theologian who had already made a name for himself as a religious philosopher, interpreter of the Greek Fathers and standard-bearer in the German-speaking world of that innovatory but largely French Jesuit movement, *la nouvelle théologie*, was writing in the post-war Austrian journal *Wort und Wahrheit*. By way of an attempt to capture the defining characteristics of Christianity, he suggested that *Christology* provides the golden rule for 'measuring' the relation between God and humankind. Here an important clue as to how we are to approach the role of the Liturgy in culture is put in our possession.

> Ultimately there is only one synthesis in which God has established his relationship to the world, namely Christ, the incarnate Word of the Father. He is the measure of nearness and distance from God; he is the analogy of being in concrete form; he is the event that took place once and for all, and at the same time the norm for all that is in the world ... God remains, even in his revelation, incomprehensible, beyond all our conception; but the access to him we are granted is no longer, as in the *theologia negativa*, a banishment to what is alien, inaccessible, dark; it means our being flooded with light, excess of light. God is love, and we can know this love and live by it; but it is in itself beyond our comprehension, flowing out superabundantly, the object of our adoration. We plunge deeper into it, and it inundates us. The more we live by it, the more we are truly ourselves. It makes us humble, for besides being absolute glory it is also absolute humility. In the abyss of divine love we are ever more profoundly united without confusion, for in God himself the three Persons celebrate, without confusion of being, the highest of unions.[8]

These words constitute perhaps the earliest announcement of that extraordinary enterprise by which Hans Urs von Balthasar would undertake, largely single-handed, the revival of theological aesthetics as the proper form of a Catholic fundamental theology, the right way to express Christianity's essential idea.⁹ Though Hodges was unaware of it, the theologian of Lucerne was beginning to answer the question of the philosopher of Reading in the very moment that the latter was putting it. For Balthasar's theological aesthetics would aim to be at one and the same time an exhibition of the symbolic structure of Christianity as an imaginative fullness than which none greater could be conceived (Hodges' 'poetic' question); a meta-physical statement of the ontological foundations of Christianity, in terms of that primordial qualifier of all being which is *pulchrum*, the beautiful (Hodges' 'philosophical' question); and an anthropo-logical demonstration of how the glory of revelation fills the finite spirit to its fullest measure and human existence, even in its most resistant areas – sin and death – with meaning (the question which, so Hodges thought, poets and philosophers could answer only by an act of collaboration). And indeed, if we take Balthasar's entire *oeuvre* into consideration, we find that Hodges' tripartite demand for the reinvigoration of Christianity is met with even more uncanny accuracy: for *Herrlichkeit*, the theological aesthetics, deals with what in revelation is beautiful; *Theologik*, the theological logic with what in it is true, and *Theodramatik*, the theological dramatics, with what in it is good for man, essentially interrelated though these three are.¹⁰ And the centre of it all is the God-man Jesus Christ, who in the logic is the Word expressing itself in human discourse, and in the dramatics is the protagonist enacting our salvation. He can be grasped as both of these only because in the aesthetics he appears as the embodied manifestation of the divine Glory, the unsurpassably wonderful divine love which, consummately in his death and resurrection, pours out its splendour into the world and calls human existence to transfiguration by its light.

Though Balthasar never fulfilled his intention of writing a full-scale study of Christian art, the sign-making that flows from the Church's reception of the gospel, nonetheless the beauty of the Liturgy – the Church's supreme sign-system – stands in a necessary relationship to theological aesthetics as he conceived it. While a natural or this-worldly aesthetics can be helpful in assisting us to make sound judgements about the form and style, excellence and appropriateness, of the media used in the liturgical setting and action, liturgical aesthetics, like Christian aesthetics at large, must take its primary cue from the supernatural or divine revelation which it is the main task of theology to describe.

This is how these matters are treated in Cardinal Joseph Ratzinger's latest contribution to the subject in his 1995 essay-collection *Ein neues Lied für den Herren* which regards disputes about the Liturgy's purpose and manner of celebration in contemporary Catholicism as not only bound up with but flowing directly from differences in perceiving and understanding the revelation of God in Jesus Christ.[11]

According to Ratzinger, the criteria for liturgical renewal are inseparable from the question posed by Jesus to his disciples at Caesarea Philippi, 'Who do you say that the Son of Man is?' (Matt. 16.13, and parallels).[12] Thus, for example, if we credit the claim that as humans ourselves we can meaningfully follow only the prophetic lead of the man Jesus whereas the divine Christ lacks existential relevance for us, then the trajectory of discipleship (what Ratzinger calls 'the Christian Exodus') will inevitably fall short of its true goal, entry into the divine life, and this cannot fail to have its effect on our liturgical theory and practice. The hope for liberation through the gospel then becomes *kitschig und kleinig*, 'kitschy and homey', rather than aiming at the heights where the Son made man, having made satisfaction for our sins, sits at the right hand of the Father.[13]

Ratzinger considers that, viewed historically, the deficient Christology which he takes as a key to an aesthetically impoverished liturgical horizontalism derives from certain flaws in the inter-war movement of *ressourcement* with whose main lines he is in other respects fully identified. One shared theme of the biblical and liturgical movements of those years when the theology that made the Council was gestating was a renewed emphasis on the humanity of Christ. One finds it in doctrinal theology in, for instance, the Tübingen theologian Karl Adam's *Christus unser Bruder*,[14] and in liturgiological mode in the claim of the Innsbruck liturgist Josef Jungmann that the Church, during her struggle against the Arianism which reduced Christ to a creature, albeit the most excellent one, relaxed her guard against an opposite danger, a quasi-Monophysitism invading the Liturgy where it left its mark in the introduction of prayers directed not to the Father but to the Son, and infecting via the Liturgy the piety of the faithful: thus Jungmann's *Die Stellung Christi im liturgischen Gebet*.[15] In Ratzinger's view both projects (Adam's and Jungmann's) unwittingly affected the Liturgy adversely by insinuating a humanistic Christ no longer capable of inserting the temporal into the eternal in his own person.

But as biblical scholarship moves on it discovers that the attempt to describe the humanity of Jesus without the incarnational narrative or to locate a Jesus of history without the full biblical portrait of the Christ produces distinctly nugatory results. As historical enquiry into the origins and development of the Liturgy advances, it finds public invocation of the Saviour before the watershed of the Council of Nicaea. And as patristic erudition accumulates, scholars have realised the decisive importance of the work of Maximus the Confessor and the Third Council of Constantinople (680–1) which canonised his achievement in its teaching that in the person of the Word incarnate two freedoms, one divine, the other human, are perfectly synthesised, so that the possibility of following Jesus' human will and bracketing his divine does not arise.

The Letter to the Hebrews calls Christ 'the same yesterday, today and forever' (13.8) and we cannot meet him, accordingly, save in all three dimensions together. Since one of them is eternal, the encounter with Christ is occluded if we fail somehow to step over the threshold of the temporal into that which is time's origin and goal. A liturgical culture centred on a Jesus presented chiefly as champion of a freer spirituality, more broadminded morality or ameliorated political structure can only be, by contrast, a moralistic affair, from which the glory has departed that once led men through the Paschal mystery to the heavenly places.

Not that the truncation of liturgical consciousness can be attributed exclusively to a reduction of the Christ who is the organising centre of theological aesthetics. The draining away of the theologically aesthetic would be, Ratzinger implies, hard enough to prevent in a world where the existence of God is deemed irrelevant to 'the shaping of human things and the forming of our life', and the very question as to what can be known shrinks to this-worldly proportions.[16] God is becoming, he fears, like the high god of many polytheisms, a *deus otiosus*, retreating to such remoteness as to be superfluous. And in any case the Christian doctrine of redemption is no longer understood: the ideas of expiation, supplication and reparatory satisfaction central to the Atonement and so to the sacrifice of the altar, the midpoint of the entire Liturgy, say nothing to the modern West. Hence the success of Christ the political liberator or the psychic healer – a reference to the much-read work of the priest-psychiatrist Eugen Drewermann. In both schemes, the one collective, the other individual, redemption becomes auto-liberation by reference to Jesus as human model, and the Church and her worship lose their salvific meaning. In this perspective, so Ratzinger had commented earlier, the degeneration of the Liturgy is an aspect of the dissolution of the Christian mystery itself.[17] The Liturgy's aim is redefined as the constitution and experience of community as such, something only too welcome in an atomised society thirsting for sociality, and the beauty of the Liturgy malforms far more than ever did the much-maligned cultus of the Baroque, into a spiritual show where the showmaster-president is concerned above all to make religion interesting in spite of the living God, encounter with whom dwarfs all humanly initiated acting.[18]

What has been forgotten (here I leave Ratzinger's text) is St Thomas' dictum in the *Commentary on the Sentences, A forma rei est decor eius*, 'From a thing's form is its beauty',[19] and the form of the Liturgy is furnished by the form of Christ himself in his Pasch, since what the Church celebrates in her worship is Christ's divine-human *leitourgia* of the Father ('Do this in memory of me') for our salvation. The visible Christ, above all in that death and resurrection which provide the Liturgy with its *Gestalt* or basic figure, renders the invisible God portrayable, for what we see in the crucified glory of the Word incarnate is not simply God the Son but deity responding filially to deity communicated paternally and taking human nature into that filial response. And if in the sacrifice for which the Word took flesh the Father initiates and the Son consents, it is the Spirit who enables that sacrifice and makes it abidingly fruitful for us, acting hiddenly in human subjectivity to make us respond to God in Christ and drawing all finite being, human persons but also cosmic nature, into relation with him.

Ratzinger's belief that decisive for our liturgical practice is our fundamental picture of Christianity – which must mean, centrally, our Christology since it is in the Word incarnate that the glory of God which measures all things makes its appearance – is echoed in the work of the American Protestant theologian of worship Paul Whitman Hoon, who writes that

> only as the precedence of divine action Christologically defined is affirmed can worship as action be authentically re-thought for our day. Otherwise the current stress on the people's active partici-pation in worship can lead to the error that what we do is of first importance.[20]

Emphasising, like Ratzinger, that the liturgical action must, to be authentic, share Christ's own time-transcending and time-transforming character, Hoon warns against a misplaced concern with immediacy, mateyness, feeling comfortable with God: 'Distance remains as important as nearness in authentic relation with the divine, and liturgical theology only falsifies the relation when it tries to speak to man's depths by removing God from the heights.'[21] Of set purpose liturgical action unsettles and disorients, for it not only embraces time but transcends or transforms it. The 'true historical meaning of the Word' with whom we have to deal in worship 'cannot be grasped unless it is dialectically illumined . . . by its trans-historical nature also'.[22]

> Liturgically to 'remember' is to experience the historical and eternal as brought together in Jesus Christ. That which happened in time is made the sacrament of that which is beyond time, and that which is beyond time is known through that which is of time. History is at once affirmed and transcended.[23]

Though fear of aesthetic élitism may deter some from admitting it, the Liturgy's capacity to signify its own time-transcending aspect derives not only from its dependence on an orthodox Christianity of an evangelically plenary kind but also – as the millenarian experience of the Church has found – from the pressing into service of what Ratzinger calls *Hochformen* ('high forms') and Hoon 'traditional forms', of which the latter emphasises the 'paradoxical function . . . in relation to time'. 'They have power on the one hand to foster a historical awareness which restrains man from escaping the life of his time and age, and on the other, they can foster a spiritual awareness which delivers him from being too much at home in any time and age.'[24] Such traditional forms, so Hoon explains, 'stabilize' man in that, just because they arose from Christian faith's engagement with the historic existence of human civilisation, they require man to 'take seriously history and the world'. But they also 'liberate' from confinement within the historical, communicating a sense of the timeless as well as the 'timeful', claiming for man a life which is more than his historical life, turning his consciousness to 'things unseen and eternal'.[25] As the Dutch phenomenologist of religion Gerardus van der Leeuw put it:

> Liturgy must hold to the ancient . . . That is no romanticism or love of the archaic, but a means of attaining objectivity. In the sermon, the language of our day is spoken or at least should be. But in the Liturgy, . . . in the Church, the difference between today and yesterday must be done away with; nothing must look as though it has its origins in the present day . . . For this reason, when the Church goes out into the world to teach and to preach, she speaks the language of the world. But when she returns to worship and fellowship with God, she speaks the language of the Liturgy in which so many generations already have carried on their conversations with God.[26]

The refusal to accept that our theological, as our worshipping, life should be aimed at the heights of Zion, when that refusal is married with a rejection of *Hochformen* (the thesis that traditional forms of high culture are indispensable instruments of liturgical expression), constitutes the distinctively Christian version of *philistinism*.

The Philistines were, historically, the plain-dwellers on the littoral of Palestine. Unlike many other Canaanite communities they refused to accept the new kind of transcendence represented by Mosaic Yahwism, preferring their old chthonic deities of Dagon, Ashtoreth and Baal-zebub. And if the threat they posed to Israel's existence was removed by David, who also laid the foundations of Zion theology by making Zion's citadel his capital (thus rooting both royal house and, eventually, the house of the Lord in Jerusalem), the Old Testament perception of the Philistine as fleshly and uncovenanted, persisting in Milton's *Samson Agonistes*, was exploited, its scope extended, in nineteenth-century Britain by such cultural commentators as Thomas Carlyle and, more famously, Matthew Arnold, in their swingeing attack on the materialistically minded.[27] Without in any way ratifying Arnold's attempt to make high culture replace the religion he feared was undergoing slow but steady extinction as the sea of faith receded in Victorian England and elsewhere, we can sympathise with him in his facing, David-like, adversaries now to be found (if one accepts the definition of specifically *Christian* philistinism given above) in positions of influence within the Church. The 'Oxford Declaration on Liturgy' speaks not without reason in this connection of forces not only 'bureaucratic' and 'secularist' but 'philistine' as well.[28]

What riposte can be made to 'forces' like these? Not, I think, that only forms expressive of high culture are worthy of baptism, but rather that such forms seem peculiarly fitted by their greater exploratory power to articulate a faith that is itself more architectonic – more comprehensive and more ultimate – than any other *Weltanschauung*. And besides, when society's cultural organism is functioning properly, high culture permeates to low and informs it, just as low contributes to high, above all by keeping its roots in the humus of the common earth.

Our particular problem in the North Atlantic civilisation today, a civilisation in some respects a global one, carried hither and thither by international markets and information technology, is that the times are unpropitious for any process of 'inculturation' in arts relevant to liturgical beauty to be Christianly helpful. Our popular culture is in a singularly deplorable state, for, as the glazier and critic Patrick Reyntiens has remarked, the media have succeeded in building up a totally horizontal culture – composed of, if not downright trivia (look at the average video library in England's villages and towns), then at any rate information which has shallow content and an evanescent, practically non-existent life within the structure of the memory.[29]

At the same time, our high culture is disoriented, and a prey to meta-physical scepticism and relativism of a disabling kind. What Ratzinger (again) has said of the great cultures of humanity (in an address to the presidents of the Asian Bishops' Conferences and their doctrine commissions entitled significantly '*Beyond* Inculturation') could hardly be claimed at the moment for our own, namely: 'It gets to the root of the great cultures to say that they interpret the world so as to order it to the divine.'[30] The issue today should be, not whether it is desirable to try to render the time-transcending as well as time-embracing reality of the Liturgy in terms closer to a consumerist, positivistic and increasingly fragmented culture in crisis, but what the divine revelation which commands the Liturgy can do to salvage that culture, by confirming certain aesthetic intimations of its patrimony and steadying its elements of rationality. I shall return to the question of the philo-sophic mission of the Church in Chapter V ('Relaunching Christian Philosophy') and to her aesthetic mission in Chapter VIII ('Resacralising Material Culture').

## Reforming the rite: retrospect and prospect

The derailing of the essentially theocentric act of worship onto sidelines of social edification and group-psychological therapy was not an intended result of the liturgical reform carried out by the papacy of Paul VI Montini in the name of the Second Vatican Council, during the twenty years or so that followed that Council's close. It is hardly necessary to add that neither was that 'entertainment ethos' in church which – sometimes for excusable though ill-judged motives of 'attracting youth' – in many parishes and chaplaincies has come to reign. And yet some of the responsibility for what befell must be laid at the doors of the liturgical reformers who, through social-anthropological naïvety, underestimated the disorienting effect of the abrupt and quite wide-ranging dislocation of the inherited rites (whether in the name of Christian antiquity, a scholarly pursuit, on the one hand, or of Christian modernity, a pastoral endeavour, on the other). Recourse to the provision of numerous 'options', not only in the choice of Scripture-reading at Mass, but in such integral features of the

Ordinary of the Mass as the Penitential Rite and even the Canon, the heartland of eucharistic praying itself, was also, it may be suggested, an imprudent measure. Intended in part to 'buy off' criticisms of the inflexibility of a fully determined rite, and to pre-empt unauthorised liturgical experimentation, the introduction into the Liturgy of a principle of choice fuelled, in many places, the fire the official reformers hoped to dowse.

Granted the normative and testimonial character of the liturgical tradition – its role as authoritative witness of faith – and the sense in which its historical development (Western and Eastern) follows a dynamism of its own (towards, for instance, the accentuation of the eucharistic sacrifice), intervention to reorder the Liturgy should, evidently, be modest and cautious at all times. Councils of bishops, popes and their curia are principally guardians of the liturgical tradition, *not* its proprietors. A power of tutelage, episcopal or papal – and it has been a feature of papal history to exert an ever higher claim to defend the Catholic integrity of Christian worship – was never intended to become a licence for the wholesale restructuring of the customary liturgical life of the Church. Not only does such radical tinkering, by drawing attention to the *constructed* character of the rite, deflect attention, by the same token, from the more important factor of the divine agency which, on the Catholic view of the liturgy of the sacraments (especially), uses these human vehicles of word and gesture, image and music, as its instrument in the purposes of grace. Further, human beings are incarnate creatures, and the Tradition of the gospel which – it is perfectly true – they can find unimpaired in the Scriptures and the doctrine of the Church must also reach them in the form of customary actions, habitual gestures, familiar images. Thus, for example, the faith of the Catholic Church in the Real Presence of Christ in the Eucharist is doctrinally speaking as well presented by her official organs now as at any time in her history. Yet, professional surveys and the more informal gathering of impressions by clergy give a clear message that among many Western Catholics, the removal – in the name of 'noble simplicity' – of much of the panoply of ritual reverence to the consecrated Host (and chalice) has had the – to sociologists, predictable – effect of diminishing the capacity of orthodox eucharistic believing to be accessible to the human imagination – even an imagination touched by grace. It is false to suppose that so long as Scripture and doctrine are preserved, disciplinary and liturgical tradition can safely be modernised at will. The assault of the 'progressive' clergy and some like-minded laypeople on the culture of custom in the neophiliac 1960s bears a marked resemblance to the priestly campaign against local religious traditions deemed superstitious and quasi-Gallican by a self-consciously modern seminary-trained clerical élite which, so recent research reports, did much to assist the de-Christianisation of rural France under the Third Republic.[31]

The situation of Latin-rite Catholic worship has been thrown into confusion not only by the persistence of manifest abuses but, more fundamentally, by the discrepancy between certain aspects of the liturgical reform, on the one hand, and, on the other, the intentions of the Council Fathers of Vatican II as embodied in that Council's Dogmatic Constitution on the Sacred Liturgy. By taking a maximalist view of the – in fact, guardedly expressed – clauses of *Sacrosanctum Concilium* on the possibility of an ongoing pastoral adaptation of the rites, the reformers eviscerated the positive statements of the bishops about, for instance, the continuing paradigmatic role of the *Latin* liturgy (with all the implications of such use of an archaic, theologically objective and precise, sacral language for the expression of liturgical style), and, more generally, their insistence that the 'substance' of the Roman rite must be preserved. Now to permit one article in a legislative document to nullify another is to render a text wholly nugatory as a guide to the Church's practice. It must follow, then, that the very *first* task of that 'reform of the reform' for which Cardinal Ratzinger has so courageously called must be the reinterpretation of the articles concerning adaptation (37–40) of the Liturgy Constitution itself to the end that they can 'no longer be used so recklessly'.[32] Not even, we may add, by the Roman Congregation for Divine Worship itself.[33]

Secondly, further changes as may be planned in the structure or content of the Roman Missal, at least in this or that monoglot region of Western Catholicism, should be at the very least postponed. It defeats the nature of a Liturgy for it to be in a state of continuous flux. The Liturgy, by its familiarity, expresses the Church's character as a maternal home – and it would be a strange home where the furniture was thoroughly rearranged every time we returned to it. Meanwhile, everything must be done to celebrate the *novus ordo* with the maximum degree of prayerfulness, dignity, correctness and, where appropriate, solemnity. I have written elsewhere by way of 'tips' in this connection:

> Here Mgr. Peter Elliott's recent provision of a rubrical directory
> for the Pauline Missal and other rites is helpful. By the quality of
> Church fabrics and metals, on the one hand, and of Church music,
> on the other, much can be done to enhance the visual and aural
> setting of the Liturgy and to convey a sense of the supreme care
> and devotion with which it should be celebrated. The liturgically

inept Jerusalem Bible Lectionary can be avoided, since copies of its Revised Standard Version competitor are still extant and make their occasional appearance in the second-hand catalogues of Catholic book sellers and can be bound and rebound until such time as the publisher be ready to risk re-issue. The liturgical strength of Latin can be invoked, at least in some sung parts of the Ordinary. Movement and gestures – of servers as well as of the officiating clergy – can be monitored. Extraordinary ministers of Holy Communion, if needed, can be suitably robed. Intrusive microphones can be removed from the sanctuary. Nor does anything in Church law prevent the recovery of the eastward or *versus apsidem* position (after due explanation to congregations!) for the recital of the Eucharistic Prayer.[34]

That is a subject to which I shall return at this chapter's close.

Thirdly, the survival of the old Roman rite, whose continuing legitimacy as an expression of the worship and spirituality of Western Catholics was acknowledged by Pope John Paul II in his letter *Ecclesia Dei adflicta* of 2 July 1988, should be welcomed as providing a valuable reference-point, a norm of tradition, which can guide priests and people in their own use of the reformed Missal of Paul VI. The continuance of this rite, if it is sufficiently visible and widespread, will impede liturgical revisionism that would push the Mass of Paul VI, as further 'adapted' or in its *de facto* celebration, towards a deepening discontinuity with the historic Roman Liturgy. For this purpose, the Pope, as Western patriarch, and in that capacity the responsible guardian of the treasures of the Western liturgy, should require bishops to allow the faithful ready access to this ritual embodiment of the Mass – on the prior condition, however, that the rite itself be (soberly!) modified to take account of the *manifest* (not conjectural) wishes of the Conciliar Fathers of Vatican II – expansion of Lectionary resources, some use of the vernacular (and hence, logically, much use of Latin!), a litanic prayer of intercession, priestly concelebration and lay reception of the chalice where appropriate. The result should be to draw the historic Roman rite closer to the rites of the East rather than, has too often been the case in recent years, toward Geneva. I hasten to add that this beneficial effect of old rite on new is only likely to be attained when the old is celebrated with that craft and care which, in the immediate past, one could find at abbeys like Ampleforth or at Westminster Cathedral, or today among the *Catholiques de tradition* in France. Younger clerics so sunk in nostalgia as to admire even the slovenliness of Anglo-Hibernian celebration in pre-Conciliar times must be allowed to sink in what is truly a *nostalgie de boue*!

## The Eastward position

The single most important act of 'reforming the reform' will doubtless be the restoration of the Eastward position for celebrating Mass.
The orientation (literally!) of church and congregation towards the
rising sun – the Sun of justice, risen with healing in his wings – is
vital to the Catholic experience of worship. As the great Austrian
historian of the Western Liturgy, Josef Jungmann, put it, recreating by
word-picture the early Roman rite, 'Now the whole congregation is
like a huge procession, led by the priest and moving towards the
sun, towards Christ the Lord'.[35] In the common orientation of priest
and people, the eschatological aspect of the Liturgy – we await the
coming One, not yet among us in his visible presence – is fused with
the cosmic. The Liturgy representatively offers praise on behalf of the
universe of animal and plant life, dependent as this is on the sun's
energy, as well as for the sake of rational beings – and in any case we
ourselves are, as the Greek Fathers liked to point out in their com-
mentaries on Genesis, mediating creatures who bridge the material
and spiritual worlds. The influential inter-war Italo-German theologian
and critic Romano Guardini, whose often quoted words, 'The Church
is coming to life in the souls of men',[36] have frequently been regarded
as the very ensign of the ecclesiological and liturgical revivals of the
twentieth century, glossed his own words by explaining that the
Church was 'regaining that cosmic spaciousness which was hers
during the early centuries and the Middle Ages . . .'.[37] And if, as
Guardini went on to maintain, the liturgical movement simply is the
ecclesiological movement in its contemplative aspect, then the Liturgy
too must have cosmic resonance: '. . . the Liturgy embraces everything
in existence, angels, men and things; all the content and events of life;
in short the whole of reality. And natural reality is here made subject
to supernatural; created reality related to the uncreated.'[38] And indeed,
if the modern Western liturgy, as commonly celebrated, appears too
frequently to be parochial in the perjorative sense of that word, brought
down to the level of a group rather than opening up that group to the
wider reality beyond it, the reason is not only the face-to-face relation
of celebrant and people – as opposed to their looking together in the
same direction. It is also the inappropriate emphasising of the natural
personality of the liturgical actors, interposing as this does a bar to the
sense of supernatural agency which the Liturgy should – effortlessly –
convey. For as the great *Supplices te rogamus* prayer of the Roman Canon
clearly implies,

the true place of Christian worship is not the church building on earth, but the temple of God in Heaven . . . The altar on high is not the altar in which the Mass is celebrated on earth, but the heavenly counterpart of that material altar in the presence of the Divine Majesty in heaven. The holy angel whom the Father is to command to bear our eucharistic offerings to the heavenly altar is none other than the 'angel of mighty counsel' . . . of Isaiah IX. 5 (in the Septuagint, Greek, Bible) who is the Son, the Christ himself.[39]

Too often we hear that the Mass as celebrated should be 'more like the Last Supper'. It is little likely that the Last Supper bore a close resemblance, in, for instance, its seating arrangements, to the idealised and 'modernised' iconography offered in such famous paintings as da Vinci's *Ultima Cena*. Was Leonardo making a covert proposal for the liturgical reordering of the eucharistic assembly? To my knowledge, no art historian has suggested this. He understood better than his later twentieth-century co-religionists that the Mass is not a repetition of the Last Supper but a celebration of what Christ instituted on that occasion – something significantly different.

Behind that appeal to render the Mass 'more like' what happened in the Cenacle there lies, one fears, a hostility to the ritual integument with which the Catholic instinct, in both West and East, has ever clothed the Church's worship. The still-Anglican John Henry Newman answered the objection well in advance:

Did our Saviour say that magnificence in worshipping God, magnificence in His house, in its furniture, and in its decorations, is wrong, wrong since He has come into the world? Does He discourage us from building handsome Churches, or beautifying the ceremonial of religion? Did He exhort us to niggardness? Did He put a slight on architectural skill? Did He imply we should please Him the more, the less study and trouble we gave to the externals of worship? In rejecting the offering of Herod, did He forbid the devotion of Christians?

This is what many persons think. I do not exaggerate when I say, that they think the more homely and familiar their worship is, the more spiritual it becomes. And they argue, that to aim at external beauty in the service of the Sanctuary, is to be like the Pharisees, to be fair without and hollow within; that whereas the Pharisees pretended a sanctity and religiousness outside which they had not inside, therefore, every one who aims at outward religion sacrifices it to inward. . . .

Persons who put aside gravity and comeliness in the worship of God, that they may pray more spiritually, forget that God is a

Maker of all things, visible as well as invisible; that He is the Lord of our bodies as well as of our souls; that He is to be worshipped in public as well as in secret.[40]

Our tongues must preach Him, and our voices sing of Him, and our knees adore Him, and our hands supplicate Him, and our heads bow before Him, and our countenances beam of Him, and our gait herald Him. And hence arise joint worship, forms of prayer, ceremonies of devotion, the course of services, orders of ministers, holy vestments, solemn music, and other things of a like nature; all which are, as it were, the incoming into this world of the Invisible Kingdom of Christ . . .[41]

These words were addressed to Evangelicals. But a century and a half later, within Catholicism itself, a primate of France, Cardinal Albert Decourtray, in an essay 'Mystère et morale', found worse: a liturgical horizontalism reinforcing and reinforced by a secularisation mentality.

After twenty-five years of conciliar reforms, would it not be as well to take stock? Can we dare accept the hypothesis that this great movement, so beneficial in itself, might partly be at fault? . . . We are turned so much towards the assembly that we often forget to turn ourselves, together, people and priests, towards God! Yet, without this essential orientation, the celebration no longer has any Christian meaning.[42]

The purpose of the Liturgy is to make present the ultimate Mystery – not to explain it away.

## NOTES

1. Cited by T. Ware, *The Orthodox Church* (Harmondsworth, 1963, 1968), p. 269.
2. W. Jardine Grisebrook, 'The Necessity of Enchantment', *Priests and People*, July 1997, pp. 266–70.
3. A. Kavanaugh, O.S.B., 'Liturgical Inculturation: Looking to the Future', *Studia Liturgica* 20 (1990), p. 98.
4. A. Kavanaugh, O.S.B., *On Liturgical Theology* (New York, 1984).
5. *The Snowbird Statement on Catholic Liturgical Music* (The Madeleine Institute, Salt Lake City, 1995), p. 1.
6. J. Hillman, *Insearch. Psychology and Religion* (New York, 1967), p. 82.
7. H. A. Hodges, *Christianity and the Modern World View* (London, 1949), p. 18.

8. H. U. von Balthasar, 'Characteristics of Christianity', in idem, *Explorations in Theology. I. The Word Made Flesh* (San Francisco, 1989), p. 177; German original, 'Drei Merkmale des Christlichen', *Wort und Wahrheit* 4 (1949), pp. 401–15.

9. H. U. von Balthasar, *Herrlichkeit. Eine theologische Aesthetik* (Einsiedeln, 1961–9); ET *The Glory of the Lord. A Theological Aesthetics* (Edinburgh and San Francisco, 1983–9) .

10. H. U. von Balthasar, *Theologik* (Einsiedeln, 1985–7); idem, *Theodramatik* (Einsiedeln, 1973–83; ET *Theodrama. Theological Dramatic Theory* (San Francisco, 1988–98).

11. J. Ratzinger, *Ein neues Lied für den Herren. Christusglaube und Liturgie in der Gegenwart* (Freiburg, 1995).

12. Ibid., p. 10.

13. Ibid., p. 19.

14. K. Adam, *Christus unser Bruder* (Regensburg, 1926; 1930²; ET *Christ our Brother*, New York, 1931).

15. J. Jungmann, *Die Stellung Christi im liturgischen Gebet* (Munster, 1925; 1962²); ET *The Place of Christ in Liturgical Prayer* (London, 1965).

16. J. Ratzinger, *Ein neues Lied für den Herren*, op. cit., p. 36.

17. J. Ratzinger, 'Preface', K. Gamber, *La Réforme liturgique en question* (Barroux, 1992), p. 6.

18. For an overview of Ratzinger's liturgical theology to date, see D. Sureau, 'La liturgie sans Eglise. La crise de la liturgie selon le cardinal Ratzinger', *Sedes Sapientiae* 56 (1996), pp. 1–17.

19. Thomas Aquinas, *In librum III. Sententiarum*, dist. 23, q. 3, a. 1, i, sed contra.

20. P. W. Hoon, *The Integrity of Worship. Ecumenical and Pastoral Studies in Liturgical Theology* (Nashville and New York, 1971), p. 131.

21. Ibid., p. 126.

22. Ibid., p. 134.

23. Ibid., p. 135.

24. Ibid., p. 98.

25. Ibid., p. 99.

26. G. van der Leuuw, *Sacred and Profane Beauty* (London, 1963), p. 111.

27. L. Beamer, 'Philistine', in D. L. Jeffrey (ed.), *A Dictionary of Biblical Tradition in English Literature* (Grand Rapids, Mich., 1992), pp. 610–11.

28. *Oxford Declaration on Liturgy* (Centre for Faith and Culture, Westminster College, Oxford), para. 1.

29. P. Reyntiens, 'All Distractions and Half-truths', *The Tablet*, 1 June 1996, p. 731.

30. J. Ratzinger, 'Beyond Inculturation', *Briefing*, 18 May 1995, p. 35. For a fuller citation, see p. 12 above.

31. See E. Weber, *Peasants into Frenchmen. The Modernisation of Rural France, 1870–1914* (London, 1979).

32. J. Mole, 'Inculturation', *The Roman Rite* 8 (1994), p. 2.

33. Cf. the Instruction of the Congregation for Divine Worship on inculturation of 4 March 1994. The appointment of the Chilean Mgr Jorge Medina Estevez as Prefect of the Liturgy Congregation has already given grounds for hoping that a more responsible policy will prevail in the future.

34. A. Nichols, O.P., *Looking at the Liturgy. A Critical View of its Contemporary Form* (San Francisco, 1996), pp. 118–19. The English 'Ceremonial' I refer to is P. Elliott, *Ceremonies of the Modern Roman Rite: the Eucharist and the Liturgy of the Hours* (San Francisco, 1995).

35. J. Jungmann, *The Early Liturgy. To the Time of Gregory the Great* (ET London, 1966), p. 138.

36. R. Guardini, *The Church and the Catholic, and the Spirit of the Liturgy* (ET London, 1935), p. 11.

37. Ibid., p. 23.

38. Ibid., pp. 29–30.

39. G. G. Willis, 'God's Altar on High', *Downside Review* XC (1972), p. 245. As Dr Willis says, it is a great pity that what may be the oldest theology of the eucharistic consecration has been replaced by others from Eastern models in the new Canons of the Roman rite.

40. J. H. Newman, 'Offerings for the Sanctuary', *Parochial and Plain Sermons VI* (London 1881), pp. 298–9, 304.

41. J. H. Newman, 'The Visible Temple', *Parochial and Plain Sermons VI*, op. cit., pp. 287–8.

42. A. Decourtray, 'Mystère et morale', originally in *Eglise à Lyon* for 5 May 1992, reproduced in *Documentation Catholique* for 21 June 1992, p. 613.

# IV

# *Reviving Doctrinal Consciousness*

## Doctrine and experience

The marginalisation of doctrinal norms in today's Church has largely happened by way of the unofficial canonising of an alternative infallibility – 'experience', which must of course mean not experience globally (there is no omnicompetent subject to entertain such experience) but some particular somebody's experience of something in particular. The idea that an individual's experience of gender or race or social location can become a *final arbiter* of truth and falsehood in the Church is no more acceptable than any of the other historically recurring attempts to make of private inspiration a supreme court for adjudicating the gospel. It is not experience we should trust but the transmutation of experience by Scripture and Tradition.

And the deepest reason for this is the nature-grace relationship without whose understanding the very idea of renewing Christendom becomes unintelligible or otiose when considered as a desirable end for human acting. Though false or misleading construals of that nature-grace relation are around, it is perhaps a process of 'dumbing down' (eloquent Americanism!) in preaching, catechesis and religious education which is here our chiefest foe. In her study *States of Grace*, Charlene Spretnak offers anecdotal but hardly atypical evidence.

> During a recent visit with a professor of British literature at my *alma mater*, a Jesuit University, he lamented the fact that many students today have difficulty grasping the thematic structure of Victorian novels because they are nearly ignorant of basic concepts of Christianity. He has to explain metaphors of the fall, grace, redemption, and so forth before he can teach the classic literature! Asked what being a Christian means, his students reply only that it means 'to be kind' and 'to love people'.[1]

41

Spretnak's deploring such evisceration of substance is the more impressive in that she describes herself as a 'retired Catholic' who has moved on, having adopted what she terms an 'inter-faith, cross-cultural approach to reclaiming the spiritual treasures that have been marginalised by modern culture'.[2] But the kind of synthesis she advocates would of course be impossible if its various constituents emptied out their own content with the alacrity shown by Church agencies that substitute the anodyne formulae of a vague moralism for their own distinctive 'wisdom traditions'. Such a fate would be an especially devastating reversal of historic identity in the case of Catholicism, since, in the words of another American commentator, 'The natural acceptance of the supernatural as real is ... the most distinctive mark of a thoroughly Catholic civilisation'.[3]

## Natural and supernatural

The difficulties which modern people have with the notion of doctrine do not issue solely from the way that the desirability of a commonly acknowledged truth, upheld in a public fashion, has, for many, ceased to be obvious. It is also the case that they do not understand what specifically *religious* doctrine is *for*. In a world where nature has been reduced, by the particular philosophical atmosphere that accompanied the rise of modern experimental science, to a condition of brute facticity, the need to interpret the sacred dimension of the cosmos has largely evaporated. At the same time, the fresh symbolic resources provided by a revealed religion – Judaeo-Christianity – are even less accessible since they serve the disclosure of a further dimension still – the gracious dimension of supernatural living, beyond the sacrality of the natural world.

Let us take each of these: the sacral, and the supernatural, in turn. The 'sacrality' of the world is, rightly seen, its naturally symbolic character – above all, its endowment with a power to gesture towards the unconditionally transcendent. All sorts of things 'transcend' each other in all kinds of ways: a lion is transcendingly strong compared with an antelope; a hedgehog transcendingly well-armoured in comparison with a mouse. We are speaking, however, of the absolute transcendence which the unspeakable divine perfection is, and for which it provides symbolic ladders of ascent in putting forth, through the act of creation, a *theophanous* world.

'Nature', declared the poet Mallarmé, 'is a forest of symbols', but it has been the unhappy consequence of a rationalistic naturalism in the Western intellectual tradition to denude the cosmos of its symbolic properties and ascribe the ownership of the garments one is thereby left holding to the culturally formed imagination (or capacity for delusion) of the human mind. Is water simply a combination of molecules of hydrogen and oxygen (or whatever, on the subatomic level, these terms may be said to convey)? Alternatively, should we think, with the French philosopher-theologian Jean Borella and a multitude of poets and artists, as well as thinkers tutored by the mythopoeic expression of reality in the archetypes of rites, myths, dreams, that there is in water a *symbolic valency* which those thinking respectfully of *all* the dimensions of the real should attempt to draw out.[4] Borella would speak of a 'semantic triangle' composed (in the case of the example under discussion) of a *signifier* – the liquid element itself; a *sense* or meaning – the idea, evoked by the image of water, of a 'matter' which in, precisely, its liquidity, can enter into all forms and yet is retained by none of them; and the particular *referent* which interpretation would assign to the symbol of water by virtue of its sense or idea – perhaps the process of the world's formation which is how water first appears in the Genesis creation account, where the Spirit 'moves over the waters' (1.1). The theophanic dimension is, however, not yet engaged. Beyond the 'semantic triangle' of signifier, sense and *particular* referent, there is the question of the *metacosmic* referent of which the three constituent points of the 'triangle' are distinct kinds of manifestation. Borella would identify it with that 'universal possibility' which belongs to God as he whose essence is the infinite source of possibilities for the world. In this way, metaphysical reference furnishes the unifying principle for the water symbol, the idea it evokes and the particular reference which interpretation might give it.[5] But how far removed is this way of mentally inhabiting the cosmos from that of secular Western man! Here, truly, are forgotten 'ancient springs' – in the title of a study by the poetess and commentator who has done most to keep alive in England a symbolic-sacral approach to the real along broadly these lines, Kathleen Raine.[6]

How did we come to lose it? The answer to this question may signal the road to regain it. The beginning of the 'crisis of religious symbolism' can be ascribed to the way the 'new physics' of the seventeenth century became linked, in the course of the next two hundred years, to a style of thinking, combining elements of empiricism and rationalism, which would culminate in the positivism – at first scientific, then simply 'logical' – of the nineteenth and early twentieth centuries. Though the intelligibility of natural science in no way demands positivism as its midwife (indeed, it is arguably hobbled, not assisted, by positivism's presence), the technical virtuosity of science's achievements and their life-transforming quality for millions of people profoundly affected, as we know, the mental landscape of the Western world. Save in counter-cultural pockets, the pseudo-metaphysics of positivism displaced the symbolic-sacral world-view which was the Judaeo-Christian revelation's natural *mise-en-scène*. Philosophy, having long accepted (since the Pre-Socratics) the honourable mission of purifying religious discourse by the tests of rational reflection, sought now to nullify the natural orientation of the human intelligence towards that divinity which, in the theophanous cosmos, had always signalled its ultimacy through the forest of symbols. The occlusion of the analogically ordered multi-dimensional reality of finite being happened by way of, first, the abandonment of a scalar ontology where all that is can be situated on the rungs of a 'ladder', and the turning away, second, from the correspondences which link beings on those diverse rungs. They link them because, in analogically ordered reality, all things participate in different ways in the being which provides the universe with its overall unity, with what makes it a 'universe'. Inevitably, then, cosmic symbols would cease to function as the epiphany of their own metaphysical reference – and indeed lose what Borella terms their 'particular' referent as well. The denial of the validity of any cosmological thinking that was not natural-scientific in character suppressed that third point of his 'triangle' which is the particular referent, just as the adoption of a 'de-mystifying' hermeneutic with the aim of neutralising religious consciousness erased the second point, meaning – for in a positivist universe, con-struals of the 'intrinsic' meaning of natural symbols is just groundless human projection. Finally, the last of the constituent points disappears as the original symbol (the 'signifier' in Borella's terminology) is first resolved into its proto-physical elements and subsequently, as scientific modernism gives way to postmodernity, loses all natural consistency in becoming a plaything of *verbal* signifiers on ever-changing cultural 'fields', as the endless process of signification structures not only consciousness but also – in this postrational world – *reason too*.

But if the *logos* or principle of intelligibility of human thinking is reduced in status to a simple effect of the functioning of such signifiers the postmoderns are of all men most to be pitied. Perhaps, as some have suggested, *logos* had to reach the term of its self-'purification' from the symbolic order of creation if it were to recognise in a speculatively satisfactory way the necessity of its relation to symbol. The revolt against symbolism leads reason, it would seem, to self-destruction. Yet the rational denial of reason is in fact reason's affirmation. We reach here an *impasse*, from which the only escape lies in entering into an understanding of the symbolic-sacred order so as to learn from receiving its light.

> Certainly we have never dreamed of proving deductively the truth of religious symbolism. On the contrary, we believe that we must maintain a hiatus of a humanly unbridgeable kind, between the understanding and symbols (analogous to that which separates the knowing subject from the object known, whether by nature or by revelation). For it is precisely by accepting this distance that the intellect realises the truth of its nature: intelligence is relation and has access to its identity only by way of consent to its ordering to the otherness of being; it only 'integrates' with that to which it submits.[7]

Leading the philosophical intelligence to consent speculatively to that submission to the symbolic is a major project in the recovery of a religious sensibility that is normally presumed by the preaching of the gospel. The gospel expects to find us as pagans awaiting conversion, not religious *tabulae rasae* on which no words are written at all. The recreation by the religious imagination of a sacred cosmology furnishing a more than merely subjective meaning to the human life-world is a responsibility of Christians who – *faute de mieux* – are now guardians of the sacrality of being in the West. Without it, the *super*natural self-revelation of God, drawing as this does on the repertory of symbol for its communication to us, falls on deadened ears, on lazy eyes, meets unalerted minds.

Divine grace means in the first place the vocation of man to the supernatural order; secondly, and in dependence on this, a gift habitually indwelling those whom God has set right with himself, and set right on course, for this supernatural goal; thirdly, the 'actual' helps, indispensable as these are in daily living, whereby we are aided to overcome the refractoriness of fallen human nature in pursuit of this wondrous goal. This elevation of our human powers of knowing and loving renders them attuned not simply to *some* awareness, *mediated* through the sensuous world, of the transcendent God but, with incomparably greater intimacy, adapts them directly to a life of everlasting friendship with the triune Lord. In the concrete order, this extraordinary transformation of our possibilities, this change in our destiny, turns on the Incarnation of the Logos as Jesus Christ when, the Father's 'Art', he who is the Expression of the inexhaustible Origin of all things, himself stepped into the realm of signs.

> The incarnate Word come into the world is not only the actual
> mediator of grace through his merit (which is only necessary
> because Adam lost this grace), but by his free coming into the world
> he makes the world's order of nature his nature, which pre-
> supposes him, and the world's order of grace his grace and his
> *milieu*.[8]

The revelation of man's supernatural vocation in Christ brings home
to us with special force the radical insufficiency or neediness which
afflicts the very substance of our being. An Augustine, a Pascal, is
needed to evoke that unquiet heart, the sense we have that our spirit is
not fully at home here, that all is not well with us (even under the
canopy of the sacred cosmos), that what we are is so much less than
what we might be.

But the sense of the supernatural is not simply this negative, yet
necessary, experience of the limitations of humanism. It is also, and
more primordially, the knowledge that 'God always gives more than
he promises'.[9] God's fulfilling our naturally unfulfillable desire in
Christ is his *super*fulfilment of it, his overwhelming it in the utter un-
measuredness of his self-gift. The mediate relation of our nature to the
transcendent God through the symbol of his creation now becomes in
Jesus Christ the immediate enjoyment of his grace – though this
immediacy means for us, as disciples, purification before illumination
and union. The pattern of resurrection not only through but in dying
whereby the incarnate Word achieved the saving revelation of the
Trinitarian Love is offered the Christian to become his or her own.

It follows that a naturalistic humanism – which by its benevolence
constitutes a shadow and simulacrum of the charity of the gospel – is
also Christian revelation's direst threat. The construal of Christian faith
as a humanism tears the heart from the faith, falsely stilling the spirit's
restlessness while simultaneously locking the marvels of divine grace
in a box and throwing away the key.[10]

Since, however, the sense of the supernatural cannot become self-
aware in us, since (that is) we cannot become reflexively aware of our
supernatural vocation, *except by grasping its object* – the realities of
faith spoken of in the Creed, the doctrinal corpus of the Church's
teaching is crucial to our being, life, identity as human creatures in the
cosmos redeemed in principle in Jesus Christ. The weakening of
doctrinal consciousness in the Church since the Second Vatican Council
is not simply, then, an unfortunate lack in the formal education of the
faithful in the Christian verities. Thanks to its necessity for what we
can call 'supernatural reflexivity' it brings with it the subversion of all
distinctively Christian living.

## Modern tolerance, apostolic rule

It is the failure to grasp this point which vitiates much contemporary criticism (within and without the Catholic Church) of the intervention of the Church's doctrinal guardians in matters of theological and moral speculation. Often enough, defence of those who depart from orthodox believing on issues of faith and morals is offered in terms of either Enlightenment notions of individual reason as the organ of truth, or liberal presuppositions about individual self-determination as the primary condition of human flourishing. Defences of doctrinal liberty couched in such terms are perhaps even more damaging to the ecclesial consciousness of those influenced by them than were the positions of the writers they are intended to succour!

Such, however, is the enthusiasm of some Christians today for pluralism and tolerance that the very concept of heresy has become (if the phrase may be forgiven) anathema. Contemporary sociologists tell us that in the present confused ideological market-place it is churches that have retained, or acquired, a clear set of truth-claims about faith and moral practice that are likely to flourish. In a situation of considerable cultural dislocation, where experience lacks clear contours and stable reference-points, it is not churches giving the impression of an anomie hardly less extensive than that of their environment which will attract.[11] The Catholic Church – not in Rome, but in many parts of the world beyond – has to beware following suit after those mainstream Protestant denominations which, in effect, have banished the concept of heresy – the idea of a departure from apostolic teaching – altogether. If there ceases to be a way even of raising the question of where the boundaries of legitimate Christian belief are situated, 'anomie' is definitely the name of the game. As Thomas Oden of Drew University Theological School has put it, in a Wittgenstein-like comparison precisely with *games*:

> This is like trying to have a baseball game with no rules, no umpire, and no connection with historic baseball. Only we continue to insist on calling it baseball because a game by the name of baseball is what most people still want to see played.[12]

But the same writer predicts that, just because this state of affairs where all constraints on doctrinal imagination, liturgical experimentation and an infinity of disciplinary and ethical relativity are removed and political correctness, multi-cultural tolerance and ethical situationism reign, is so thoroughly lacking in coherence, the time will come, and is in fact hard on our heels, where the more reflective laity and clergy will raise the issue of criteria for orthodoxy.

> The rediscovery of boundaries in theology will be the preoccupation
> of the twenty-first century of Christian theology. Some within the
> Church – a party I call postmodern palaeo-orthodoxy – are increas-
> ingly gaining the courage to enquire: Is pantheism heresy? Is
> reductive naturalism as reliable as any other assumption? Can
> Christianity make friends with absolute relativism? What would
> the Church look like if it were apostate?[13]

These are remarks made by a Protestant theologian about (one
supposes) the historic Protestant churches, but Catholics would delude
themselves if they thought that the analysis in no way applied to their
own communion. One only has to think of the knee-jerk reaction in
the correspondence columns of such church magazines as the London
*Tablet* whenever news comes of the investigation of some theological
figure by the Congregation for the Doctrine of the Faith to realise
that! Of course the identification of *lacunae* in the form or substance of
such proceedings is not what is objectionable but the assumption of
folly in their happening at all. Even allowing for the possibility –
probability – that a sizeable proportion of the *Tablet's* individual
subscribers and readers are Anglicans, what has happened to that
'jealousy of error', that instinctive repugnance toward heresy so crucial
for John Henry Newman in his account of the *consensus fidelium*? That
jealousy of error was, for Newman, but the other side of the medal to
'instinct' for supernatural truth, 'direction' by the Holy Spirit and divine
response to the prayer of the Christian people for right faith. Only as
all of these – negative abreactions and positive attractions – together
does the 'consensus fidelium' furnish its testimony to the fact of the
apostolic teaching.[14] Here the inroads of secular awareness and its
attendant criteria into the heartlands of Catholic consciousness have
gone deep – and augur ill for any simple appeal to majoritarian
consensus should some analogue of the Arian crisis (when a substantial
part of the episcopate opposed evangelical and Catholic truth) again
transpire. Fortunately, in assessing the response of the faithful in the
discernment of what counts as authentic doctrine, votes are weighed
as well as counted.[15]

Those who, in some regard already determined as crucial, have
rejected the apostolic rule of faith, with its authoritative interpretation
of the Canon of the apostolic Scriptures as accredited by the discipline
of apostolic teachers, can hardly expect to be included among what the
historic eucharistic prayer of the Western Liturgy calls 'those who hold
and teach the Catholic faith, that comes to us from the apostles'. The
identity of the Church is crucially bound up with the identification of
right doctrine.

Christian doctrine has as its aim the appropriate naming, by the Church, of the Triune God whom it worships and serves. Its primary function is not the satisfaction of human curiosity, nor even the explanation of human experience; it is, rather, the giving voice to that reality made known in creation, encountered in Jesus Christ and poured out through the Spirit. It is a story-telling, a passing on of the narrative which has called the Church into existence. Through telling its story in doctrinal terms the Church seeks to tell the truth about God and about itself.[16]

To this excellent statement of that interrelation by a Methodist author one can only add Catholicism's belief, that, owing to the promises of Christ and the accompanying presence of the Paraclete, this 'aim' has indeed been fulfilled, and this 'seeking' found its goal.

We cannot overestimate the depth and the range of the sense in which, when received in heartfelt fashion, doctrine, dogma *changes our minds*. As I put this in a 'theological introduction to Catholicism':

Dogma is the fruit of that process whereby, within the communion of the Church, the thinking mind adores the self-revealing God and thinks within the mystery of grace in a renewed way. Paul told his hearers that their minds were to be renewed by the grace of Jesus Christ. This was not just a moral exhortation, encouraging people to be good, though it has moral implications and conditions. More than that: the Fathers, at any rate, understood Paul to be speaking about the difference made to the very way the human mind operates by the redemption and transfiguration of the world through Jesus Christ and his Spirit. Outside the sphere of salvation, reason is adapted to the fallen state of humankind. It is often happily and successfully so adapted, but adapted nonetheless it is. Fallen reason can generate truth – speculative truth in pure reason, truth about conduct through practical reason, and that other truth for which we have no name in productive reason (i.e. in making things, from pots and pans to states and governments). Yet it remains fallen reason, and the telltale signs are scattered throughout the history of thinking. Our apparently inextinguishable urge to locate ourselves in relation to reality as a whole, to go beyond what experience alone can tell us, ends up frequently enough either in hubris or in impotence. Thought either leaps into speculative delusions about how much it can know or else falls back into a state of supine resignation to not knowing. And so the history of philosophy is a history of reaction against metaphysics, and of reactions against the denial of metaphysics.

The Christian message insists that thought cannot go beyond the limits of fallen humanity, of a fallen world, unless it undergoes a death and a resurrection. The 'death' in question is a discipline, an asceticism, provided for the human mind by ecclesial experience (worship, meditation on the Scriptures, prayer, religious love) all of which purify little by little the eye of the human intellect. The 'resurrection' involves the transformation of fallen reason into that understanding which mirrors the Word of God, in whose image and to whose likeness we were originally made. In this resurrection of the mind we rise into the life of the Holy Spirit. The mind becomes spiritual, penetrating into the ultimate significance or bearing of things, as it becomes attuned to the Spirit of God.

Doctrine, then, together with dogma, its most hard-won form, and the theological thinking these stimulate, is the vision of the world that results from this Easter 'passover' of the mind from death to life. It is the festival of the mind celebrating the mystery of existence in God. It is a wondrous medium that permits us to see in Christ, by the Holy Spirit, the final truth of the world beyond the illusions (be they hyper-metaphysical or antimetaphysical) of what the Bible calls this *aiôn*, this age of the world.[17]

It is, then, quite false to regard submission to the Church's public doctrine as a barrier to personal spiritual development. The contrary is the case. Rather, the acceptance of doctrine – as Chesterton indicated in *Orthodoxy* – ushers the self into a wider room where, in the words of St John of the Cross,

> Mine are the heavens and mine is the earth; mine are the people, the righteous are mine and mine are the sinners; the angels are mine and the Mother of God, and all things are mine; and God himself is mine and for me, for Christ is mine and all for me. What, then, dost thou ask for and seek, my soul? Thine is all this, and it is all for thee.[18]

The apostolic tradition – which makes all this possible – is not endlessly plastic. As the detective novelist, Dantist and lay theologian Dorothy L. Sayers lamented (in a typical understatement) to a correspondent, 'We have been so anxious to avoid the charge of dogmatism and heresy-hunting that we have rather lost sight of the idea that Christianity is supposed to be an interpretation of the universe.'[19]

Modernity, like all periods and world-views, stands under the judgement of the norm that historic orthodoxy has applied to false or inadequate ideas of reality in all ages. And if the foundational responsibility to preserve and pass on that faith is given in the sacraments of initiation, and so belongs to all the baptised as members of the universal and royal priesthood of the household of faith, an especially heavy burden of duty falls on those who, by virtue of the ministerial priesthood, have been commissioned by a further sacrament to represent and proclaim that faith in a public fashion. When departure from the apostolic confession comes about – as often nowadays – through misplaced allegiance to ideologies that are dying (rationalist humanism and liberalism, radical feminism, Marxism-Leninism), that collapse of apostolic confidence is notably tragic.

Bishops often fear that insistence on the boundaries of doctrinal consciousness will generate unmanageable conflicts in the Church. One could as cogently argue that it is the failure to demarcate limits that creates conflict. The seeming erasure or non-observance of boundaries creates dismay and anger among some, and false expectations that can never be satisfied among others. Where limits are permeable not only do they lose their function of identifying the Tradition, they also create unending and insoluble controversies (for a controversy could only be solved and brought to an end by the establishment of a fresh limit that was *not* permeable in this way). There is freedom of discussion for ways of improving the Tradition's transparency – but this must be judiciously distinguished from the obliteration of Tradition's lines.[20] That is the necessary negative counsel: but positively – and here is where the emphasis should fall – we must do all in our power to stir up doctrinal consciousness, a Christian sensibility, by all the means – preaching, catechesis, apologetics, art and the novel, hagiology – that are in our power.

## NOTES

1. C. Spretnak, *States of Grace. The Recovery of Meaning in the Postmodern Age* (San Francisco, 1993), p. 3.

2. Ibid., p. 8.

3. T. Storck, *The Catholic Milieu* (Front Royal, Va, 1987), p. 12.

4. J. Borella, *La Crise du symbolisme religieux* (Lausanne, 1990).

5. Ibid., pp. 9–10.

6. K. Raine, *Defending Ancient Springs* (London, 1967).

7. Borella, *La Crise*, p. 8.

8. K. Rahner [S.J.], *Nature and Grace, and Other Essays* (ET London, 1963), p. 23.

9. J. Borella, *Le sens du Surnaturel* (Geneva, 1996²), p. 12.

10. I allude to Matthias Joseph Scheeben's masterwork *Die Herrlichkeiten der göttlichen Gnade* (Freiburg, 1863) whose contents, it may fairly be said, will seem to a secularised Christian to be sheer Chinese.

11. T. C. Reeves, *The Empty Church: the Suicide of Liberal Christianity* (New York, 1996).

12. T. C. Oden, 'Can we talk about heresy?', *Christian Century*, 12 April 1995, p. 390.

13. Ibid.

14. J. H. Newman, *On Consulting the Faithful in Matters of Doctrine*, edited with an introduction by J. Coulson (London, 1961), p. 73.

15. On the principles involved, see my *The Shape of Catholic Theology. An Introduction to its Sources, Principles and History* (Collegeville, Minn. and Edinburgh, 1991), pp. 221–31.

16. R. Clutterbuck, 'Our Doctrines', *Epworth Review* 24.3 (1997), p. 24.

17. A. Nichols, O.P., *Epiphany. A Theological Introduction to Catholicism* (Collegeville, Minn., 1996), pp. 55–6.

18. *The Complete Works of Saint John of the Cross*, translated from the critical edition of P. Silverio de Santa Teresa, C.D., and edited by E. Allison Peers, III (London, 1943), p. 244.

19. B. Reynolds (ed.), *The Letters of Dorothy L. Sayers II. 1937–1943: From Novelist to Playwright* (Cambridge, 1997), p. 158.

20. As the American Dominican Fr Benedict Ashley has written,

> The term 'dissent' has become very ambiguous. I think it is most properly used to mean giving one's own theological opinion an authority superior or equal in certitude and practical value to that of the church's magisterium, especially if this is made public and used to discredit and promote resistance to the theoretical or practical force of the magisterial pronouncement. Hence, it is *not* dissent for a theologian to point out defects or suggest corrections or improved formulations in fact or argumentation in magisterial documents with a view to sound doctrinal development, nor to debate the exact authoritative weight of a document, provided this is done prudently in a forum where a genuine search for truth can be reasonably expected and faith and objectively good consciences fostered.

B. Ashley, O.P., *Justice in the Church. Gender and Participation* (Washington, 1996), p. 32.

# V

# *Relaunching Christian Philosophy*

IT has long been the conviction of the Catholic Church that theology cannot suitably be written without some underpinning of philosophy. Grace, after all, builds upon nature, while nature is open (of its nature!) to grace. So a defective philosophical culture is a source of potential disaster for the intellectual life of the Church.

## Analytic philosophy

Contemporary philosophy in English-speaking countries is not, by and large, a supplier of helpful handmaids to theology. For, in the first place, still dominant yet showing signs of dislodgement from its once unquestioned supremacy, comes analytic philosophy. Helpful in setting out a coherent grammar of discourse, analytic philosophy could be of benefit to the Church by disposing of objections to Christian belief – as well as clarifying the logic of Christian language. Though in and of itself, analytic philosophy does not commit the practitioner thereof to any particular set of *credenda* – it is, as one distinguished Catholic member of the school, Elizabeth Anscombe, has remarked, 'more characterised by styles of argument and investigation than by doctrinal content' – *de facto*, analytic philosophers can usually be expected to hold any number of opinions that play havoc with a Christian metaphysic.[1]

Miss Anscombe has usefully tabulated these. They fall into three categories: those that concern man (anthropology), those that concern the good (ethics), and those that concern the cosmos and God himself (cosmology or general metaphysics, and natural theology or the philosophy of religion). Being alive, she explains, is what it is for a human being – a living thing – to exist at all. Hence the enormous importance of determining the start and close of life, and not postponing

53

human status until a human being develops sufficiently to become a person (a human being *is* a person simply by virtue of existing, and hence of living), or prematurely depriving someone of human personhood (i.e. life) by declaring that since they are not (apparently) carrying out fully personal actions they are reduced from 'selfhood' to merely biological status. Actually, biological status is what is all-important here, since the connection of personhood with our membership of a biological species is far more securely established than is the well-foundedness of that (definitely slippery) language of the 'self'. A prejudice against natural kinds is philosophically unhelpful, and no amount of rhetoric about the supposed horrors of 'essentialism' can disguise that simple fact.[2]

So much for anthropology. A comparable range of misunderstandings reigns in ethics too. The fact/value divide is so taken for granted that ethics is considered to be formally independent of such outstanding givens of human life as physiology. The consequent divorce of ethics from real being, in favour of an exclusive bond with rational being, explains the curious fascination of analytically-minded ethicists with the appeal, in considering moral obligation, to imaginary cases fantastically beyond physical possibility for men. Substantively, the ethics analytic philosophers commonly practise deals, on the one hand, in a calculation of consequences (no absolute moral prohibitions always in force here!). On the other hand, the currency of moral approval is restricted to such outcome terms as 'right' and 'ought' (or for moral disapprobation 'wrong' and 'ought not'). The language of the virtues and vices which composes the necessary intermediate terms between such words and the life-situations the moralist considers is strikingly absent. Or, if the language of the virtues and vices *be* used, it is interpreted in an 'emotivist' way: taken, namely, as expressing the 'pro' or 'con' feelings of the observer to the action (or omission) in question.

And where ethics takes a wrong path, so cosmology and the philosophy of religion may follow. The common assumption is deterministic: causation just means necessitation, and so the will's freedom is either delusion or to be understood in a way compatible with total naturalism in explanation of the world. If a God be allowed into this cosmos it is as one subject to its rules, and conceived on the model of a magnified human agent, mutable, the subject of frustration, and given to gathering evidence to enable the best possible decision he can.

And all of these are challengeable assumptions or views from which the tradition of analytic philosophy needs to be purified so as to become, in Christendom, a serviceable tool. Its concern with argumentative strategies for clarifying conceptual geography is fine so far as it goes. But its disconnection from the sapiential tradition of Western philosophy leaves it without an overall goal, a unifying end. For philosophy should be not simply an exercise for the sharpening of wits but, as Professor John Haldane has remarked, a highroad to speculative and practical truth.

## Postmodernism

Other philosophies which do not lack a doctrinal content of a sort largely inimical to Christianity figure most prominently, as the twentieth-century West draws to its close, under the blanket denomination 'postmodernism'. Its breathtaking advance not only in the discourse of high culture, but in academic theology too, poses peculiar problems for Catholic thought.

Postmodernism, we can say, is a revived Nominalism on its way to nihilism, though this movement of thought has *some* goods to deliver en route. *Au fond*, postmodernism rejects not only all foundations but even all form. It is characteristic of late mediaeval Nominalism to regard the form-bearing principle no longer – contrast the ancients and early and high mediaevals – as first and foremost *nature* – whereas for traditional philosophy the cosmos itself mediated truth, nature communicated reality, and what we today would call 'culture' constituted a further shaping of what is given to man. As the centre of Western philosophy shifts from Descartes' Paris to the Königsberg of Kant that form-bearing principle is increasingly reidentified not so much as nature but as *mind considered apart from nature*, the human subject over against that object which is the world. And as cosmic intelligibility vanishes, so does the link – through analogy and participation – between God and creatures, the link that *is* creaturehood itself. For post-Kantian voluntarism, indeed, nature becomes the *enemy* of freedom. No longer the nurturing, if also at times demanding and perilous, mother, nature becomes the strait-jacket that would paralyse the form-bearing principle before it can get to work. Now postmodernism comes to complete this process by a thoroughgoing rejection of the ontology *both* of the cosmos *and* of the subject.[3]

The assault on what postmodernists term 'foundationalism' is of a piece with this. (Here they join hands with such systematic relativists as the American philosopher Richard Rorty.) Human finitude, the socio-cultural 'embeddedness' of human judgements and the fact that all exercise of human reason has its context, rule out any establishing of

universal norms or standards which could reflect the universal structures of being. This move is especially disruptive of the Catholic
intellectual tradition for which the soteriological and ontological orders
(salvation and creation, grace and nature) are joined by a basic
continuity. Opening a fissure – indeed, a chasm – between theology
and ontology creates particular problems for notions of gospel truth,
which is why such Catholic foundationalist thinkers as Karl Rahner
and Bernard Lonergan (themselves no great friends of Cartesianism
and the Enlightenment) insisted that Christian thought cannot surrender
to notions of pure historicity, sheer historical flux.[4] As Thomas Guarino
has written:

> A move towards non-foundationalist ontology means either a turn
> toward significant mutability and flexibility in fundamental
> Christian teachings or, conversely, a fideistic assertion of the
> immutable truth of the gospel, prescinding from any attempt to
> establish this immutability reasonably. Without a foundationalist
> ontology of some sort, there is no possibility for logically sustaining
> the stability of textual meaning or a referential notion of truth,
> which appear to be essential principles for traditional under-
> standings of doctrine.[5]

With the postmodernist attack on foundations and forms, the issue of
truth itself is irremediably entangled. Classical and modern notions
of truth are deconstructed in the belief that truth – if the word still
be used – is dependent on social norms and cultural warrants. To
suppose that truth is anything so simple as the grasping of actual
states of affairs is regarded as quite naïve. Inevitably, the spectres
of esotericism and 'privatism' (each culture, each place, each individual has a truth 'for them') raises its head. 'In its extreme forms,
deconstructive post-modernism declares that meaning itself is
impossible, except as relative and essentially arbitrary choices we decide
upon and act out in ironic performance.'[6] It was to conjure away such
spirits that the German post-metaphysical thinker Jürgen Habermas
launched his project of universal neo-pragmatics where the ethics of
the democratic consensus enjoys the authority once held by the sacred,
by God.[7]

The anti-foundationalist, anti-referentialist attack on both the
substantiveness of the knowing subject and the reality and intelligibility
of the essences that subject can know is itself founded on exaggeration
– a postulate of 'extreme groundlessness' – for which it needs, for
epistemological therapy, appropriate referral. There is no difficulty in
co-recognising, with the recognition of the epistemic subject, its (his or

her) presuppositions, background beliefs and ideological engagements which, of course, colour deeply its (their) noetic acts. That is simply to say what St Thomas long ago acknowledged (though with less awareness of historical and social 'placing' than ourselves) that what is known is always known in the mode proper to the receiver of that knowledge. As Fr Robert Sokolowski has written, 'Natural wholes are displayed to us in the thick of human custom, making and culture.'[8] And if that is so for natural kinds, it is not less so for that unique whole which is the historic divine revelation: it too, supernatural though its origin be, follows the law of the Incarnation in its transmission, as such writers of the school of *la nouvelle théologie* as Marie-Dominique Chenu, Jean Daniélou and Henri de Lubac emphasised as early as the 1940s. Still, in the encompassing web of contingencies, it really is *wholes* – essential forms, and above all the form of divine revelation itself – that are made known to us. Historicity is not so constitutive of knower and known that 'knowledge' is mere human construct. Certainly, the knower brings his own contribution – and often fruitfully so, for some limitations are matreutic. (Without selection of focus we should be, epistemologically, all at sea.) But more fundamentally, the knower is receptive of reality in its intelligible structure – for his mind, a mind that is, as the ancients put it, *capax mundi*, 'capable of the world' is essentially co-natural with the structure of a world made through the Logos of God. As the English Catholic philosopher Hugo Meynell has insisted, following in the steps of Lonergan, the marvels of technology would hardly be possible without such a pre-harmonised 'fit' between nature and mind. Without such a primarily receptive view of mind's relation to nature, it is hard to see how an understanding of divine revelation as God's enduring gift of truth to the Church can get off the ground.

A crucial respect in which deconstructionist approaches to truth must collide with orthodox Christianity comes into view when we consider the question, Is there such a thing as a 'true' interpretation of a text? It may well escape current practitioners of the historical-critical method in biblical studies, innocently guarded as these can be by a wall of circumambient scholarship protecting them from the blasts of philosophical currents without, that options for or against 'foundationalism' have an unstoppable repercussive effect for their subject-matter. The founders and continuators of this discipline took for granted as a 'given' what was in fact a metaphysical commitment of Christianity, made on the twofold basis of classical rationality and the biblical doctrine of man – namely, that human nature, abiding in all essentials through the changes of history, is basically one. A 'shared ontology', as Guarino puts it, 'grounded a recoverable and representable textual meaning'.

> If, however, as postmodernity claims, there is no fundamental human nature, shared essence, transcendental consciousness, or invariant structure of knowing, then one cannot speak of a common matrix for reconstructive thought (scholarship, i.e., which can reconstruct original meaning). Without some universal nature 'rooting' objectivist hermeneutics, one cannot logically defend a stable and recoverable textual content.[9]

That the same meaning could be found, expressed and re-expressed in a variety of clothings according to context was a conviction that united Catholic theologians on both sides of the divide between the more subtle Neo-Scholastics and the masters of *nouvelle théologie* in that great debate over theological method in Catholicism which preceded, and formed a significant portion of the background to, the Second Vatican Council.[10] It was part and parcel of the conceptual baggage of that Council itself. It remained the firm belief of mainstream post-conciliar writers like the German Walter Kasper, the American Avery Dulles.

Rejection of the content/context distinction in any form which such rejection may take carries with it the threat of hermeneutical anarchy. For if the content/context distinction is irredeemably naïve, then with a change of context – so imperious logic demands – a change in content necessarily follows. That is why the influential German theorist of interpretation, Hans-Georg Gadamer, in abandoning, as impossibly 'Romantic', the notion that, by such means as philological analysis and the study of earlier societies and their historic cultures, the original meaning of a text could be fully retrieved (leaving for our contemporaries only the task of 'applying' to ourselves that understanding) sought to fend off unlimited pluralism in interpretation by his notion of the 'fusion of horizons' in all 'correct' reading of a text. Here, so it is said, the perspective of the original writer and that of the modern reader intersect, while never wholly coinciding. But while this stratagem restores the importance of tradition (hence the dislike of Gadamer's thought by the more radical disciples of his master, Heidegger),[11] the latitude in acceptable interpretation it leaves is still so wide as to render distinctly Pickwickian any notion that 'true' interpretation remains our goal.

Where modern hermeneutics *is* helpful is in reminding us of two salient features of the age-old process of interpreting texts and other monuments of tradition. First, as the distinguished Dominican theologian William Hill has opined:

> Truth and its form or expression can never be separated – as if one
> could peel away the outer appearance and discover a disembodied
> and transcultural truth at its core. But the impossibility of a real
> separation is no denial of grounds for a *distinction*.[12]

Let us note, however, that precisely that extreme difficulty of recasting
true meaning in fresh idioms of expression should engender in the
service of truth – above all, of truth in its highest office, *revealed* truth –
a prudent conservatism. To hand down authentic Tradition while manifesting *insouciance* towards the forms in which Tradition is embodied
(the immemorial rites and customs that compose Catholic Christianity's
received culture) has been, in recent decades, the somewhat contradictory policy of numerous representatives, some highly placed, of the
Latin church.[13]

And secondly, an objective hermeneutic need not be understood as
licensing only wooden repetition of a meaning from whose resources
no fresh accessions of significance can ever be gained. The original
meaning, precisely in its genesis, can show itself rich enough to present
new facets, hitherto unnoticed dimensions, as new questions are put
to it, aspects of reality juxtaposed with it for the first time. That is what
makes 'development of doctrine' possible.

If texts have been regarded as mediators of knowledge (or indeed of
falsehood, which is the other side of the coin of truth, and dependent
on the validity of the concept of truth for its own value), it is hardly
deniable that texts themselves are made up of *words*. The crisis of
interpretation is deepened by the turmoil into which, with postmodernism, the philosophy of language has entered. What a postmodern author such as Jacques Derrida maintains is that the non-
capturable otherness of life requires that we abandon linguistic
representationalism and any such plain stratagems of explanatory
speech as ostensive definition ('That's a chair!'). Derrida emphasises –
indeed parodies, grotesquely over-emphasises – the playful character
of language (the 'play of signifiers' that at one and the same time 'refer
and defer' – defer endlessly, that is, any fixed point for their referring).
The world is always more *different* than naming by language would
have it seem. Behind this lies a deadly (to Christian theism a *literally*
deadly) seriousness.

> If the representational force of linguistic and semiotic systems can
> be deconstructed, then the logos structure of reality, and ultimately
> the One who undergirds this cosmos, the Transcendent Signified,
> may be deconstructed as well. For Derrida, God has become the
> ultimate totalizing agent, the Signified who unites the metaphysical

idea of cosmic intelligibility with the ostensive view of language. It is the Transcendent Signified, especially as exemplified in the Logos [the second divine Person, in whom, for Scripture and the doctrinal tradition, all things were made] that weds Western representational thought to signifiers.[14]

The Word incarnate renders the absent God present; in Christ the signifier *par excellence*, God the signified (equally *par excellence*) is perfectly expressed. Such a supremely successful act of the sensuous 'presencing' of an absence, an act duly represented in the language of the New Testament, furnishes the final validation of a logorhythmic world where the patterns of language give access to nature in its actual order and course. Derrida attacks the gospel not by frontal attack on theistic or incarnational belief but by hacking away at one of its crucial mooring-ropes: the notion that the sign really is a signifier for the absent-now-present.

Since Derrida's theory of the word is intended not merely to disturb the metaphysical tradition, awakening it to a clearer sense of its limitations, but rather to destroy that entire ('onto-semio-theological') tradition root-and-branch, to give a lodging to his philosophy, even in the ante-chamber of theology, produces more than simply a renewal of that 'apophaticism' – negative theology – practised in their different ways by both the Greek Fathers and many of the Western mediaeval divines. The classic theologies of the Church have all shunned conceptual idolatry where the divine mystery is concerned, but that is not to say that they have wished to sever the bond between human language, in its referring power, and what God is. It is notable that Jean-Luc Marion, the one contemporary Catholic theologian, otherwise unmistakably orthodox in his thinking, who went furthest to meet what is acceptable (concern for genuine 'otherness') in Derrida's work, has found himself obliged to backtrack under criticism from (in particular) the French disciples of Thomas. To say that the God of Being has been made, historically, the 'prisoner' of Being can readily be shown to be a travesty; rather, the language of Being is placed precisely at the service of the divine liberality.

The Other proclaimed by postmodernism, whether in its atheistic form, with Derrida, or in its theistic form, with Emmanuel Levinas, a believing and practising, if theologically unconventional, Jew, is fairly flaccid, indeed, when compared with the being, whether divine or worldly, of traditional metaphysics, and the ethics that flow therefrom. As Gabriel Josipovici has remarked, shrewdly if sardonically, on Levinas' exalted reputation in the 1990s:

[t]he ... mixture of banal modernist postures and the apparent retrieval of long-buried Jewish traditions had been music to the ears of French and American intellectuals with a bad conscience and the desire to embrace an Other who does not actually require too much readjustment of their own intellectual and affective lives.[15]

Though the language of alterity is lacking, there is as much if not more marvelling at 'others' in so unpretentious an expression of the *philosophia perennis* as Aristotle's *De partibus animalium*. Distinguishing the 'heavenly bodies' (the eternal world) from those kinds of things (here below) that 'are brought into being and perish', Aristotle in his praise of both is the very opposite of a 'homogenising totaliser' who would smother otherness by the capriciousness of his own ego.

Each of the two groups has its attractiveness. For although our grasp of the eternal things is but slight, nevertheless the joy which it brings is, by reason of their excellence and worth, greater than that of knowing all things that are here below, just as the joy of a fleeting and partial glimpse of those who we love is much greater than that of an accurate view of other things, no matter how numerous or how great they are.

And on the lowlier beings among whom we live, the same note of wonder is struck:

So far as in us lies, we will not leave out any one of them be it ever so mean; for though there are animals which have no attractiveness for the senses, yet for the eye of science, for the student who is naturally of a philosophic spirit and can discern the causes of things, Nature which fashioned them provides joys that cannot be measured ... Therefore we must not betake ourselves to the consideration of the meaner animals with bad grace, as though we were children, since in all natural things there is something of the marvellous. There is a story that tells how some visitors once wished to meet Heracleitus, and when they entered and saw him in the kitchen, warming himself at the stove, they hesitated; but Heracleitus said, 'Come in; don't be afraid; there are gods even here'. In like manner, we ought not to hesitate nor be abashed, but boldly to enter upon our researches concerning animals of every sort and kind, knowing that in not one of them is Nature or Beauty lacking.[16]

Certainly the lack of a philosophical doctrine of nature consigns these postmodern asystematic 'systems' in their ethical respects to the mercies of a Kantian formalism whose injunctions, now recast in terms of respecting alterity in general, seem remarkably vague.

## With Aquinas to metaphysics' heart

In times of philosophical disorientation (not to say near-insanity), the Catholic tradition has instinctively turned for steadying to Thomas Aquinas. The present juncture is just such a time.

We can begin by noting the sanity of Thomas' approach to the entire philosophy/theology relationship. On the one hand, barely above water as the human race is in a sea of conflicting philosophical currents, revelation lets down a life-craft by indicating to us an ontology and epistemology – an account of being and mind – compatible with truth since compatible with itself. It is up to theology, in this sense, to elaborate a philosophy consistent with revelation. On the other hand, human nature, even wounded human nature, is not incapable of reaching valid metaphysical truths, even truths about divine being. The Church as teacher encounters in culture already recognised truths that are congruent with her wisdom, just as Christ, *the* Teacher, met scribes who answered him well and whom he declared to be not far from the Kingdom. It is up to theology, in this sense, to accept graciously, as from without, philosophy's *freely rendered* services as handmaid. (Thus the axiom *ancilla theologae sed non ancilla nisa libera*: philosophy is theology's handmaid, but only if she is *free*.)[17]

Coming on to the substance – the word is apt – of St Thomas' philosophy, the service Thomas can still do for the life of the mind is well captured in these words of an erstwhile pupil at his school:

> In his theological ordering of truth as a whole, Thomas proceeded as a metaphysician, so that his theological order exhibits not only the surface structure of a formal, logical kind, but also a deeper order of a metaphysical kind . . . What things really are is capable of being understood as an intelligible order, an order of subordinate orders. What makes Thomas permanently valuable is his recognition that . . . being, truth and meaning are indefinitely diverse and yet (this is the ultimate mystery) that being does disclose itself in meaning. . . . Thomas' genuine and permanent originality was to display the internal consistency of a view of the world in which the world effortlessly shows itself for what it is, flowers into the light.[18]

A rebirth of ontological thinking, after this manner, is what we need, and it is St Thomas' peculiar gift of drawing together the master-idea of creation with the *oeuvre* not only of Aristotle but also of Plato (a more primordial yet sometimes neglected element in the presentation of his thought) that enables him to be, in successive ages, its midwife. 'The True, The Good, the One, Being Itself, Beauty: these are the eternal lamps of Platonism, which alone make possible human thinking, even the kind of thinking that denies them.'[19] To the *truth of being*, that pre-eminently Platonic theme, Thomas added Aristotle's characteristic concern with the *becoming of being* – where the concept of causality is pervasively invoked as a humble newcomer to the circle of the transcendental ideas, those 'eternal lamps'. The mystery of being as this founds becoming makes itself present to the world, and to our awareness, in a fashion at once hidden yet expressive, through *causality*. But the idea of causality, once disengaged in its full dimensions, is also pertinent to discourse about the truth of being too – for it helps us to think through the greatest problem encountered by such discourse, the issue of the one and the many, being's unity and multiplicity, its differentiated yet unified *order*.

The reality of the multiple, the reality of becoming – these are explicable only in terms of a radical novelty in being, the idea of which enters philosophical thought with the revealed doctrine of creation. In modern times, such 'novelty' which springs in fact from the divine liberty, has been ascribed rather (above all in Hegel's philosophy) to awareness where it reappeared as the spontaneity of 'spirit'. After the failure of Hegel's panentheism, philosophy renounced concern with the truth of being, a renunciation variously expressed in neo-positivism, dialectical materialism and atheistic existentialism. But beyond all crassly deterministic (and all merely analytic) accounts of finite reality (manifold, ever becoming) lies still to be accounted for the source of such being in a synthesis of unity and multiplicity, plenary being and becoming. And this is the moment of free genesis which is to be found only in the creative act of God.[20]

The notion of participation which, as recent Christian metaphysicians have stressed, is as key to a sound ontology in general as it is to Thomas' work in particular, expresses the mode of being of finite beings. If we ask, in what do finite beings participate (precisely by being in the finite mode) the answer must be in that creative Source from which causal efficacy in the universe flows and to which final causality (the causality of the intrinsic purposiveness of things) draws us back. Western thought has managed to reduce ontology to a philosophy of knowledge – an account of the status of objects of knowledge (in Hegel 'being' is the self-awareness of the experiencing subject – the absolute impersonal subject of his system). Actually, it is *relation to the divine Logos* that establishes the truth of beings, whereas Western thought now recognises only that derivative sense of truth and falsity which belongs with the examination of what is created. Truth, like Christian orthodoxy, is rooted in the doctrine of creation.[21]

Not to know this is to forget the nothingness which the creature is 'before' and 'outside' the divine creative act, i.e. what the creature would be were that act for even one instant to fail. Such nothingness attests the infinite indigence of the creature – and the infinite power of God, as also his infinite reality whose dynamic richness alone can overcome the creature's poverty. That is what Kierkegaard famously called the 'infinite qualitative difference' between the Creator and the creature. Thomism alludes to that difference by its distinction between *esse* and *essentia*, being and the way being is found in limited form in concrete things. By participation, creatures depend wholly on the gift of *esse*, on which the created order is founded. The 'act of being', *actus essendi*, is intimately present to essences: this is the 'inside' of that relationship whose 'outside' we describe as 'creation' or the total dependence of the finite on the Infinite. *Esse* expresses either the fullness of the act whereby God possesses himself by essence, or (in the case of creatures) the quiescence at the heart of every existent of the participated primordial energy which raises the creature above nothingness.[22] This primal act that is being is the act at the heart of every other kind of acting: transcendental participation in being unifies in diversified fashion all the multitudinous action that goes on at every level – from the behaviour of a subatomic particle to the most delicate movements of mind and will that a novelist with the fastidiousness of a Henry James could chronicle.

While being is in one sense utterly straightforward and incontrovertible (perception, after all, already puts us in immediate contact with existence or reality), in another sense being is in its multiform expression bewilderingly profuse. Caught in the webs of a huge variety of languages – those for instance of logic, mathematics, and the sciences; of prose and poetry and common speech – its full determination belongs with a metaphysic open to the foundational creation event. The Italian Thomist ontologist Cornelio Fabro has written:

> This *esse* is the point of convergence, of completion and foundation, of every other aspect of being in its relation to reality. It is for this reason too that *esse* receives the essential and distinctive qualification of first and last 'act'. It is the single act which can and must exist 'separately': it is thus God himself . . . Creatures are inasmuch as they have participated *esse*, that profound and motionless act, not directly accessible either perceptually or formally.[23]

What is immanent is precisely the transcendent (the opposite of pantheism).[24] This Chesterton grasped.

Elder father, though thine eyes
Shine with hoary mysteries,
Canst thou tell me what in the heart
Of a cowslip blossom lies?

Smaller than all lives that be,
Secret as the deepest sea,
Stands a little house of seeds,
Like an elfin's granary.

Speller of the stones and weeds,
Skilled in Nature's crafts and creeds,
Tell me what is in the heart
Of the smallest of the seeds.

God Almighty, and with Him
Cherubim and Seraphim,
Filling all eternity
Adonai Elohim.[25]

The Aristotelian account of causal becoming had really been limited to sensuous becoming – the becoming of sensible things that come into existence only to pass away again. Plato's thought – through the key concept of participation – enabled Thomas to incorporate the Aristotelian account of becoming into a structure of transcendental causality held together by the primordial universal Origin of all forms, all activity. Beings are dependent on *esse*, the many on the One, just as correlatively the explanation of the existence of beings which in their multiplicity become what they are turns on the prior reality of the transcendent Good in its desire to communicate itself to what is not (the Form of the Good in Plato re-conceptualised, in the light of the biblical disclosure of God). The doctrine of creation enabled Thomas to surmount both the closed transcendence of Plato, and the closed immanence of Aristotle. The Platonic 'Idea' becomes the active principle of things in God, while the Good becomes the origin of all causality.[26]

Though created beings are true causes at their own level of operation, transcendental causality – as its name suggests – goes beyond this or, if one prefers, precedes it, is presupposed by it. It has three moments: creation; conservation; and the divine moving of creatures according to their own proper operations. The truth of the creation idea imposes itself once it is realised how *esse* is the supreme intensive act, what is most universal, most common yet most formal, most intimate yet most profound in whatever is and acts. It is *sheer gift*, for the presence of *esse* in creatures is absolutely gratuitous.[27] Yet all immanent causality – all the causal power that creatures can exert – is founded upon this giftedness. That is true of spiritual causes, the causal activity of beings endowed with intellect and will, quite as much as it is of material causes. The causal activities of spirited beings can be said to be 'necessary' inasmuch as the formal object of intellect and will is pre-given – it is the real as the intelligible and the real as the good, respectively. But their activities are free in that they choose their last ends. No particular good – which is also a good by participation – can, however, move the will to seek the universal unparticipated good which is God, so here the freedom of the will that would do just that must itself be set in motion by transcendental causality. The distinctively human world of causation cannot be fully described, therefore, without reference to God's *grace*.

## Metaphysics and morals

If a renewed metaphysic is the chief blessing that a 'fourth Thomism', which has learned the lessons of the postmodern assault on modernity, can teach us, it needs always to be remembered that for Thomists being and action are intimately one. *Agere sequitur esse*, asserts Thomas' maxim, and so ethics for Thomists – as for orthodox Christianity at large – are not to be regarded as a non-ontological aspect of philosophy. On the contrary, the truth of acting (moral truth) cannot be had without the truth of being (ontological truth) just as the effect of the Incarnation of the Word and the outpouring of the Spirit was the provision for fresh resources for human activity (including of course worshipping and therefore contemplative activity) in the world.

The most popular form of the assumption that moral truth is simply not to be had was seen off quite some while ago by Chesterton – that formally untutored yet incomparably intuitive admirer of St Thomas. To reject the idea of moral truth on the grounds that opinions about it are varied and manifold is no more reasonable than to take the fact that some people thought the earth flat, others round, as ground that one is 'free to say that it is triangular, or hexagonal, or a rhomboid', or 'has no shape at all, or that its shape can never be discovered'. 'The world must be some shape, and it must be that shape and no other; and it is not self-evident that nobody can possibly hit on the right one.'[28] So too with the moral life. The 'shape' of that life is best laid out as a pattern of virtues that truly human living should unfold – and the revival of 'virtue ethics' in contemporary moral philosophy (here the convert to Catholicism Alasdair MacIntyre is perhaps the outstanding name) amounts to a vindication of the classical Christian approach in these matters. But just as MacIntyre has insisted that the point of the good, and the rationale of the virtues, cannot be fully seen except within a corporate tradition where that good has been exhibited through the actual flourishing of those virtues (and this is the foundation for his version of the call for a renewed Christendom, linked in his work with the hope for a new St Benedict), so, in the light of the Thomist tradition we can say that a metaphysics (and not just a social politics) of morals is needed in order to demonstrate how in drawing on the virtues the human person invests their being in the moral *act* (hence the pertinence of the analogous hope for a new St Thomas as well!).

In current culture, the nerve of moral effort often seems semi-severed by such factors as: assumptions of scientific and social determinism (so people cannot be different from what they are); the politically correct absolute of respecting individuals by forbidding interference with the life-options of others (so we should not try to make people different from what they are); and the saturation of awareness by the mass media (so people are in any case unsure of what they are). It thus becomes imperative to bring out (as the ethics of Pope John Paul II has tried to do) the 'decisional character of ethical life': how it is 'deliberately lived-out human action', and this requires from a realist metaphysics that we come to grasp how the person is a 'causal originator of ethical action', without which our experience of responsibility is inexplicable.[29] And the vital importance of all this is that it is by ethical acts that persons become good – or, through unethical actions, evil. Yet it is hard to see how persons could become morally realised – qualified in a new way in their own reality – unless the being of the good became *synthesised with themselves* in a new mode. Metaphysical realism is needful if human beings are to take nobility as their natural goal. In a morally debilitated age (one only has to think of the often reported absence of a moral dimension from much State education), a Christian philosophy has to put such nobility – the natural analogue of sanctity – before people with all the persuasiveness it can command.

As we saw in the last chapter, on 'reviving doctrinal consciousness', it is never sufficient for a Christian thinker to remain perpetually on the philosophical level – the level of what is accessible by way of metaphysical analysis and phenomenological exploration of our common humanity alone. In the economy of the saving revelation centred on Jesus Christ, the triune God deepens our human interiority by opening it to himself. 'In the communion of grace with the Trinity, man's "living area" is broadened and lifted up to the supernatural level of divine life.'[30] In this, a special place is held in the Catholic under-standing by the Mother of God who, thanks to her unique receptivity to the triune God's gracing man in Christ, formed the locus of these changed dimensions. By her faith 'first at the Annunciation and then fully at the foot of the Cross, an *interior space* was opened up within humanity which the eternal Father can fill "with every spiritual blessing".'[31] So far from producing an 'acosmism', a denial of the goods of creation and history, our engracement – because it is a deeper radication in the divine love – expands the outreach of human beings to their fellows and all creation. In the next chapter we shall see how the biblical revelation, read in the light of tradition and with philosophy's help, affects our understanding of that wide form of community that is civil society, and the State.

## NOTES

1. G. E. M. Anscombe, 'Twenty Opinions Common among Anglo-American Philosophers', in A. Ansaldo (ed.), *Persona, verità e morale* (Rome, 1986), pp. 49–50.

2. See H. T. Engelhardt, Jr, 'Some Persons are Humans, Some Humans are Persons, and the World is what we Persons make it', in S. C. Spiker and H. T. Engelhardt (eds.), *Philosophical Medical Ethics* (Boston, 1977), pp. 183–94.

3. L. Dupré, *Passage to Modernity. An Essay in the Hermeneutics of Nature and Culture* (New Haven, 1993).

4. T. Guarino, *Revelation and Truth: Unity and Plurality in Contemporary Theology* (Scranton, 1993), pp. 38–56.

5. Guarino, 'Postmodernity and Five Fundamental Theological Issues', *Theological Studies* 57.4 (1996), pp. 659–60.

6. C. Spretnak, *States of Grace. The Recovery of Meaning in the Postmodern Age* (San Francisco, 1993), p. 12.

7. See, e.g. J. Habermas, *Postmetaphysical Thinking* (ET Cambridge, Mass., 1992); D. S. Browning and F. Schüssler Fiorenza (eds.), *Habermas, Modernity and Public Theology* (New York, 1992) .

8. R. Sokolowski, 'Knowing Essentials', *Review of Metaphysics* XLVII.4 (1994), pp. 691–709, and here at p. 696.

9. Guarino, 'Postmodernity', p. 669.

10. Guarino, *Revelation and Truth*, pp. 166–78.

11. J. Caputo, 'Gadamer's Closet Essentialism', in D. F. Michaelfelder and R. E. Palmer (eds.), *Dialogue and Deconstruction. The Gadamer-Derrida Encounter* (Albany, 1989), pp. 258–64.

12. W. Hill, O.P., *The Three-Personed God* (Washington, 1982), p. 246.

13. G. Hull, *The Banished Heart. Origins of Heteropraxis in the Catholic Church* (Sydney, 1995), p. xii.

14. T. Guarino, 'Postmodernity', p. 674.

15. Reviewing M.-A. Lescouret, *Emmanuel Levinas* (Paris, 1994), in *Times Literary Supplement*, 27 January 1995.

16. Aristotle, *De partibus animalium*, I. 5, 644b23.

17. A failure to realise what may be called this 'asymmetric equilibrium' (for assuredly revelation, and so faith, enjoy priority vis-à-vis the human sciences) damages (along with similar unilateralisms) Géry Prouvost's *Thomas d'Aquin et les thomismes. Essai sur l'histoire des thomismes* (Paris, 1996).

18. C. Ernst, O.P., 'Seven Hundred Years of Thomas Aquinas', *The Listener*, 10 October 1974, p. 480.

19. N. D. O'Donoghue, O.C.D., 'Edwin Muir: the Untutored Mystic', *Chesterton Review* XIII 4 (1997), p. 469.

20. See C. Fabro, *Participation et causalité selon s. Thomas d'Aquin* (Paris, 1958).

21. W. Kasper, *Theology and Church* (ET New York, 1987), pp. 135–6: the ontological truth created by God grounds the finite grasp on truth of humankind.

22. *Summa Theologiae*, Ia., q. 61, 1: 'Every thing that is by participation is caused by that which is by essence' – an argument, in context, that the holy angels, despite their lack of matter-form composition, must have been created by God.

23. Fabro, *Participation et causalité*, p. 76.

24. See my *Epiphany. A Theological Introduction to Catholicism* (Collegeville, Minn., 1996), pp. 11–13.

25. G. K. Chesterton, 'The Holy of Holies' in *Collected Poems* (London, 1937⁶), pp. 343–4.

26. *Summa Theologiae*, Ia, q. 49, a. 4.

27. Ibid., q. 104, a. 3.

28. G. K. Chesterton, *All Is Grist* (New York, 1932), pp. 7–8.

29. K. L. Schmitz, *At the Center of the Human Drama. The Philosophical Anthropology of Karol Woytyla/Pope John Paul II* (Washington, 1993), pp. 44–6.

30. John Paul II, *Dominum et Vivificantem*, II.4.59.

31. John Paul II, *Redemptoris Mater*, II.1.28 with an internal citation of Ephesians 1.3.

# VI

# *Reimagining the Christendom State*

THE hymn *Te saeculorum principem*, used at first Vespers on the feast of Christ the King, was mysteriously deprived of several of its verses in the reform of the Liturgy of the Hours which followed the Second Vatican Council. They include the following stanzas:

> May nations' rulers you profess
> And in a public worship bless;
> May teachers, judges, you revere,
> In Arts and Laws may this appear.
>
> Let every royal standard shine
> In homage to your power divine;
> Beneath your gentle rule subdue
> The homes of all, their countries, too.
>
> All glory be, O Lord, to you,
> All earthly powers you subdue;
> With Father and the Spirit be
> All glory yours eternally.[1]

Lest it should be thought that the reasons were stylistic or otherwise fortuitous, the same principle of emendation – the removal of reference to the 'social reign of Jesus Christ', the Christendom State – has been applied to the Matins hymn *Aeterna Imago Altissimi* (now found at Lauds), the original Lauds hymn of the feast of the Kingship of Christ (a version of the *Vexilla regis*, now suppressed in its entirety) and the Collect of the day, where it is no longer the 'families of nations' (*familiae gentium*) over whom Christ is called to rule but *tota creatura* – 'every creature', or perhaps, as the official English translation has it, 'the whole of creation'. The conversion of the political into the cosmic is not, of course, a retrenchment of the reign of Christ – quite the contrary! And yet the modulation – from polis to cosmos – merits its own comment.

71

## Biblical foundations

As the Anglican Evangelical theologian – close to Catholicism on moral teaching – Oliver O'Donovan has pointed out, the 'ground' for speaking of human political authority in the biblical revelation is *the divine rule*.[2] For Scripture, God's rule is what gives authority to those actions in which men and women are summoned to act on behalf of others in their name, as well as for themselves. Those acts are precisely *political* acts, acts where we engage the destinies of fellow-members of the polis in what we say and do. O'Donovan is clear, however, that this *biblical* concept of political authority is not to be counterposed to that more universal concept which the speculative tradition in the Church has rooted in *natural law*. The history of the divine rule, unfolded in the historic revelation, is disclosed as both a safeguarding and a redeeming of the goods of creation. More weighty, then, than issues of structure and office in a Christian political theory (though these are not negligible) is the matter of the conditions of such political acting, its purpose, and its *modus agendi* or way of being exercised.

The New Testament was not addressed to a polis – a city or nation, but to a diaspora of communities of the Church. The Old Testament, by contrast, envisages a people. Discontinuities, needless to say, rupture any seamless passage from the Elder Covenant to the Gospel. Yet these discontinuities must be read within that ampler continuity which makes the New Testament to be 'Sacred Scripture' only within the unity of the Canon – and so in its relation to the Old (just as the Elder Covenant is, for Christians, Scripture in that fashion too). Christian tradition has been justified, accordingly, ever since the patristic period, in seeking in the Hebrew Bible illumination for a theology of the polis. Or as O'Donovan puts it, in terms indebted perhaps to Balthasar with his 'theodramatics', it was Israel that constituted for Jesus, as for his followers, 'the theatre of God's self-disclosure as the ruler of nations'.[3] Commenting on the discussion of Israel's hope in Romans 2, O'Donovan continues; 'The public tradition of Israel carries an unrealised promise for the full socialisation of God's believing people, the appearing, as another prophet puts it, of the New Jerusalem from heaven.'[4] Like many writers on these topics, O'Donovan distinguishes between authority and power. 'Power is our broadest term for the capacity to get things done, be this by force, by persuasion or by "authority"'. 'Authority' is an altogether more interesting term. Without ceasing to be a means of power, it is also, and fundamentally, a mediation of the good – a most mysterious mediation whereby the good appears to us as imposition or constraint (for it may well prevent our following ends of our 'private' action that are clearly good for us), and yet for all that is really our good, the intelligible end of our free acting.

When the ancient people of God proclaimed that 'The Lord is king', so O'Donovan explains, political and religious meaning were inseparably united in an implicit concept of authority which did not suffer from the deficiencies of the Western secular notion thereof since Rousseau, nor from the failings of the (very different) theistic idea of the late Middle Ages and on. The cry 'The Lord is king' summoned Israel to a fulfilment that was at once beyond her yet corresponded to the *true end* of human beings. As such it was not alien to the human – unlike the 'absolute power' Ockham ascribed to the Deity (a fair enough description of God 'before' he puts forth his creating activity, but a travesty of his Providence, where he is always faithful to his creative purpose). But equally, such authority does not imply, as Rousseau's civil authority does, a human will divided against itself, my will at once consenting to institutions and yet chafing against their demands. The early kings of Israel – Saul, David – were, O'Donovan suggests, actually only 'kings' in Israelite thought because of some relation to the divine exertion of authority thus understood.[5] In other words, the human title 'king', not the divine one, may be, in this context, the more strictly metaphorical of the two. The divine judgements, disclosed by God in revelation history, are possessed and pondered on by the faithful people or their representatives and become in this way a resource for future action. And this leads O'Donovan to his central assertion in a scripturally based theology of the political: 'Political authority arises where power, the execution of right and the perpetuation of tradition are assured together in one co-ordinated agency. When one of the three is separated from the others, there can be no authority.'[6] Merely intending to unite these three factors does not of itself guarantee, of course, that they will be so united. A role must be left here for divine Providence, the regime of history – of world history, as well as of any intra-societal history – to take a hand. The task of a society is to acknowledge when this coincidence occurs – to *recognise* due authority, *not* to constitute it, for in the axiom of both Bible and natural law thinking, long part of the Church's teaching, such authority is more fundamentally *bestowed* by God. As Professor Stephen Clark has put it, 'State-authority is what emerges when households, clans and crafts first recognise a sacred centre in their lives together and then forget where the centre gets its authority . . . The voice of the High God reminds us that the land is his.'[7] That connection between politics and religion never, in human culture, entirely goes away. For O'Donovan the doctrine that *we* set up political authority, as a device to secure our own essentially private, local and unpolitical purposes, has left the Western democracies in a state of pervasive moral debilitation, which, from time to time, inevitably throws up idolatrous and authoritarian reactions.[8]

A regime's authority is a mediation of divine authority but we also note how for the Hebrew Bible any human regime is subject to the *law's* authority, which furnishes independent testimony to the divine command. Though, for O'Donovan, Israel did not generate a concept of 'natural law' (it was through Israel's own prophetic vocation that God revealed his will to her), nonetheless, as the prophetic writings witness, she knew of a law which could and did bind the Gentiles in a universal way. (A Catholic writer, more willing to give the sapiential books of the Old Testament their full place in the Canon, would expect to see some discussion of the Wisdom literature here, and explain the 'witness' to natural law thinking of such prophets as Isaiah of Jerusalem by their access to the kind of understanding that literature represents.)

A law that embodied that divine will and way could find expression among the ancient people of God by other routes than the policies of rulers. That ampler law could emerge, for instance, as individuals presented their grievances, or thanks to the wise insight of good counsellors, and last but not least through the figures we call 'prophets'. The conscience of such individuals constitutes a repository of the moral understanding which formed their community in the first place, and in a situation of breakdown, partial or quasi-total, may enable a community to renew itself and survive. The 'sovereignty' of the State or of the people in modern theories, in so far as they correspond to valid principles, do so as expressions of fragments belonging within what is properly a theological whole.

O'Donovan's discussion of how, in Israel, the community becomes actively related to the shaping power of the divine righteousness could easily seem, as hitherto expounded, somewhat individualistic in tenor. Is it never the sense of the community at large and that of its customarily recognised leaders which is the bearer of justice? Doubtless so as to dispel this negative impression, he warns against the idea that Scripture might support a doctrine of diffused authority in the civil order if this is understood to mean that Scripture ratifies, or even connives at, the establishment, as some kind of ideal, of multiple centres of competing power.[9] The excessive diffusion of power like the lack of power are just as much evils as are power's over-concentration or abuse. (A point which Western liberalism, whose representatives rarely live in societies hamstrung in the former fashions, has difficulty in comprehending.)

With the Incarnation, and the appearance of Jesus as the Christ, all the hopes and expectations once vested in the *re*-appearance of the traditional monarchical leadership became, for his disciples, focused on him. The rule of God as power exercised against such enemies of community as disease, want, and angelic evil; judgement against the governing establishment of Israel in favour of the poor (in various though allied senses) and such 'lost sheep' as the tax-collectors; and the reconstitution of the community through the mission of the disciples and the new ethos which they were, as professional rememberers of Jesus' teaching, to proclaim: all this was dawning in his person.

## A post-Ascension State

As we know, the aims of Jesus the incarnate Word of God to humankind were achieved only by the cross and resurrection in which the Father, by his all-wise plan, brought them to fulfilment. The traditional teaching of Catholicism that the polis – the organised community – has the duty, as has each individual, to resituate itself in terms of this climax of the Creator's redemptive plan (the Catholic, or, as I prefer to phrase it, the *Christendom* State) raises the question of whether this transcendent fulfilment of the hope of Israel, at once spiritual and cosmic, has anything to do with the political as usually understood. Secular (O'Donovan terms them 'classical republican') theorists would deny it. But, as he asks:

> By what right is the term 'political' claimed exclusively for the defence of social structures which refuse the deeper spiritual and cosmic aspirations of mankind? The price to be paid by classical republicanism is that of pitting political order against human fulfil-ment, of making the polis constitutionally hostile to philosophy, theology, and artistic vision . . . A 'pure' political theory which can make it a matter of intellectual conscience to disinterest oneself in the transcendent is not one that any humane thinker need feel guilt about rejecting.[10]

That would be, indeed, the primary apologia I would offer for a post-Liberal State. O'Donovan adds two further considerations, one negative, the other positive. Negatively, a civil order open, even in its govern-mental apparatus, to the strange victory of crucified Love in the seating at the Father's right hand is an order open at the same time to the prophetic criticism of all existing human arrangements – which can only be provisional until we catch up with the Exalted One at his Parousia. Speaking more generally we can say that before the twentieth century the higher reference which political communities have recognised – Arab caliphates, Western nations, the Chinese empire – not only sustained and justified governments. It admonished them as well. More positively, O'Donovan goes on, public recognition of the *Sessio* – the crown rights of the Redeemer – draws the attention of those governing to the way God's rule is realised in the Church, Christ's body, for this, as the organ of his redemptive, indeed, recreative reign cannot now be omitted in any statement of the ends of man. The kingly rule of the divine-human mediator, representative of God to men and of men to God, is 'God's own rule exercised over the whole world . . . visible in the Church . . . but not only there'.

And so the question becomes, if the authority of the risen Christ is present in the Church's mission, 'to what extent is secular authority compatible with this mission and, so to speak, re-authorised by it?'[11] For should not secular authority now simply *give way to* that of Christ-in-the Church, granted that his universally representative, redemptive act climaxed in his Ascension when, by sitting at the Father's right hand, he was publicly vindicated (before angels and men) as bearer of the definitive rule of God? Here at last is a public community-related authority that *increases* freedom rather than taking it away, just because it is eschatological, salvific. Political representation should, to some degree, always achieve this, multiplying freedom not subtracting from it. But that arithmetic, so often deficient, is now at last supremely exemplified in the kingship of Jesus Christ. And so the argument will be of course that civil authority, after the Ascension, must bear *some* relation to this event.

'The subjection of the nations' is Professor O'Donovan's account of these further implications – and one readily sees with how much greater seriousness he takes the crown rights of the Redeemer than did the reformers of the Roman Liturgy in the 1960s and 70s. 'Nations shall come to your light and kings to the brightness of your rising' (Isa. 60.3). The Church's primary *credendum* about the State is, in Paul's words in Colossians (2.15), 'He [God] disarmed the principalities and powers and made a public example of them, triumphing over them in [Christ].' This may mean *either* a relative marginalisation of the State whose function becomes now primarily the uncomplicated one of judging its citizens by appropriate praise or blame (Rom. 13.1–7), and through its peace and order, not least in international relations, providing suitable space for the Church's development (1 Tim. 1–3); *or*, as Balthasar has developed so powerfully in the closing volumes of his *Theodramatik* an infuriated self-apotheosis by the civil authority, faced as this is with the alternative of submission to the reign of God in Christ (very much the perspective of the Johannine Apocalypse).

The gospel truth in that *terminus technicus* of Latin ecclesiology, the notion of the ecclesial body as a 'perfect society', is that the Church has her own independent authority, derived directly from the ascended Christ, and not at the disposal of any earthly ruler – as the mediaeval papalists, by their essentially Christological doctrine of the pope's authority vis-à-vis kings and governors, affirmed. The grace given by Christ in the Spirit to the universal episcopate under its papal head is on the Catholic view a chief – though not the only (any of the people can prophesy!) – key to the maintenance of this autonomy. So a Catholic cannot concur in O'Donovan's view that 'the identity of the Church is given wholly and completely in the relation of its members to the ascended Christ independently of Church ministry and organisation'.[12]

A Catholic can agree with O'Donovan, however, when he writes that the 'power' of the Church is her 'effective enablement to be . . . the community of God's rule, manifesting his Kingdom to the world'.[13] Should it not be a consequence of her missionary vitality that those who bear civil rule in post-Ascension society should bow to the throne of Christ? The secular power belongs with the order of creation. It is a helpful and even an indispensable condition of natural sociality. But its time is limited, its dispositions provisional, for the Kingdom of God is coming in fullness with a view to the comprehensive transfiguration of humankind, our ultimate flourishing. And should not Christians rejoice if the carriers and representatives of political power become attentive beforetime to the final disposition of the human good? If they seek to realise that good by anticipation within the limits that the contingency of the world and the continuing effects of sin allow?

Let us distinguish this position from 'neo-mediaevalism'. Whatever the possibilities of successful evangelical awakening among the churches, it is unlikely that the national society of, for instance, the United Kingdom will not in the future be more credally heterogeneous than any mediaeval society in the West. We are not speaking of a fully homogeneous society which simply possesses two foci of authority – *regnum*, 'the kingdom', and *sacerdotium*, the 'priestly', i.e. episcopal, power. And in any case, the more subtle awareness of not only the need but also the intrinsic interest of working out a public relation of Christian authority to, for instance, rationalist agnostics at one end of the spectrum, followers of the Eastern religions at the other, which has characterised the modern epoch in the Church would forbid so undifferentiated a scheme. (The positive relation of a Christendom State to Jewry would be especially important here.) That notion of a multiple, differentiated responsibility of the rulers of a post-Ascension society to citizens variously placed vis-à-vis the natural and supernatural orders would also tend to absolve such rulers from the temptation of assuming a proprietary attitude towards the Church herself. No one who loves the Church, with her full range of institutions founded by Christ, would want to see her subjected to a new Babylonian captivity by publicly Christian lay rulers. On the other hand, within the totality of Spirit-given charisms in the Church, may not some be bestowed on Christians with the (natural) vocation of servants of the common polis? If so, this would be precisely with a view to maturing the judgement of such men (and women) in exercising the royal and universal priesthood of the baptised in an age of salvation where the State has no full consistency save in relation to Christ. And could not the (natural and supernatural) prudence of such statesmen be appropriately engaged in the deliberations of bishops and popes? Professor O'Donovan would make a sharp separation here between 'vocation', defined as a social situation within which someone is called in Christ, and 'charism', seen as a spiritual gift which forms part of the Spirit's working in the Church. Yet *Apostolicam actuositatem*, the Decree of the Second Vatican Council on the Apostolate of the Laity, speaks of the reception of charismata as generating for each believer the 'right and duty' to use them not only in the Church but 'in the world', 'for the good of mankind and for the upbuilding of the Church' – giving as ultimate *raison d'être* of this state of affairs the fact that 'it has pleased God to unite all things, both natural and supernatural, in Christ Jesus "that in all things he may have the first place"'.[14] The coronation rite, as still used in O'Donovan's own communion, the Church of England, points in this same direction – and in a culture where the symbolism of Christian monarchy was functioning healthily it would act as a sacramental archetype of all consecrated service of the natural community made through the Word and made for its own super-fulfilment in him incarnate.

What could be the gains of strengthening or reintroducing elements of a Christendom order? Do they include gains which even those who only have an imaginative or sympathetic, not a confessional and committed, attitude to Christian virtues and *credenda* might welcome? First, secular authority requires truth of some kind to ground its claim – and here at any rate is a possible truth! If the State is merely a massive administrative enterprise, those who wield the State power can hardly expect anyone to die for it. Only if the State is also a sacred guardian of beliefs and values that are precious could such a demand reasonably be made.[15] Second, there may well be virtues – compassion, say or co-responsibility – which may be hard to commend outside of the Christian narrative since their ontological underpinning is only given conspicuously with particular aspects of revealed understanding: the divine pity, for instance, or the communion of saints. Equally important here are the vices that Christianity finds special rationale for discouraging – one of which, *pleonexia*, the tendency always to want more, may yet cripple modern civil society, after all.[16] Alasdair MacIntyre, indeed, has argued that Western people did not first cease to believe in God and subsequently withdrew their consent from the morality defended by the Church. Rather, they lost any global agreement on their manner of living together and only subsequently rejected the authority of the Church.[17] Of course, if this be true, then, not only will it be the case that the response to the gospel's preaching which is a Christendom society requires (as already conceded) the re-evangelisation of majorities; it will also be the case that only putting (or retaining) in place *some* features of a Christendom society, with its particular configuration of practical reason, can render evangelical believing possible again on a demographically massive scale. Third, by dint of its convictions about both the aboriginal created order, on the one hand, and, on the other, the ultimate end of man, God in Christ, an effective Christendom society could free the modern democratic State from the debilitating consequences of its own history and nature – of, indeed, its own success.

## Saving the State from itself

How so? The modern democracies (with the exception hitherto of Britain which seems poised, however, to exchange its own legitimation narrative, based on the common law and the historic evolution of the Crown in Parliament, for one on the American or French Revolutionary model) look back for their genealogy to the ancient republics, from which they draw their democratic charter, and the empire of Late Antiquity from which they take their theory of sovereignty. It is precisely the amalgamation of the two into the concept (and practice) of popular sovereignty which produces that most dangerous of all monsters – a tyrant with the force of a majority behind him. For the early twentieth-century Thomist philosopher of the civil good, Jacques Maritain, by contrast, the 'prince' of St Thomas' political writings was precisely *not* called a 'sovereign' because the latter term – properly used only of the Lordship of the divine rule achieved in the exalted Christ – conflates the human and the divine, the natural and super-natural orders in an illegitimate way.[18] The omnicompetent State, technically efficient, of modern times, has the effect, so thought Maritain's contemporary, the Jewish convert to Catholic belief, Simone Weil, of deracinating people by tending to replace, rather than confirm, other attachments – the extended family, one's profession, village or town, county or province.[19] Her work on the uprooting force of modern State ideology was taken further by the American social analyst Christopher Lasch, in a variety of penetrating studies on the weakening of the intermediate realities between State and individual.[20] The disappearance of traditional forms of sociability – its symptom the rise of a rhetoric of 'communitarianism' – is to be reckoned among the greatest challenges to a State order that is peaceful, harmonious, socially in flower. Breakdowns in the ordinary context of living in neigh-bourhood or city are a greater preoccupation of modern electorates than are (even) their 'consuming passions' – always having more.

In any case, secularism can scarcely be acknowledged by Christians as a good *per se* since the good of the creation (which Christian secularists claim to uphold) is only available to us within the resurrec-tion order where it is found restored and then (not a chronological but an ontological 'then') transfigured. Secularism (something far more radical than anti-clericalism) was never *voted in* at all. It is simply what happened when traditional societies entered a liberal thought-world. Liberalism is the imposition on the person of the priorities of secularity and prosperity over against deeper needs, and why should that supinely be accepted? To a duly functioning Christian sensibility it can only be an impossible project, for it results from the extreme separation of the supernatural from the natural when in fact these realms interpenetrate utterly.[21] It is the message of MacIntyre's *After Virtue*[22] that we are thus placed in an impossible situation where the city of man despises the city of God, even though nature is only safe through grace, just as the city of God, absolutising grace, may despise the city of man, though grace only maintains itself via nature. Thereby politics becomes liberal in substance and not only in mode, that is, becomes indifferent to the fate of the soul, while by the same token, faith may become discarnate, indifferent to the fate of the body. In rejecting nature sixteenth- and seventeenth-century heretics – Calvinists, Jansenists – not only aroused secularism but, in spite of themselves, rejected grace; liberalism finished their work by expressly expelling grace from the city, in that way destroying nature likewise. Hence our present unstable situation, alternating between a moral relativism and a religious fundamentalism equally ill-based.

Is all, then, lost? The 'chair' of the department of political science at the Catholic University of America, writing in 1990, claims to have felt the first faint zephyrs of some wind of change: 'The conception of a secular society, existing without reference to any transcendent source, and drawing its legitimacy entirely from humanity's autonomous self-determination, has begun to lose its appeal.' And David Walsh goes on to register some 'glimmerings that, perhaps, it is only through participation in the order of this transcendent source that the existence of individuals in society and history partakes of goodness and truth and reality'.[23] What is not visible on the Cam may nonetheless be espied on the Potomac. Undoubtedly the influence on American political thinking of such figures as Leo Strauss, Hannah Arendt, Eric Voegelin, (all in a Central European tradition of marrying sociology and history with metaphysics because thinking through the presuppositions of the human good) accounts for much of this disparity. For Walsh's method in his study is to confront those 'problems of order today' that lead to realisation of truths in both philosophy and religion – rather in the manner that Borella's study aimed to show how the problems rationality encounters when separated from the religiously resonant symbol bring a rediscovery of the latter's truth-value. We can compare with this some words of Walsh's fellow-American, Thomas Molnar:

> The separation [of Church and State] effected by such medieval thinkers as Simon of Bisignano, William of Ockham, John of Paris, Marsilius of Padua (and others) weakened the status of the spiritual authority, but . . . it also undermined the power of the very state that the separation was to make independent of the spiritual. . . . No community can stand unless the spiritual element (which is also the civilising element) is integrated with its existence and structure. The secular state as such, whether the medieval or the modern, the liberal or the Marxist, is able to generate only an ersatz spirituality (ideology), which works not at its preservation but at its destruction.[24]

For the desacralisation of the State leads to its 'desymbolisation' (the proposed modernisation, at the time of writing, of the ceremony of the royal opening of the British Parliament is a case in point), and desymbolisation leads in time to loss of legitimacy – a process whose results we already see in the disaffection and cynicism which so many modern citizens manifest toward the State power. Since virtue is the formative element of the community and the human flourishing to which it leads its goal, Aquinas, the classic thinker of the Christian West, did not imagine that the State could dispense with the active presence of the Church: *civil* religion would furnish at best a national, provincial or otherwise partial rendering, merely, of the virtues, while 'another "religion" [if the Church be rejected] is bound to fill the vacuum which inevitably forms by the fact that no community can exist without an active moral authority'.[25] In effect, secular humanism is now, in what were once Christian nations, that religion.

Today, the legislatures of all previously Christian nations enact laws which erect sin into the norm, and they do so in a social climate which is either largely indifferent to the intrinsic moral issues or, indeed, accepts and promotes immoral solutions . . . The problem before the Christian citizen is new: Can he survive morally in a state that recognizes no spiritual transcendence that 'competes' with itself (except in falsely pious lip service to 'traditional values', best kept undefined), that is desacralized even in its function as protector of the common good and usurps, in a caricatural way, many functions of the Church, for example, in the moral order? . . . Today the state is not indifferent; it has a quasi-official ideology in secular humanism, which it takes for granted, and enforces in the public and increasingly in the private sphere as well.[26]

Naturally, in a desacralised civilisation, civil society tends to drag down the Church to its own level – hence the confusion which reigns in many Church leaderships in matters not only external, on the interface with the State, but internal as well. The recovery of clarity and coherence on the part of the Church is a necessary precondition for its exertion of moral and spiritual leadership. That leadership, once communicated to secular agencies and the State itself, will inevitably confer a degree of mundane power – civilly recognised spiritual authority – on the Church itself. It is a Manichaean temptation to flee such power, which is simply that of acknowledged indispensability in a patchwork civilisation where the State easily drifts from its moorings. A postmodern civilisation that 'affirms its own aimlessness cannot long serve as the cement that holds society together'.[27] The lack of any other institutional authority with which the State can share its powers is damaging to the State itself, leading to what Molnar has termed a 'delirious' mode of exercising powers that information technology, and other wonders of modern life, render ever expansible. To ask that the Church disavow the term 'pluralism' when used as a euphemism for the neutralisation of her spiritual and magisterial gifts (the Republic of Ireland offers an instructive example of this today) is not to seek the Church's self-aggrandisement. It is to provide a source of help for society and State in consolidating their ability to fulfil the tasks for which they were (through the creation of the human species) made. Too often the State fails to protect the community by dereliction of powers it should uphold, while simultaneously arrogating excessive powers of direction where the principle of subsidiarity would restrain its hand.

It has largely been forgotten that the common good of society does not consist *principally* in economic prosperity. Our social worlds are becoming exemplars of what the influential Cistercian monk and spiritual commentator, Thomas Merton, called the 'society of salesmen'.[28] Mutual service, the pursuit of truth, and the worship of God touch more closely, however, what should be the shared social substance.

## The form of the State

Orthodox Christians with a sense of responsibility for both the propagation of the gospel and the good of the polis are faced, accordingly, with the search for a form of political society which will confer on the total human good held out by revelation in its fullness the degree of intelligibility that it requires. This will be chiefly a matter of the virtues that State inculcates by its legislation, and the manner in which it does so. (Not that the soul of the citizen is the direct concern of the State, but what *does* concern the State is the virtuous quality of the co-ordinated conduct of the civic life at large. As we have seen, no State can afford to be emptied of all meaning save the material satisfaction of its clients.) Crucial also will be the repristinisation of what Walter Bagehot called the 'dignified' part of a constitution – those institutions which arouse and preserve the respect of the population for fundamental laws (as distinct from the 'efficient' part, which consists of those who do the actual work of assuring society's well functioning).[29] More widely, that multiform participation of groups and individuals in the social good which corresponds, in the well-ordered polis, to the sacramental and charismatic economies of the Holy Spirit in the Church, as also to that basic religious metaphysic of Catholicism with its holding together of the One and the Many in differentiated unity which we considered in Chapter V, strongly suggests the desirability of a multiform State order – as commended in the last hundred years in England by (especially) such Catholic-minded Anglicans as J. N. Figgis and the late David Nicholls of Littlemore.[30]

A multiform State order is appropriately capped by a monarchical rather than republican institution. Where there are plural authorities there are many opportunities for tension, and it is characteristic of a republican polity to produce an antagonistic ethos where tensions are with difficulty contained.

I have said so far that the embodiment of the shared aims of a Christendom society cannot be separated from the need to enact the foundational norms of such a society in the civil law, for the re-creation of Christendom as State. Whereas in traditionally republican polities, a supreme court might be regarded as the appropriate institution for testing proposed legislation against the public criterion of the Judaeo-

Christian revelation, I wish to concentrate in conclusion on the possible role of a revived (national and also international) monarchical institution in this regard.

In Western Europe, the difficulty of even articulating the concept of a religiously sanctioned monarchy derives from the peculiar ideological circumstances of the early modern period (the seventeenth and eighteenth centuries). In England, for instance, Anglican Royalism was an extraordinary mish-mash of theological and philosophical ingredients, ranging from defence of the ancient Constitution (of which the monarchy was the preponderant part), through a patriarchalism stressing indefeasible hereditary right, to a sacramentalism based on the royal anointing by the rites of the Church. In Continental Europe, Jean Bodin's new-fangled theory of princely absolutism, by identifying ultimate authority with the will of the prince, both falsified the character of the mediaeval monarchy, and, in generating the concept of political sovereignty, contributed unwittingly to the fathering of popular democracy.

The significance of a religiously sanctioned monarchy lies in the fact that it alone of all possible State forms represents the essential notion that authority descends. *A me reges regnant* ('By me kings reign') is the subscription of the Christ image on the crown made in *c.* 962 for the Holy Roman emperor Otto II and still preserved in the Viennese Hofburg.

The need for such an institution derives from the need to recognise the existence of a natural law, antecedent to political power – a natural law made more precise, and richer by the Judaeo-Christian heritage – in, for example, precepts of tempering justice with mercy and loving especially the poor founded as these precepts are on the work of God in Israel and the Christ. Every society experiences the need for some basic norms, whereby to live; norms which can be refined, or reapplied in the light of new situations, but which are inappropriately made the subject of parliamentary vote.

Catholicism, as Orthodoxy, has, historically, regarded the monarchical institution in this light: raised up by Providence to safeguard the content of the natural law in its transmission through history as that norm for human co-existence which, founded as it is on the Creator, and renewed by him as the Redeemer, cannot be made subject to the positive law, or administrative fiat, or the dictates of cultural fashion. Let us dare to exercise a Christian political imagination on an as yet unspecifiable future. The articulation of the foundational natural and Judaeo-Christian norms of a *really* united Europe, for instance, would most appropriately be made by such a crown, whose legal and customary relations with the national peoples would be modelled on the best aspects of historic practice in the (Western) Holy Roman Empire[31] and the Byzantine 'Commonwealth' – to use the term popularised by Professor Dmitri Obolensky.[32]

Such a crown, as the integrating factor of an international European Christendom, would leave intact the functioning of parliamentary government in the republican or monarchical polities of its constituent nations and analogues in city and village in other representative and participatory forms. As the Spanish political theorist Alvaro D'Ors defines the concepts, power – that is, government – as raised up by the people can and should be distinguished from authority. Power in this sense puts questions to those in authority as to what ought to be done. It asks whether technically possible acts of government, for co-ordinating the goals of individuals and groups in society, chime, or do not chime, with the foundational norms of society, deemed as these are to rest on the will of God as the ultimate giver of the shared human goal. Authority, itself bereft of such power, answers out of a wisdom which society can recognise.[33]

## Mission to the polis

Christendom belongs with mission and, unless the notion of mission be so defined that the wholesale conversion of society is *a priori* excluded from its ambit, mission entails the possibility of Christendom. But, so Professor O'Donovan points out, successful mission does not simply result in extending the Church's influence; it also involves witnessing to the triumph of Christ by the unmasking of evil. But, as O'Donovan stresses, this – with its possible outcome in martyrdom – should not be thought of as an *alternative* to taking principalities and powers captive for Christ. As he writes in an especially fine passage of his helpful study:

> Since true martyrdom is a powerful force and its resistance to Antichrist effective, the church must be prepared to welcome the homage of the kings when it is offered to the Lord of the martyrs. The growth of the church, its enablement to reconstruct civiliza-tional practices and institutions, its effectiveness in communicating the Gospel: these follow from the courage of the martyrs, and the church honours them when it seizes the opportunities they have made available to it. No honour is paid to martyrs if they are presented as mere dissidents, whose sole glory was to refuse the cultural order that was on offer to them. Martyrdom is, as the word itself indicates, witness, pointing to an alternative offer. The witness is vindicated when it is carried through in a positive mode, saying yes as well as saying no, encouraging the acts of repentance and change by which the powers offer homage to Christ.[34]

The point is that the Church has a message for the State just as it has to civil society as a whole, and if a society in very great part hears the message, and takes heed of it in setting out the conditions of social existence, it is only the rankest neo-liberalism that would deem it very wicked to express that large measure of agreement in political conventions or ceremonies or laws. In St Thomas' account in the *Summa Theologiae*, the making of laws and their execution for a community which grasps their pertinence is pre-contained within an architectonic concept of law as a 'unified structure finding its source in God's creative decrees for universal existence'.[35] And here the revelation of God's ultimate design for the universe in Christ can only be relevant.

> The legislative activity of princes . . . was not a beginning in itself, it was an answer to the prior lawmaking of God in Christ, under which it must be judged . . . Even those Christians who defended most determinedly the supremacy of the sovereign over earthly courts understood well enough that the sovereign's decree had no legal substance if it ran counter to divine law, natural or revealed.[36]

For before the seventeenth century in Christendom, sovereignty, the *suprema potestas*, referred to that office of State which, by *presiding* over other offices, ensured the lawfulness and authority of all – something not only compatible with but even dependent on the rule of divine law over the State. Only with the reconceiving of the notion as an act of popular will does sovereignty come to be thought of as the *source* of all law and constitutional order. A universal law was being replaced by a nationalist positivism, itself to be rendered precarious by the globalisation of economics and the revolutions in communications which the end of the twentieth century has witnessed.

Those who consider that social relations in a pluralist society can only take the form of endless debate have in effect surrendered the unity of society as a now anachronistic concept. That is not an option which Christian hope can take, for that hope is for life not death, and the destruction of the social bond means social death.

We notice too that the present chaos of beliefs or non-beliefs, and the massive disruption of religion are not the result of immigration into largely Christian societies from elsewhere, but of the collapse of a predominantly Catholic people in, for instance, Ireland or Spain. The passing of the Christendom State (as also its possible revival) shows the truth of Eric Voegelin's thesis that 'the order of society that man seeks to structure through politics depends on the experience of order he is capable of realizing as part of the order of being . . .'.[37] A society whose public rhetoric has rejected the revelatory experience of Israel, the 'metaphysical' experience of ancient Greece and the soteriological experience of Christianity will have a different – a more diluted – participation in the order of being, and consequently, if Voegelin's fundamental intuition is justified, construct a different political order as well. In the words of two English commentators:

> The trouble is that the public square is not neutral, as modernists had hoped, but operates on the basis of fundamental meta-physical assumptions about the nature of reality, about what it means to be human, about the *telos* of human society. Far from offering freedom from any particular faith and moral system, secularism simply replaces one system with another as the basis of our common life. When schools teach secular values detached from their roots, they are not so much preserving neutrality as asserting the marginalisation of religion to the private fringes.[38]

But the Church is not 'a privatised utility dispensing a franchised commodity called religion'.[39] We must turn now to an early victim of this development: the family.

## NOTES

1. I take this translation from *Breviary according to the Rite of the Order of Preachers* II (Dublin, 1967), pp. 900–1.

2. O. O'Donovan, *The Desire of the Nations. Rediscovering the Roots of Political Theology* (Cambridge, 1996), p. 19.

3. Ibid., p. 23.

4. Ibid., p. 25.

5. George Every makes a point of much the same kind when in accounts of the religion of the Ancient Near East he proposes that the differing political structures of the civilisations of the Euphrates and Nile basins reflected their religious systems – rather than the other way round.

6. O. O'Donovan, *The Desire of the Nations*, p. 46.

7. S. L. R. Clark, *Civil Peace and Sacred Order* (Oxford, 1989), p. 90.

8. O'Donovan, *The Desire of the Nations*, p. 49.

9. Ibid., p. 94.

10. Ibid., p. 122.

11. Ibid., p. 146.

12. Ibid., p. 169.

13. Ibid., p. 189.

14. *Apostolicam actuositatem*, 3 & 7, with a citation of Colossians 1.18.

15. As Alain Besançon writes, 'The democratic principle would have it that the citizen obey himself in function of interests and preferences he himself defines. In this sense, the democratic ideal is inferior to that of the cities of antiquity and monarchical regimes which in principle did not lose sight of the education of the citizen in virtue and the search for a common good transcending individual interests.' Thus his *Trois tentations pour l'Eglise* (Paris, 1996), p. 98.

16. See M. Atkins, 'Can We Ever Be Satisfied?', *Priests and People* 12.2 (1998), pp. 45–9.

17. A. MacIntyre, *A Short History of Ethics* (New York, 1966), pp. 110–20.

18. J. Maritain, *Oeuvres complètes* IX (Fribourg, 1996), pp. 513–39.

19. S. Weil, *L'Enracinement* (Paris, 1949).

20. See Chapter I above, note 1.

21. See above, Chapter IV.

22. A. MacIntyre, *After Virtue. A Study in Moral Theory* (London, 1981).

23. D. Walsh, *After Ideology. Recovering the Spiritual Foundations of Freedom* (San Francisco, 1990), p. 1.

24. T. Molnar, *Politics and the State. The Catholic View* (Chicago, 1980), p. 22. So the question is, what kind of society could permit a form of satisfactory action? See on this D. Emmet, *Function, Purpose and Powers. Some Concepts in the Study of Individuals and Societies* (London, 1958; 1972).

25. T. Molnar, *Politics and the State*, p. 98.

26. Ibid., pp. 103–5.

27. Ibid., p. 112.

28. T. Merton, *New Seeds of Contemplation* (New York, 1972), p. 84.

29. W. Bagehot, *The English Constitution* (London, 1867; 1964), pp. 59–66.

30. D. Nicholls, *The Pluralist State. The Political Ideas of J. N. Figgis and his Contemporaries* (New York and Basingstoke, 1975; 1994).

31. The model of that empire was crucial to J. N. Figgis' development of the idea of the plural State: see M. Goldie, 'J. N. Figgis and the History of Political Thought in Cambridge', in R. Mason (ed.), *Cambridge Minds* (Cambridge, 1994), pp. 177–92.

32. D. Obolensky, *The Byzantine Commonwealth* (London, 1971).

33. A. D'Ors, *Presupuestos para el estudio del Derecho Romano* (Madrid, 1943).

34. O'Donovan, *The Desire of the Nations*, p. 215.

35. Ibid., p. 234.

36. Ibid.

37. W. C. Havard, Jr, 'Notes on Voegelin's Contribution to Political Theory', in E. Sandez (ed.), *Eric Voegelin's Thought. A Critical Appraisal* (Durham, North Carolina, 1982), p. 101.

38. L. Bretherton and J. Casson, 'Politics in Denial', *Demos* 11 (1997), p. 36.

39. C. Greene, 'What Sort of Story – What Sort of Church?', *The Bible in Transmission. A Forum for Change in Church and Culture* (Spring, 1998), p. 8.

# VII

# *Reconstituting a Society of Households*

A<sup>S</sup> is well known, the foundational cell of civil society in Catholicism's view is the *natural family*, itself centred around

> a man and a woman bound in a socially approved covenant called marriage, for purposes of the propagation of children, sexual communion, mutual love and protection, the construction of a small home economy, and the preservation of bonds between the generations.[1]

So conceived, the family is in sharp decline in the West, to the point that some commentators even envisage its effective disappearance as a significant presence in culture, under the impact of both mounting marriage breakup and declining rates of marriage. This process, one may suppose, would hardly have reached its current extent on the basis, simply, of changing morality – developments, as it were, in theoretical ethics. Not only is it the case that, through the widespread availability of contraception and the reduction of sexuality to pleasurable contact, the bond linking the unitive and procreative aspects of sexual union has snapped in people's minds, and the concept of lifelong monogamous union as the proper setting for conjugal relations accordingly weakened in its appeal. More than this, the wider social, economic and educational setting whereby what I have termed in the title of this chapter 'a society of households' underpinned the natural family has itself melted away. Certain social trends, in other words, must themselves be diverted, *subverted*, if a renaissance of the family – as distinct from a renewal of thinking about the family – is not to be stillborn.

When key functions of the family are hived off to other agencies, its material and psychological foundations begin to give way. It can hardly be a coincidence that families are strongest in societies of free peasants and craftsmen, and weakest in modern industrial societies with mass State education and State-organised care for the old. Modern industrialisation carries the possibility of far greater prosperity than was known on the subsistence farm or in cottage industry, just as State provision of education and nursing of the elderly alleviates burdens that are demanding and even hard to bear. But the price paid in terms of diminishing the solidarity and independence of the family is itself a heavy one – and only at the end of the twentieth century, as the chickens come home (or, in point of fact, *fail* to come home) to roost is its cost being counted up. When the productive small home economy is, in Allan Carlson's words, 'stripped of its tasks' – even to the point of losing those of home cooking (in favour of fast foods) and child care (in favour of play groups), it is hardly surprising if the centre cannot hold. Too much weight is placed on the role of moral exhortation to couples, children and wider family members, and not enough on the wider strategies that must underpin the moral structure of the family in a post-lapsarian if also grace-permeated world. (Grace, however, is not restricted in its epiphanising to touching and transforming hearts; it can also have, as the sacramental mysteries of the Church make manifest, a social face.)

One reason for the allergic reaction of Catholicism to both industrial capitalism and industrial socialism is the awareness that, on this issue, there is little to choose between them. The efficiency of the market, on the one hand, and of the centralised economy on the other, is likely to run counter to a society of households, just as are the wish of the State, liberal or socialist, that children should be educated in those particular ranges of skills it considers desirable (hence State education) and its reluctance to lose good workers to the demands made by the care of children and the elderly (hence State provision of these services likewise). Of course, public authority has the duty to see that these essential tasks are performed when households fail. But that is very different from the effective marginalisation of the household in these its historic roles.

The idea of the 'family wage' served, in the late nineteenth and early twentieth centuries, to preserve a modicum of household autonomy within the factory system of that epoch. Wage levels were assessed by criteria which included the imperative that wages paid to one family member (normally, the father) should be computed as given to the head of the household (and bonuses, determined by the number of children, make up a shortfall). It takes, however, a philanthropically minded employer or corporation not to prefer to such a practice direct access to the labour pool of married women – with its likely consequence of depressing the average industrial wage. For working mothers to be the norm, however, schooling could not be done, even for infants, at home, and the consequent invasion of public schooling into even tender years further sapped the family structure. The more that family members become decreasingly useful to each other, and likewise with the relation of one family to another in a neighbourhood, the more the centripetal power of family and community life begins to fail. Today, working hours for men and women are going steadily up, for a home without a clear rationale is stressful, work often fun. Thus the house is deserted while work *becomes* home. The 'refunctionalising' of the family turns on its ability, then, to recover ground from the exterior agencies to whom too many of its tasks have too often been transferred.

The teaching of Catholicism that the family constitutes the basic unity of that ordered multitude which is civil society is not fully dissasociable from the economic doctrine of the late nineteenth- and twentieth-century papal magisterial tradition, favouring as that doctrine does a proprietary or distributivist society where men would be economically free through their ownership of capital and land.

It is in this context that one should see the Distributism which was the specifically English Catholic contribution to the relaunching of a society of households this century.[2] In the same inter-war period, the Russian economist Alexander Vasilevich Chayanov, later shot by the Soviets, was arguing for the superiority of a sustainable family-centred agriculture to industrial farming. Revalorisation of the role of the mother – written off in both classical liberal and Marxian economies as an economic irrelevance (yet domestic skills have precisely economic value) – restored something of the original meaning of the word 'economics': *oikonomia*, the management of a household.

In the encyclical *Laborem exercens*, Pope John Paul II spoke of the family wage as 'a concrete means of verifying the justice of the whole socio-economic system'.[3] It is not the task of a Roman pontiff to design an economy, but it may be his responsibility to formulate principles in whose light economies can be judged. Among these are the importance of family-centred unpaid labour in the home, essential as this is, owing to its effect on family development, to the good ordering of society. It is deeply regrettable that civic authorities dedicated to 'population control' frequently discourage the emergence of patterns of smallscale productive ownership precisely because of their tendency to increase family size, and pressurise countries (such as Mexico) typified by the development of family-centred economies to revert to an industrial model. Too often also, the State authority ignores the way tax laws can reward – or penalise – marriage and the 'stay-at-home' mother.

The spectacular rise of 'home schooling' in the United States and Canada must count as a cognate development which bureaucracies in State and (one regrets to add) Church also may view with alarm. Plainly, not all parents will have the desire or ability to follow this lead; yet the phenomenon of home schooling has the benefit – even for those who do not take this way – of strengthening the position of the family vis-à-vis society at large.

## A spirituality of the household economy

How should 'material things and processes be managed'[4] in Christian households that could serve as energising exemplars for a wider society? Francis Mannion, writing under the inspiration of the Rule of St Benedict, suggests five facets of the good economic household – all of which turn out to be anti-modern and counter-cultural in greater or lesser degree. Whereas in a market-*driven* economy (evidently, economic life must *have* a market-place!), we find a competitive struggle for resources, that small-scale *oikonomia* (household management) which reflects the 'Great Economy' of the Kingdom of God revealed in Scripture will tend to be *stewardly* in its attitude to things. The head of the household – in the monastic context, the abbot – will be a wise steward of the possessions of his house and the way through skill and craft they are augmented, conscious not only of the needs of members and those beyond but, above all, of the God 'to whom he will have to give an account of his stewardship'.[5]

Secondly, the good household economy will be sacramental. Whereas in our culture the material order of manual work and kitchen service in the home is treated as, generally speaking, without spiritual significance, as indeed are processes of production and work at large, Benedict regarded prayer and labour as intimately connected. In a household whose ethos was governed by the ethos of the Holy Rule, contemplation and worship – and recreation too – would refresh the human spirit for return to that work whose fruits are enjoyed in these other periods or aspects of the daily round. In the Augustinian tradition – to which the present writer, via his Dominican profession, belongs – labour and *sacrum otium* (contemplative leisure, literally, 'holy indolence') form a symphony, while in modern economies the prevailing psychology is rather for work to be abandoned as soon as sufficiently remunerated: not surprisingly, if it has lost that 'sacramental' character which once lent it honour and even joy.

Thirdly, on Francis Mannion's analysis, the exemplary Christian household should be typified by a certain *frugality*. This is not simply a matter of avoiding waste and extravagance. On the principle that 'less can be more', genuine frugality (the word is connected with *fruges*, 'fruits') enables the fuller enjoyment of a creation whose gluttonous consumption satiates and makes the fruits of the earth pall. Frugality is linked to a certain simplicity (not to be confused with meanness or ugliness, on the contrary) whereby the way of life of a household focuses its members' attention on things that really matter, and keeps the elements of a good human life and the objects of an uncluttered mind in due proportion.

A society of households that took the Rule of Benedict as its inspiration would give great prominence, fourthly, to the virtue of *hospitality*, which shows forth the receptivity of a host to, especially, the needy poor – in their various manifestations, not all of them simply pecuniary. We live in an epoch of unprecedented State welfare but not an age of hospitality. The danger that one will offer people politics but not access to a home necessarily afflicts a Church that takes its cue from the secular agenda.

> It is probable that systemic concern for justice in the world has never been as intense in the church's consciousness as it is today. However, one of the criticisms made of some modern theologies of justice is that they seem too abstract, generalized and inordinately focused on structural reform in society. One hears of a desired move in the modern Church from charity to empowerment, or from charity to justice. Certainly the configuration of the modern world is such that the church cannot minister to the poor and needy oblivious to the need for institutional reform.

And yet:

> in the concern for institutional and policy reform, the Church and its constituent communities can lose their souls. To abandon the understanding that the soul of justice is charity in which Christ is received and served is to reduce the Church to a secular social service institution . . . Christian action for justice in its fundamental structure is a matter of the hospitable economic reception of the other.[6]

Hospitable solidarity of this sort can only be furnished by people *to each other*.

Finally, if the Rule of Benedict praises *stability* of life – over against, in its own context, the itchy-footed monk who would wander from one monastic setting to another without ever making that demanding commitment to the local and particular – Mannion suggests how papal social teaching on respect for 'subsidiarity' is little other than the appeal for a 'stable economy' by analogy with that Benedictine virtue.

> Subsidiarity allows for intensive living in a definitive social space, in relation to a definite set of people, a particular history, and a set of common projects. In the area of economics, the principle implies value in local ownership, local management, and local responsibility. It suggests . . . that many little economies are preferable to large centralized economies.[7]

The common history and culture that has hitherto surrounded economic processes and rendered them humanly habitable turns to a considerable extent on precisely this.

## The family as social cell

A stable society (in the sense sketched above but also in the common-or-garden meaning of the adjective 'stable') depends on a sufficiency of traditional families, as distinct from *ménages* constituted by passing sexual liaisons. This is because such families are bonded by a shared history, and ties of mutual help and loyalty that resist easy slippage. The theological, cultural and legal defence of the family is integral, therefore, to a humane and harmonious social order where the qualities of a sane and Christian economy suggested above might find fuller instantiation. This is something G. K. Chesterton saw plainly.

> [Chesterton's] thought about the family arose in the context of his social doctrine . . . The serial monogamist who is always remarrying can never know any of his wives more than superficially. Like the supercapitalist who can never enjoy all his property, he wants more than his proper share.[8]

No modern Christian writer has done so much to identify a *virtue* of domesticity as Chesterton. 'Domesticity' is the disposition whose active prosecution tends to the flourishing of the family, the smallest of polities, or what Chesterton himself called

> the small state founded on the sexes [which] is at once the most voluntary and the most natural of all self-governing states. It is not true of Mr Brown [with a reference to W. S. Gilbert's patriotic lyric] that he might have been a Russian, but it may be true of Mrs Brown that she might have been a Robinson.[9]

The vow made most freely to establish this polity – the marriage vow – is also the vow which must be kept most firmly since uniquely weighty consequences are attached to it in the form of children. Owing to its link with procreation, the marriage covenant that brings this miniature yet irreplaceable polis into existence is unlike any mere contract. 'There is no contract . . . that can . . . bring cherubs (or goblins) to inhabit a small modern villa.'[10] The virtue of domesticity makes us tend to practice the loyalty this altogether exceptional promise requires for its fulfilment.

And here we must add that if, normally, a virtue, or an interlocking chain of virtues, is required for sustaining some cultural practice good for man, it is also true, reciprocally, that virtues themselves can be and are sustained by institutions congruent with the human condition. Thus in *What's Wrong with the World* Chesterton remarks with soberingly down-to-earth realism:

> [I]n everything worth having, even in every pleasure, there is a point of pain or tedium that must be survived, so that the pleasure may revive and endure . . . In everything on this earth that is worth doing, there is a stage where no one would do it, except for necessity or honour. It is then that the Institution upholds a man and helps him onto the firmer ground ahead.[11]

A decent marital relationship is worth having, unlike the sex that is divorced from it which soon degenerates into anticlimax, with other people reduced to masturbatory aids. Men need the warmth and comfort that flow from a relation where matters of 'performance' are altogether secondary; women need motherhood and children more radically than they do those professional outlets in work so euphorically seized in the 1960s and 70s. And as for children, a household where both father and mother are absent from early morning to late-ish evening is scarcely much of a home. The feeling of being valued, essential to sanity, is a direct result of parental care. Absent in childhood, it is extremely difficult to gain in later life; once gained, subsequent trials have trouble to destroy it.

Yet in the last analysis, Chesterton's account of marriage and family was not pragmatic and earthbound but mystical and heavenly. (Perhaps it would be better to say that, for him, only an account of the family that was 'mystical' would work in practice, only a 'heavenly' perspective on family would keep it on the good earth.) As he writes in *The Everlasting Man*:

> The old Trinity was of father and mother and child, and is called the human family. The new is of child and mother and father, and has the name of the Holy Family. It is in no way altered except in being entirely reversed, just as the world which it transformed was not in the least different, except in being turned upside-down.[12]

But since in the Holy Family heaven has in fact come down to earth by the Incarnation, the natural virtue of domesticity is not cancelled out but lifted up by the action of its supernatural counterpart. This – the Christianisation of the natural family – does not go against nature's grain since, according to Chesterton, domesticity is in any case open to the transcendent. The home is the 'one wild place in the world of rules and set tasks'[13] – despite, or because of its finitude, something he regarded as actually a necessary condition for all genuine creativity. As he remarks in *Orthodoxy*, 'The artist loves his limitations; they constitute the *thing* he is doing'.[14] In a home, homemakers act as artists, and in a Christian home, the capacity of the homemaker-artist to gesture toward the sacred is taken up into an art of homemaking that is sacramental, that expresses the divine Mystery at work in the Christian economy.

The increasing obscuring of such a vision of the family is owed to the mutually reinforcing factors of ideology and institutional change. Once the dogmatic framework of revealed religion ceases to be of public relevance in civil society, the virtues which that revelation pinpointed will naturally tend to be lost to view, and the cultural practices suggested by those virtues will vacate the secure housing they possessed in institutional life. That a family should have two parents of different genders bonded to each other by a lifelong vow is knowledge largely possessed now only in churches. But, as already indicated, institutional change works its own transformation on ideology: it is not simply that, somewhere between the Enlightenment and ourselves, the Church lost, in this area, a battle of ideas. The economic marginalisation of the family undermined its cultural practice, called into question the virtues which found in the excellence of that practice their own proper point and in this way created a climate where divine revelation appeared otiose and unpersuasive. It has been, accordingly, by a profound instinct that the Catholic Church in the last hundred years has sponsored or supported a variety of initiatives for reversing the peripheralisation of the family economically – distributism, Back-to-the-Land, co-operatives, Schumacherian intermediate technology economics. In England, where farming land is owned and exploited in large, industrial-style units, it is more difficult to create the distinctively rural life (only 4 per cent of our population works on the land) in the way still feasible in regions of the United States. But in many countries, parishes are capable of creating food co-operatives – even in Third-World 'mega-cities', since three-quarters of the food consumed in such conurbations is still produced in home gardens and small poultry operations in those cities themselves. In the cities of the developed world, analogously, family gardens and allotments could conceivably serve as foci for a common family enterprise. The Church can help by linking parishes in such a way as to connect urban and rural families for the direct acquisition of fresh produce, by stimulating the creation of community banks and credit unions, and even by creating pools of start-up capital for small family-centred concerns in agriculture, manufacturing and the service sector. (In Italy, mutual guarantee schemes for such businesses have proved a remarkable success.) Moreover, Christians can use the much vaunted 'consumer sovereignty' of the modern market-place to choose to sustain local, family-run producers, retailers and providers of services.

In the broader picture, the giant corporations which have dominated the world economy for the last 150 years are increasingly regarded as dinosaurs: they are moving to contract out many of their functions to independent, home-based consultants; one of the most successful European economies, that of Germany, is based in part on a *Mittelstand* of small and medium-sized companies in manufacturing industry – a phenomenon to be found in the United States as well; and there is evidence that, fairly widely in Western countries, a new type of educated craftsman is making his appearance in response to a widely felt dissatisfaction with bland, machine-produced artefacts. There are even proposals in England for a new version of the mediaeval guilds to help such designer-producers in marketing their work, guaranteeing standards of quality and using finance and equipment more effectively.

Beyond these developments, there is also the possibility of well-drafted State legislation in favour of small enterprises – not only via changes in the taxation system but by such devices as limiting the opening of superstores and prohibiting their receiving volume discounts or selling below cost. The Church does not hold, with the Enlightenment political economists, that property rights are absolute and economic individualism inevitably, if only in the long term, benign. She holds with the great Archbishop William Temple of Canterbury, that in the words of his *Christianity and the Social Order* (1941) 'wealth [is] essentially social and therefore subject at all points to control in the interests of society as a whole'. Exactly fifty years later, in his 1991 encyclical *Centesimus Annus*, pope John Paul II stressed how economic life should so be patterned as to succour the family, for this very reason. It is worth recalling that, in the view of modern historians, the failure of family businesses in the late 1920s and 30s in Europe was a major factor in the advent of Fascism. People knew something was deeply wrong; alas that the only solution to hand hurt more than healed.

Economics must be about morals since it is about human beings – who are ineluctably moral creatures. Both Marxism and Liberalism – which share an origin in the Enlightenment – make the mistake of trying to give an account of society on the basis of some *a*moral underlying dynamic. This may be substantive, as with the Marxian claim that society is driven forward by the interplay of natural resources with the means of production, distribution and exchange, or formalistic, as with the Liberal claim that only a morally neutral procedural type of reasoning can generate a rationally acceptable – a 'fair' – political, social and economic order.[15] The lack of the most basic social virtues reported dejectedly by those concerned with rebuilding civil society in the East after Communism's collapse is paralleled in the democratic West by a spiritual neutrality and passivity that is peculiarly vulnerable to what has been termed 'soft totalitarianism' – the non-violent exercise of invasive power over institutions, culture, life and thought by ideology-driven governments and *dirigiste* bureaucracies. It is as necessary for 'soft' totalitarianism as it is for hard to do away with those genuine absolutes that limit its range – hence the peculiar animus it is likely to show towards the remnants of Christendom.[16]

## NOTES

1. A definition I draw from A. C. Carlson, 'Towards a Family Centred Economy', *New Oxford Review* December 1997, pp. 27–8. See the same author's *From Cottage to Work Station. The Family's Search for Social Harmony in the Industrial Age* (San Francisco, 1996).

2. D. Quinn, 'Distributism as Movement and Ideal', *Chesterton Review* XIX. 2 (1993), pp. 157–74. For the case that the technological and economic environment is now more favourable to one aspect, at least, of Christendom economics then it has been for centuries, see R. Sparkes, 'The Recovery of the Guilds', *Chesterton Review* XIX. 4 (1993), pp. 499–513.

3. John Paul II, *Laborem exercens* 89.

4. I take this phrase from M. F. Mannion, 'Benedictine Economics and the Challenge of Modernity', *American Benedictine Review* 47:1 (1995), pp. 14–36, and here at p. 19.

5. *Rule of St Benedict* 64.7, citing Luke 16.12.

6. F. M. Mannion, 'Benedictine Economics and the Challenge of Modernity', art. cit., pp. 30–1.

7. Ibid., p. 33.

8. S. Gilley, 'Chesterton, Catholicism and the Family' in S. Barton (ed.), *The Family in Theological Perspective* (Edinburgh, 1996), p. 137.

9. G. K. Chesterton, *The Superstition of Divorce* (London, 1920), p. 23.

10. Ibid.

11. G. K. Chesterton, *What's Wrong with the World* (London, 1910; 1912), p. 53.

12. G. K. Chesterton, *The Everlasting Man* (London, 1925), p. 62.

13. G. K. Chesterton, *What's Wrong with the World*, p. 58.

14. G. K. Chesterton, *Orthodoxy* (London, 1908; 1996), p. 51.

15. A. Basile, 'Crucified between Two Thieves: Catholic Social Teaching vs. Marxist and Liberal social theories', *Culture Wars* 17.2 (1998), p. 28.

16. M. O'Brien, *The Family and the New Totalitarianism* (Killaloe, Ont., 1995).

# VIII

# *Resacralising Material Culture*

'MATERIAL culture' is something of a vogue phrase for the physical yet man-made surroundings of our lives, of which human settlement, in its relation to land and sea, has *buildings* – and so architecture – as its primary instantiation. The 'modern movement' which has dominated twentieth-century architecture hitherto (including, at accelerating pace from the Second World War onwards, the building of churches) has itself, in recent decades, come in for a little – and more than a little – deconstruction. What is in question is the capacity of a modern movement building, where functionality is key, to express – never mind the sacred – but even those basic aesthetic principles which render a building worthy at all. For unless a building arouses visual delight and satisfies a thirst for order – two foundational features of any material environment congruent with man's nature as a sentient yet rational being – it is most unlikely that it will have the wherewithal to function as a sacramental sign. Deprived of such necessary characteristics, it will hardly serve successfully as a sacred space, a focus for that plenary being and meaning of which the sensuous and intelligible orders alike are hint and promise.[1] 'From Stonehenge to Chartres, from the Parthenon to the Pantheon, buildings have given us as profound an understanding of the spiritual as any text or picture. Even in the most profane societies we still need the measure.'[2] A building is not just a solution in engineering to a problem about pragmatic use. The technical knowledge must serve a *form*, and the form can outlast many uses. In a sacred building more than anywhere else form will absorb function, or to put the same point in a different way, the building will only function if it *is* a form.

The specifically Christian version of the sacred is the sacramental. For a church must reflect not just any sacral cosmos but that of the

Christian economy. Hence, for instance, the tradition's clear preference for the cruciform church over the central plan church. It is the former, not the latter, which best articulates in terms of visual space the form of the Church itself: the sanctuary where the celebrant offers the holy Sacrifice represents the Church's head, Jesus Christ; the body of the transept (the traverse crossing aisle) and the nave (the aisle on axis with the altar), the Church body – the Mystical Body – of that head. A rich sacramental aesthetic, however, was never going to be easy to combine with the minimalism of architectural Modernism, with its austerity and absence of image. As one American Catholic critic of *stylus modernus*, Professor Duncan Stroik of the School of Architecture at the University of Notre Dame, has put it:

> Aesthetically, Modernist architecture was inspired by works of engineering including bridges, industrial buildings, and temporary exposition halls which were large, economical and built fast. An essential paradigm was the machine: Swiss architect Le Corbusier claimed the plane, the boat and the car were models for a functional architecture. Just as a plane was designed efficiently for flight, so a house was a machine for living in. Just as the anthropological, spiritual and traditional aspects of *domus* for dwelling and raising a family were stripped away in the 'house as a machine for living in', so would ritual, icon and sacrament be purged from the 'church as machine for assembling in'.[3]

Though the 'liturgical design establishment' has been remarkably deaf to criticisms of architectural Modernism – whether in general or more specifically as an aesthetic incompatible with the Liturgy's demands of a building – *memory*, *symbol* and *meaning* became major elements in the assault on Modernism from other architects and architectural critics themselves.

The chapters in the *Catechism of the Catholic Church* which touch on this subject paint a very different picture from that given us by the capitulation of too many episcopal or parochial authorities in the West to this wave of abstract functionalism beating on the walls of the house of God.

> Visible churches are not simply gathering places, but signify and make visible the Church living in this place, the dwelling of God with men reconciled and united in Christ.
>
> In this 'house of God', the truth and harmony of the signs that make it up should show Christ to be present and active in this place.[4]

And the rite for the dedication of a church, as found in the post-Conciliar 'Pauline' reform, explains:

> a church . . . stands as a special sign of the pilgrim church on earth
> and reflects the Church dwelling in heaven.
>
> It . . . should stand as a sign and symbol of heavenly things.[5]

A church needs to be recognisable at once as a sacred building even from the outside. Within it must reinforce the sense of sanctuary and display the themes of Catholic belief, worship and ethos by deploying forms and images from the bimillenial tradition in architecture and iconography for this purpose. The shapes and volumes of the basic historic forms of a church are already redolent with associations. Moreover, the iconographic tradition ranges from geometric symbol to the most intimate pictorial detail in its articulation of doctrinal meaning – and the renaissance of figural art means that the latter need in no way be set aside, even by art-world sophisticates, in exclusive favour of the former.

It cannot be said too clearly that a minimalist functionalist architecture with a non-iconographic church interior acts as a real subversion of the Catholic tradition – just as Modernist city planning, and Modernist buildings within such city plans, were conceived by their makers as exercises in social engineering, not simply reorganising such functions as housing, work, recreation and traffic but systematically redefining the social basis for each. Their revolutionary building types and urban structures were meant to change existing forms of collective association and indeed personal habits, predicated on an absolute break with the past – the instrument of which would be the *deliberate decontextualisation of the new environment*. By quite consciously obliterating what was familiar in an environment, and the employment of shock effects, a considerable repertoire of which was available through avant-garde art, the Modernists proposed to make the city strange, all with a view to creating a new type of urban public. Maximalising the corporate domain of the State, minimising the familial domain through changing the environmental conditions of residence and domestic organisation, health care and education, the aim was to impose a master-plan, comprehensive, State-sponsored, in which many features of the traditional city would become, quite simply, architecturally invisible and thus (it was hoped) socially irrelevant. The comparison with the ecclesial realm is plain. The designing of Modernist churches for new liturgies, in a spirit of hostility to the inherited liturgical and devotional practices of the Latin clergy and faithful is the ecclesiastical equivalent of the blueprint utopias of the secular city.

Of course material culture extends beyond the shell of the church building. It includes not only the iconography within the church space (a subject to which I will turn in a moment) but also the decoration of a Christian home – and that home is, after all, the *ecclesia domestica*, the basic cell of the Church. We do not need to be environmental determinists to agree with Colleen McDannell when she writes:

> The symbol systems of a particular religious language are not merely handed down, they must be learned through doing, seeing, and touching. Christian material culture does not simply reflect an existing reality. Experiencing the physical dimension of religion helps *bring about* religious values, norms, behaviours, and attitudes. Practising religion sets into play ways of thinking. It is the continual interaction with objects and images that makes one religious in a particular manner.[6]

Such things are needed – above all by an incarnational faith – to anchor a world-view in the world. 'If we immediately assume that whenever money is exchanged religion is debased, then we will miss the subtle ways that people create and maintain spiritual ideals *through* the exchange of goods and the construction of spaces.'[7] It is a mistake to suppose that Catholics, say, who habitually make use of particular objects and images in their devotional lives, or act as though there were a geography of salvation, with some places being more spiritually imbued than others, are necessarily weak believers, needing props for faith. Indeed, the capacity of ordinary Christians to define and express themselves through the repertoire of material culture – over against a high culture or a mass culture of a more hegemonic kind, it may be – is an impressive manifestation of the virtue of faith. Among Protestants too, while churches may be aniconic, images are often permitted, or even encouraged, in home, tavern, school. Moreover, it is frequently educated believers who are key to the production of distinctively Christian goods and the construction of peculiarly Christian landscapes, e.g. the Church's cemeteries.

Images fuse the visible and the invisible. In the prologue to St John's Gospel, the Word incarnate's glory, full of grace and truth, is *seen*, not – as the title 'Word' would more naturally suggest – heard. In New Testament religion, seeing came into its own long before the emergence of a Christian pictorial art. But then, with the coming of that art, what radiance is shed on earth! In the smaller domed churches of the middle Byzantine period, the gospel of the Incarnation is wonderfully expressed in the Christos Pantokrator, Christ the All-ruler, of the dome, not, as some would have it, a distant and judgemental figure, but 'the High God who bends to earth, in a gesture of breathtaking intimacy, to listen to the prayers of the humble and afflicted'.[8]

Fergal

Fergus       9064 2228

764

Such a theological art, convinced that it can join heaven and earth, is able to insinuate how beyond the sensuous glory that we see lies a greater glory still – and by far. That implies not only the Incarnation – though that first and foremost – but, as a necessary presupposition of the Word's communication with us through the flesh, the metaphysical eloquence of being in art. A Christian sacral art – a sacramental art – has to build on a metaphysical art that is resistant to trivilisation, un-fixated on such modes as parody and pastiche, which can get beyond irony, is rooted in the body even as it moves out to embrace all that is of the spirit, and converses with eternity.[9] It is hardly coincidental that Western art entered into crisis in the late nineteenth and early twentieth centuries – precisely when the great narrative of Judaeo-Christianity and the cosmology which it shaped were in process of disappearing from public culture.

The loss of power of the Christian world-view does not derive only from the variety of intellectual assaults made on it since the seventeenth century. Some may find the gospel incredible but more find it un-imaginable. To significant degree, it has ceased to clothe itself imaginatively in symbols that speak to people and make them respond, 'Yes, this has the feel of reality about it, the ring of truth is there.' The imagination must rise again with Christ if a living faith is to be reborn.

In this perspective, to recover – in the spirit of Chapter III of this study – the 'splendour of the Liturgy' (invoking in that phrase the English title of a once celebrated and many times reprinted commentary on the Mass of St Pius V by Maurice Zundel),[10] to regain a sense that the ultimate orientation of the arts (the original French title of Zundel's book was, far from accidentally, *Le* poème *de la sainte Liturgie*) must be theocentric and doxological: this can only aid artistic culture in its present wilderness wanderings. For the influential English theoretician of the visual arts Clive Bell, 'significant form' is form behind which we catch some glimpse of ultimate reality. For the sculptor Henry Moore, formal devices have to be expressive of moral and spiritual life if the art in question is to be of any stature.[11]

The difficulty facing the arts ever since the Romantic movement is that the rise of that sophisticated reflection on artistic making we call 'aesthetics' happened simultaneously with the gradual withdrawal of revealed religion from the public space of culture. For Immanuel Kant, we gain in aesthetic judgement the best possible understanding of how things *seem*. At most, then, in the words of Professor Roger Scruton, we see the world 'as it really seems'.[12] The secular artist, encompassed by metaphysical scepticism, cannot bring himself with any facility to that desirable condition where, as the poet Wallace Stevens has it, in words Thomas Aquinas would surely approve, we 'let "be" be finale of "seem"'. As Scruton writes:

> It is through aesthetic contemplation that we confront that aspect of the world which was the traditional concern of theology. We cannot prove, by theoretical reasoning, that there is a God; nor can we grasp the *idea* of God, except by the *via negativa* which forbids us to apply it. Nevertheless, we have intimations of the transcendental. In the sentiment of beauty we feel the purposiveness and intelligibility of everything that surrounds us, while in the sentiment of the sublime we seem to see beyond the world, to something overwhelming and inexpressible in which it is somehow grounded. Neither sentiment can be translated into a reasoned argument – for such an argument would be natural theology, and theology is dead. All we know is that we can know nothing of the transcendental. But that is not what we *feel* – and it is in our feeling for beauty that the content, and even the truth, of religious doctrine is strangely and untranslatably intimated to us.[13]

That is a statement by an agnostic philosopher who is himself *anima naturaliter christiana*, and he is citing a thinker, Kant, who, if his concept of Christian philosophy, never mind orthodoxy, left much to be desired in Catholic terms, spoke nonetheless from a more than residual Lutheranism. As Scruton's words show, the truth of the revelation given in the Incarnation and resurrection of the Lord is desperately needed, so as to give, by way of a Christian metaphysics, more solid flesh to these transcendental 'intimations'. Meanwhile, however, many in the philosophical world have moved on, beyond not only the father of modern philosophy but modern philosophy itself. Here the task of Zion is to save Athens from the novel philistinism called 'postmodernism', which, as we saw in Chapter V, would wreck both revelation and reason (including there aesthetic reason) too. The removal of 'authors' from not just texts but *the world*, in what Roland Barthes calls an activity truly revolutionary since it refuses to allow that inherent meaning can exist, is also, as the same postmodernist prophet argues, an 'anti-theological activity' of the purest dye, refusing God and his 'hypostasis' in reason, as well as science and law.[14] How foolish those Christians who have rushed to hail postmodernism, on the ground of its hostility to the Enlightenment, as their saviour, forgetting that the enemy of my enemy is not necessarily my friend!

What, then, tutored by the beauty of the Liturgy, can the artist learn from the Judaeo-Christian revelation? First and foremost, a theocentric view of all created things. The Impressionist painter Edgar Dégas wrote, 'Everything, everything has a sacred meaning' – a fine, if tacit, statement of the doctrine of creation. God creates the world so that he may be expressed in it, as his superabundant life is imaged and enjoyed by creatures. Inevitably, therefore, the artist has to do with God as from the creation he selects his raw material and transforms it by the bestowal of what the poet Paul Valéry termed 'harmonious and unforgettable shape'. He or she acts thereby as a kind of sub-creator, continuing God's primordial work in dependence on the Creator Spirit. Professor George Steiner has written:

> The arts are most wonderfully rooted in substance, in the human body, in stone, in pigment, in the twanging of gut or the weight of wind on reeds. All good art and literature begin in immanence. But they do not stop there. Which is to say, very plainly, that it is the enterprise and privilege of the aesthetic to quicken into lit presence the continuum between temporality and eternity, between matter and spirit, between man and 'the other'. It is in this common and exact sense that *poiesis* opens on to, is underwritten by, the religious and the metaphysical.[15]

It is in this area of creation theology that the balance between Platonic transcendentalism and Aristotelian empiricism of St Thomas has proved so useful to Catholic aestheticians like Jacques Maritain and Etienne Gilson this century. 'The beauty of the creature', said Thomas, in his commentary on Denys' *Divine Names*, 'is nothing else than the likeness of the divine beauty participated in things.'[16] Because such beauty is earthed in the forms the Creator has bestowed on his works, it can be experienced by us as a radiance or attracting splendour attached to things – and persons. As a modern student of Thomas has remarked of the dictum 'Everything is beautiful in proportion to its form':[17]

> Things stand out for us by their forms. They are the aspects under which things appear to us, the 'looks' they give us, so to speak, and by which we recognise them. They enlighten us as to what things are; and so it is natural to think of a form as a kind of light to which we must be open if we are to perceive or understand a thing.[18]

But since form depends on being for its perfectness, the deeper source of a thing's beauty lies in the 'act of being' by which it reflects the glory of God as *ipsum esse subsistens*, very Being itself. The 'metaphysics of Exodus', the revelation of God as He Who Is, is almost a necessity for any art that has lost its first innocence, if it wishes to use the things of this world as a vocabulary for the sacred. It can learn the essence of that metaphysic from the doxological action of the Liturgy as Paul Claudel did.

It is Peter's vision, when the Angel showed him all the fruits and
the animals of the creation, let down from heaven in a cloth
so that he might freely enjoy them,

And all the images of nature have also been given to us, not like
beasts to be hunted and flesh to be devoured,

But so I may create them in my spirit, using each to understand
the rest . . .[19]

It is because this message must not be obscured that the human artefacts
used in the Liturgy should always be well made of good materials (be
it stone, metal or wood; paint or mosaic; fabric, language, or musical
sound), and not traduce by lack of form the creation they continue
and, in continuing, representatively sum up.

The second sort of intelligible beauty which the artist can learn from
the Liturgy pertains to the possibility of redemption, and so derives
more intimately from the Liturgy's paschal character, its basic form. In
a world where human beings have huge potential but also suffer from
their own and their neighbours' limitations and alienation, it is not by
chance that the Liturgy's beauty is sacrificial. The transcendent cosmic
atonement to which it points in hope comes by means of a sacrifice.
The Liturgy knows true tragedy, which is indeed the arena of our
fallen condition, but it knows it more specifically as the ground of
resurrecting sacrifice. Even or especially at the 'extreme verge' of the
most precipitous 'cliffs of fall' (Hopkins) what Karl Rahner called the
'absolute future' of God-with-man is incipient. This J. S. Bach learned
from the Church's worship when in all the *Matthew Passion*'s portrayals
of suffering he created by musical means the sense that it is not just
brute, it is for a purpose. At the arrest in the Garden, the words 'Behold,
the hour has come!' are accompanied by a note sequence that in Bach's
musical vocabulary means victory. That the death on the cross is not
meta-history's final word is signified by the strange sense of expectancy
at the end of the aria 'O Golgotha' where the singer's final note is not
the tonic but the leading note, leaving the cadence unfinished. Here is
suffering pregnant with hints of glory and joy beyond.

The liturgical life, then, can tutor the artist as to not only the theocentric and doxological character of finite being, but also the possibility
of the redemption of existence through the transfiguration of its negative
component in that fashion we call 'eschatological', when all is right *in
the End*. It is by its transgression of this canon that liturgical sentimen-
tality (denying the negative, and the need for the End) is such a sin.

The reaffirmation of a theology of Zion and the repulse of the
Philistines should have beneficent consequences not only for the

surrounding culture, and especially for the arts in confirming theo-centric orientation and the possible redemption of suffering by sacrifice. It should also help the Church as well. In a rationalist world where praxis is all and that depth to existence which poets, artists and musicians have explored flattened out, it is tempting for Christians to take their cue from the age and interpret their faith in terms of a blood-less rationalism or a 'practical' Christianity unconscious of its own pre-suppositions. But in thus levelling the mountain of Zion where the Holy One dwells high and lifted up we would be denaturing the biblical faith itself. 'The God of the Covenant and the Kingdom is not only the "true" God and not just the "good" God; he is also the "beautiful" God.'[20]

The Church needs artists and craftsmen in all the relevant media, so that she can enact liturgically what a theological aesthetics of revelation recommends, and indeed surround the Liturgy with that penumbra of liturgically inspired and liturgically related artistic activity which may not be seen or heard in church, yet which provides a vital context for what *is* seen and heard there. We cannot summon up such artists and craftsmen from the vasty deep, but we can keep alive a sense of their ecclesial vocation, their inalienable place in the Church, by reminding ourselves of the task their predecessors performed. We need, though, to work at a theological critique of the history of the Christian arts, and identify more fully those elements in the Christian theophany which can and must receive imaginative expression. Certain art-forms and individual artists, in whatever medium, will come, in such a process, to acquire a canonical, normative and paradigmatic status. I can offer two examples, corresponding to my distinction between liturgical art and a Christian art that leads into the Liturgy. And they are: the art of the Byzantine icon and the poetry of Claudel.

Absent in Byzantine art are the concerns for the ethos of human society and the individual's existence before God common in Western mediaeval art – the portrayal of occupations and the characteristic labour of the seasons, the personification of virtues and vices, allegories of the liberal arts, and the expression of eschatological hopes and fears. Instead, the heart of the Christian faith is laid bare: the Church's Christological dogma, with all its saving implications. Here, other historical subjects from Old and New Testaments, as well as the apocrypha, find their place not so much by any independent narrative value as for their testimony to the truth of the central dogmata, while the saints, as refractions of the 'only Holy One', Jesus Christ, can easily be brought under the same rubric.

If we were to make an inventory of features commonly adduced to explain the character of art, the list we would come up with would surely include: its authors' aim of establishing intimate relation between the world of the beholder and the world of the image; its comparative simplicity as figures identified either by unmistakable attributes or plain inscription are placed frontally before us, or, in more dramatic contexts, face each other on a curved or angled surface; the way it beckons us to enter dialogue or action within the typical 'hanging' architecture of a cupola-crowned, cross-in-square, church building, expressive as that is of *katábasis*, the downward movement of the divine economy of grace. But is there a master-key to its interpretation?

The late nineteenth-century Russian rediscoverer of the iconographic tradition, Evgeny Trubetskoy, believed that there *was* such a single key, and he identified it as the essential *Gestalt* of the Liturgy, the Paschal action itself.[21] The attenuated, ascetic figures painted nevertheless with such chromatic brilliance convey the fact that the joy of universal resurrection is found only through the life-giving cross.

It is noteworthy that in the so-called 'querelle de l'art sacré' which troubled French Catholicism and the Roman authorities between 1945 and 1955, an objection to the art of Georges Rouault, in other respects one of the more acceptable of the artists who worked on the celebrated church of Assy in Haute-Savoie, was that, powerfully as his *Christ aux outrages* expresses the suffering of Christ, 'the Christ of the Resurrection tends to be passed over in silence'.[22] In other words, it failed to pass a canonical test inherent to a specifically liturgical aesthetic.

More satisfactory as an art that induces to the Liturgy, though not itself liturgical, is, in the medium of words, the poetry of Claudel, of which du Sarment wrote in his study *Claudel et la Liturgie* that 'jubilation' there has its source in 'sacrifice joyously consented to'.[23] In that poetry, the Liturgy appears as cosmic praise. In a creation in a wide sense sacramental, every being has a voice, even if it takes a sacerdotal humanity to assemble the voices and make them resonate in the conscious worship of God. And that is not all, for to such creaturely praise, 'the perfect "praiser", the Christ, has added by his Sacrifice a divine character, and an incomparable splendour'.[24] As Claudel put it in *Conversations dans le Loir-et-Cher*: 'The redeeming Word must make himself heard by everything that the creating Word has brought to be, so that nothing will be alien to his revelation in glory.'[25] As the instrument of integration for a creation whose unity sin has destroyed, the cross bears for Claudel a cosmic character. Hence the importance to him of John 12.32: 'When I am exalted, I shall draw all things to myself', the two arms flung wide along its beams reaching, as the eternal Wisdom, from end to end of the world. In such works as *Corona benignitatis anni Dei* on the liturgical cycle or *La Messe là-bas* on the rite of Mass, not only does Claudel re-express the content of the Liturgy, centred on the glorious cross, so that we may see its transfiguration of nature and human existence for what it is. The Liturgy also impresses its own qualities of form – ultimately, its paschal quality – on his poems in their realism, 'sobriety, clarity, detachment (the hard Good Friday qualities), yet also ardour, *suavitas*, splendour (the glorious Easter ones).

It is typical of Claudel, as in Britain of his contemporary David Jones, that, like not only Byzantine art but all the great styles of historic Christendom, he could deal in symbolic analogy because he accepted intellectually the existence of multiple, interconnected planes of reality. The Thomist principle of analogy, which both Claudel and Jones recognised, posits internal relations between the different orders of the real thanks to their orientation to a common source, centre and goal. As Trubetskoy's modern successor Paul Evdokimov has pointed out, a materialist art is, by contrast, doomed finally to loss of form, as in much impressionist and abstract painting and their literary equivalents where a fragmented outpouring of physical images or sense expressions is divorced from a wider context of meaning.[26]

But the world embodies, or can embody, epiphany, and the more sublime the form given to such manifestations of transcendent meaning, the more we find those forms to express something intimately our own, answering our deepest needs. Only in the wedding of form to content achieved by a signmaker is that perception brought (mystical experience aside) within our range.

Balthasar, however, goes beyond such 'traditional' – classically, Thomist – ontology in his assertion that the analogy of being *is* Jesus Christ, who is thus the 'concrete universal' sought by Hegel: a claim of theological metaphysics which represents in philosophical style the implicit claim of the Liturgy itself that the axis on which the God-world relation moves is the Passover of the Lord. It is because in such different ways the liturgical art of Byzantium and also the para-liturgical poetry of Claudel (and Jones) grasped this that they serve the beauty of the Liturgy so well.

In conclusion, then, we return to that wider agenda which, as set by Hodges, figured in Chapter III of this book. As Peter Taylor Forsyth, the Scots Congregationalist theologian so much admired by Balthasar, has it, it is improbable that a great Christian art – and so the serving in signs and symbols of the eschatological beauty in the Liturgy – will arise once more

> till the condition of its existence in the Middle Ages is again realized, and we possess a theology which is not only tolerated by

the public intelligence, but is welcome for life, commanding for
the reason, and fascinating for the imagination of the age.[27]

So there is much to be done, not only for the worshipping life of
Catholicism but for its intellectual culture, and its art. And if, in the
words of W. S. Gilbert in the Savoy opera *Patience*,

> Though the Philistines may jostle,
> you will rank as an apostle,
> in the high aesthetic band[28]

that will be, should the thesis here presented have anything to
recommend it, because of that creation-consummating mystery of the
Trinitarian Incarnation in the glory of the cross from which the Liturgy
– and in its wake, all the 'material culture' of Christendom – borrows
its beauty.

## NOTES

1. These are the most basic criteria involved in Roger Scruton's *The Classical Vernacular. Architectural Principles in the Age of Nihilism* (London, 1995).

2. P. Davey, 'Faith in Buildings', *Architectural Review* 198. 1185 (1995), p. 5.

3. D. G. Stroik, 'Modernist Church Architecture', *Catholic Dossier* 3, 3 (1997), p. 7.

4. *Catechism of the Catholic Church* (London: Geoffrey Chapman, 1994), paras. 1180, 1181.

5. *Rite for the Dedication of a Church*, Paragraphs 2, 3.

6. C. McDannell, *Material Christianity. Religion and Popular Culture in America* (New Haven and London, 1995), p. 2.

7. Ibid., p. 6.

8. P. Brown, 'A More Glorious House', *New York Review of Books*, 29 May 1997, p. 20, commenting on H. C. Evans and W. D. Wixom (eds.), *The Glory of Byzantium. Art and Culture of the Middle Byzantine Era, AD 843–1261* (New York, 1997).

9. I take these terms of set intent from the manifesto of 'The New Metaphysical Art' associated with Dr Peter Abbs of the Institute of Education at the University of Sussex.

10. M. Zundel, *The Splendour of the Liturgy* (ET London, 1945).

11. P. Fuller, *Theoria. Art and the Absence of Grace* (London, 1988), pp. 158, 191.

12. R. Scruton, 'Modern Philosophy and the Neglect of Aesthetics', *Times Literary Supplement*, June 1987, p. 616.

13. Ibid., p. 604.

14. Cited in S. Prickett, *Words and the Word. Language, Poetics and Biblical Interpretation* (Cambridge, 1986), p. 26.

15. G. Steiner, *Real Presences* (London, 1989), p. 227.

16. Thomas Aquinas, *In divinis nominibus*, c. 4, lect. 5, n. 337.

17. Ibid., c. 4, lect. 5, n. 349; cf. idem, *Summa Theologiae*, Ia., q. 5, a. 4, ad i.

18. A. A. Maurer, C.S.B., *About Beauty. A Thomistic Interpretation* (Houston, 1983), p. 9. Cf. ibid., pp. 6–19 and 105–22 on the ontological foundations of beauty in Aquinas.

19. P. Claudel, 'Cinq grandes Odes', in idem, *Oeuvre poétique* (Paris, 1967), p. 281.

20. B. Quelquejeu, 'Le Christianisme comme poétique', in *Le beau Dieu. Christus* (Paris, 1980), p. 18.

21. E. N. Trubetskoy, *Icons. Theology in Colour* (ET Crestwood, N.Y., 1973).

22. Cited in G.-J. Auvert, *Défense et illustration de l'art sacré* (Paris, 1956), p. 61; cf. W. S. Rubin, *Modern Sacred Art and the Church of Assy* (New York and London, 1961), pp. 84–8.

23. A. du Sarment, *Claudel et la Liturgie* (Bruges, 1946), p. 72.

24. Ibid., p. 12.

25. P. Claudel, *Conversations dans le Loir-et-Cher* (Paris, 1935⁸), p. 258.

26. P. Evdokimov, *L'art de l'icône. Théologie de la beauté* (Paris, 1970).

27. P. T. Forsyth, *Religion in Recent Art* (London, 1905), p. 148.

28. *The Savoy Operas. Being the Complete Text of the Gilbert and Sullivan Operas Originally Produced in the Years 1875–1896, by Sir W. S. Gilbert* (London and New York, 1967), p. 174.

# IX

# *Rethinking Feminism*

FEMINISTS are a more ancient breed than the feminist *movement*. Women who wished to obtain legal rights identical to those enjoyed by men could be found, for instance, among the liberal-bourgeois households of the French Revolution – although the 'Declaration' on the rights of 'the woman and citizeness' addressed by Olympia de Gouges, on behalf of the 'Third Estate', to Marie Antoinette in the declining months of the Bourbon monarchy in 1791, got short shrift from the subsequent revolutionary Convention which sent her to the guillotine in 1793.[1] The feminist movement of the late nineteenth and early twentieth centuries derives either from a matrix centred on constitutional law, with a leadership upper class in Europe, middle class in America,[2] or from an origin in revolutionary socialism which in its Marxian form proclaimed the necessity of freeing women from the tyranny of the 'holy family'. However, few proletarian women seemed inclined to accept this offer of liberation from husbands and children – the improvement of their working conditions was more to the point. The Saint-Simonian socialism of the mid-nineteenth century, with its capacious package of demands – for the legal equality of women, their social and economic emancipation, and a liberty to change sexual partners unstigmatised and at will – more truly anticipates the character of the 'neofeminism' of the Western world after the Second World War.

Armed with such scriptures as Simone de Beauvoir's *The Second Sex* and Betty Friedan's *The Feminine Mystique* and ideological ammunition of various kinds (from the civil rights movement, the revisionist cultural Marxism of the Frankfurt School, the rhetorical and confrontationist manoeuvres of 'black power', the theoreticians of the sexual revolution), neofeminists, in the 1960s and 70s chiefly American, went on the offensive in the name not so much of 'emancipation', which had connotations of gradualism, but of 'liberation', which did not.[3] A major distinguishing feature of the new feminism would be its aspect of 'gender war'. A fresh emphasis on not so much the parity of women with men but their diversity, and therefore on the specificity of the womanly, might well be benign. But it rapidly ceased to express a humanism conscious, and respectful, of gender difference when it carried war into the enemy's camp by a deliberate devaluation of the masculine. A characteristic speculative development in neofeminism is the notion of a specifically female *nature*, of a radical fissure, then, within the human race creative effectively of a duality of species, and so of an absolute difference in origin between men and women.[4] One aspect of such claims is, unsurprisingly, the attempt at a theoretical justification of lesbianism.

Perhaps owing to the activity of the guardian Angels, it cannot be said that such notions have generated a great deal of conviction, even among those for whom sexual orientation is a disturbing or confusing topic. In the feminist literature of the 1980s the theme of gender specificity was taken less as an excuse for a vengeful isolationism and more as an invitation to recognise the enrichment which difference brings.[5] That is not to say that the thesis of two irreducibly competing and essentially non-communicating human natures is no longer encountered. It remains in favour with some radical feminists, just as, for that matter, there are still representatives of the older feminism of the late eighteenth, nineteenth and early twentieth centuries which, from its Enlightenment origins, was interested in penny-plain equality between men and women, not the colour of their complementary differences.

If radicalisation of feminist demands, and the accentuation, some-times extreme, of female difference, are typical traits of neofeminism, so, thirdly, is the primacy it gives to what we might call sexual inventiveness over against the biologically given. A woman's freedom in relation to her own body is used to support the ever greater extension of the legal right to abort the *conceptus*. The co-responsibility of man and woman in sexual relations is denied in favour of what one Spanish theologian has termed *una desresponsibilización sexual de la mujer*: a willed suppression on the woman's part of any exercise of responsibility.[6] Alternatively, by a very different strategy, the gestation of the fruit of sexually expressed love in the woman's body may serve as a basis for the inference that the decision whether to abort or not is the mother's alone. The subversive effect of such patterns of thinking and feeling on the institution and ethos of the family is obvious – and frequently deliberate, for the claim of Friedrich Engels, Marx's literary collaborator, that the family is an engine for the oppression of woman, through the privatising of her emotions and thus her inevitable subordination in the public world, is widely accepted in radical neofeminist circles.

## Feminism and Christianity

The definitely mixed ancestry of feminism at large has not prevented the rise of a specifically Christian version of feminism whether neo- or palaeo-, radical or moderate. Until the Second Vatican Council the Catholic women's movement was, with few exceptions, moral and educational in character. Eschewing the political ambitions of secular feminism, it aimed at enhancing the dignity of women, not only by removal of the less defensible inequalities in the civil law of various societies, but also by giving women a sense of their role in the missionary task of spiritually reconquering society for the faith.[7] The emergence from Catholic backgrounds of women theologians deeply affected by ideological neofeminism introduced an alien, jarring note. Thus in 1968 Mary Daly, lecturer at the Jesuit Society's prestigious Boston College, published her *The Church and the Second Sex*, originally a doctoral thesis defended at the University of Fribourg, in which the Catholic Church appears as the last redoubt of patriarchalism, itself the seminal source of the *machismo* by which men make women suffer.[8] By 1973, Daly had discovered Christianity to be irremediably tied to the patriarchal and Catholicism itself beyond redemption.[9] Her declaration *intra Ecclesiam nulla salus*, however, left her academic tenure rights unaffected and this remained the case as in subsequent writings she developed a syncretistic 'religion of the goddess' – at once inner feminine principle and earth mother (hence the buzzword 'ecofeminism' or, as Daly prefers, 'gyn-ecology').[10] Crucial to the revival of 'goddess religion' among feminist theologians in Western Europe and North America alike was the rediscovery of the nineteenth-century Swiss historian of ancient religion, J. J. Bachofen. His *Mutterrecht und Urreligion* argued for an aboriginally matriarchal social order – whose restoration, then, would require the reactivation of gynocentric symbolism for the divine.[11] Soon 'Wicca', a revived witchcraft, conceived as the peculiar skills of 'wise' women, added spice to the brew – though the worship of 'Lilith', a demoness figure of Jewish legend, hostile to both God and men, was fortunately reserved to anti-Christian, rather than simply post-Christian, feminist circles.

Most of the writing that issues from those quarters of radical feminism that retain an attachment to gospel and Church hardly merits the name 'theology' at all. The ground for that harsh-sounding judgement is *not*, however, its feminism. (Nothing has yet been said in this chapter about what sort of understanding of woman Catholic theology might nurture.) Rather, doubt as to the wellfoundedness of calling much of this literature 'theology' stems from the minor place, infrequent reference, and casual tone which, in these works, the idea of revelation is accorded. Such books and articles present themselves, in overwhelming measure, as reflections on women's experience – and so for the reasons outlined in Chapter IV of this study it is owing to the naturalistic liberalism of their presuppositions that they fall outside the canon of recognisably Catholic divinity – along with all other 'non-dogmatic' theology of whatever stable (most of it, of course, written by men).[12] Feminist scholars with admirable mastery of the data of the sources exist, and their learning and intelligence conspire to send out shafts of light here and there. But, viewed as contributions to the theological tradition of the Church, Elisabeth Schüssler Fiorenza's exegetical work, for instance, or the occasional revisiting of patristics by Rosemary Radford Ruether (in her pre-feminist period, a fine student of the fourth-century Greek doctor St Gregory Nazianzen) fall at the first hurdle.[13] The decision to submit the biblical Canon to the extraneous judgement of feminist orthodoxy, and to propose its reconstitution on that basis, like the refusal to accept the authority of the patristic consensus as a constitutive moment in the Church's reception of the biblical revelation, disqualifies any continuing claim of these writers to membership of the specifically Catholic Christian theological sorority/fraternity.

As a somewhat rueful English Catholic feminist, Angela West,[14] has argued at length, the false universalisation of personal experience which forms the methodological basis of much Christian feminist reflection does not only produce theology that is unrecognisable, often bizarrely so, by the canons of Catholicism. It is also potentially extremely damaging to women themselves. Leaving aside the danger to the authenticity of Catholic doctrine (and so consciousness), there is a menace here to the humanity – the sanity – of feminism-influenced women from which, she thinks, a grasp of that least popular of the Church's dogmas, original sin – itself reaching us, of course, from the biblical Canon patristically interpreted – could save them.

In *Deadly Innocence, Feminism and the Mythology of Sin*, West argues that it is deeply unhelpful to women to convince them of their own essential innocence. Not for them the burden of guilt about human life and its history for which men, as orderers of patriarchal society, are in fact responsible and which they would, if they could, unload on to women, the Eve figures, primal temptresses, of the human world.

Notions of the quintessential peacefulness of women, and their infallible instinct, if left alone by men, to protect and nurture generated a 'euphoric feminist utopianism'. These notions could not survive, however – and here if you will, is 'personal experience' with a vengeance – their attempted exemplification in the women's 'Peace Base' at Greenham Common in Berkshire where a saga of descent into rivalry and recrimination, followed by thousands of radical women in Britain and Europe, dealt a death blow to *faux naïveté*, to 'simple faith in female solidarity and salvation by sisterhood'.[15] And this prompted in West's case a rather wider investigation, via academic literature, of how women behaved under the Third Reich, the classic 'sinful situation' of our time. The result was the discovery that women in National Socialist Germany were quite frequently victimisers – perpetrators, or at least accessories – rather than victims. The feminist archaeology of history, considered as a moral tale, was fable, fantasy.

Human realism, no less than theological, had eventually to revolt against the thesis of Everywoman's holy and immaculate conception. And West comes to rediscover not simply the doctrine of an aboriginal fall encompassing in advance both genders and all cultures in all phases of history (there is in other words, no natural paradise to be found). By pondering the implications of the search for 'liberated' sex this century, and especially among feminists, she finds a peculiar plausibility in Augustine's notion that it is 'our sexuality, as it issues in the process of generation, that provides the most intimate and powerful experience of the flawed will that undermines our idealism'.[16] And that not simply because sexual concupiscence is an extraordinarily graphic illustration of the way post-lapsarian passions escape an enfeebled will but also for the reason that, as parents pass on the scars of one generation to the next, they know themselves, with sickening certainty, to be that process's co-opted agents. It is, West concludes, the judgement of God – and no natural resource – that alone can ground liberation from guilt and that wider righteousness which women (and men) seek, and for an understanding of this the doctrines of Fall and Redemption are indispensable. They are, in fact, indispensably salutary.

## A probe of tradition's resources

If the shriller feminist theological writing is what West calls, uncomplimentarily, 'matronizing claptrap', we may be encouraged to look again at the resources, in this area, of traditional Christendom.

Sensitive historians of the role of women in past society, civilisation, spirituality, and Church can contribute much to amplifying the profile of specifically ecclesial woman – and so bring out the distinctively female contribution to catholicity. One thinks for instance here of the American mediaevalist Caroline Walker Bynum who, while occasionally seeming to deplore the ability of mediaeval women to rise above 'gender wars' in the interests of *humanitas*, argues that these are still authentic female voices (even though men had to permit, and help along, their finding public and literary expression).

> The determination of medieval women writers to speak of themselves more as human than as female, while nonetheless also utilizing rich domestic and female imagery, has no direct connection with current feminism, although the late Middle Ages may be the first time in history when we have large enough numbers of women's voices to be sure we are hearing characteristically female concerns.[17]

And Bynum vigorously repulses the suggestion that, because those concerns as expressed by thirteenth- and fourteenth-century Latin Catholics differ (unsurprisingly) from those of secular or neo-paganising radical feminists today, *therefore* mediaeval women were pitiable victims of patriarchal consciousness. As she writes, 'A focus on women as oppressed or as outsiders obscures the extent to which women – particularly in the late Middle Ages – were the actual creators of some of the distinctive features of mainstream Christian piety.'[18] And in contrast to bland or superficial assumptions about women's history (in the excruciating but widely favoured pun in the less distinguished examples of such studies, 'her-story'), Bynum concurs with the German sociologist Max Weber that 'the gender of the deity or of leaders of cult does not determine the presence or absence of either religious or social opportunities for either gender'.[19] By about 1320, she calculates, women account for nearly three-quarters of lay saints.

The reputation of holy women in the mediaeval period rested on, above all, their charismatic authority – symbolised especially in the matter of visions. Their mysticism was more historical and incarnational – more *fleshly*. They felt less need for structured living as found in the Orders or conventual houses of men – hence the multitude of *béguines* and (at first hardly distinguishable from these) tertiaries. Their apparently extravagant world-rejection and mystical yearning was often married with an utterly practical charitable care for others in society. The contrasts of action and contemplation, world-fleeing and world-serving break down in the lives of the holy women: typical is Catherine of Genoa's implied assertion that, since human suffering can enjoy integration with Christ's eternally valid sacrifice, asceticism, mysticism and charity are ultimately one single act.[20] 'Women understood the suffering that lay at the core of their lives to be both mystical ecstasy and the active, innerworldly service of their fellow human beings.'[21] It will be seen that Caroline Bynum's exemplarily meticulous and sensitive research is far from confirming the conviction of both a secular and a Church-alienated religious feminism that historic Christendom simply stereotyped women and, once having done so, deposited them firmly on its margins.

## Woman and the two societies

How in the perspective of a reconstituted Christendom should we be reimagining woman in the twin societies, the civil one and that of the Church? The story of modern feminism is, in part, the revindication of women's full contribution to these two communions, the social and the ecclesial, by an honouring of their gifts that is not only more conscious, more self-aware, but also more public and effective. But it is also the painful relearning of lessons that Christendom already knew. The fatigue many professional working women now report would seem to derive *au fond* from depression, resentment and exhaustion at having to fill *simultaneously* too many roles. Most women give highest priority to family obligations – exchange with neighbours, and their own children. Indeed, speaking now more generally (and this comment throws light on the caritative activities of the mediaeval women mystics described by Bynum), most women find themselves, almost without thinking, closely bound up in other people's lives. That greater need (and capacity) for self-involvement with others indicates that 'double career coupledom' is not – even irrespective of the effects on children – a desirable norm for the great majority of women. (A small minority will pull it off, and a rather larger minority, perhaps, prefer not to be home-builders at all.) As Christopher Lasch remarked in a collection of posthumously published essays on this topic: a feminism worthy of the name would not disparage housework, motherhood, or unpaid civic and neighbourly services; it would reject the mystique of an exigent and intrusive technological progress and economic development which impedes that refunctionalisation of the household I discussed in Chapter VII.[22] The recognition is gradually dawning that it is useless for politicians to wring their hands about the decline of the family while maintaining 'politically correct' support for those women who have chosen – in approved new-style fashion[23] – not to include a father in the upbringing of their child. This is not simply because society needs stable families (though it does). It is also because women themselves need the co-operation of men in the bringing up of children. Nor is cohabitation an answer: women also need that fixity of status which guarantees them against instant replacement by another sexual partner – and this assurance is only available where divorce (as distinct from separation) is either impossible or at least difficult to obtain. A case should be made too for the general preferability of traditional divisions of labour within the unity of those responsibilities which family and home bring: that prevents rivalries from poisoning the relations of the couple on which so much turns.[24]

In and out of the home, a woman's dignity cannot in the long term be advanced, as Angela West rightly says,

> solely on the basis of how she and her sex have been wronged. Her dignity is in her calling whatever it may be, how she makes her profession; not on how she claims her debts but on how she pays her dues to the community that she belongs to. Thus, it ought to be possible to judge a true feminist not by the purity of her theory but by her fruits of sisterly compassion, loyalty and co-operation. The phoney virtue through victimhood is a continuation by other means of that attitude which feminism has so consistently and rightly deplored – that women can be seen as less than full moral agents – that they are to be somehow excepted from the moral standards we use to judge other human beings.[25]

West's book ends with a plea for the recovery by feminists in the Christian tradition of the orthodox soteriology of the Church. As she puts it:

> the scale of the outrage by humanity and against humanity is so vast, our ability to repair or restore or compensate so negligible, that all our little busy-ness for justice is just so much froth on the ocean by comparison. If we are not redeemed, then we are wholly abandoned, truly lost.[26]

The mystery of the redemptive Incarnation reveals 'a gracious kind of dealing, unlike that in our world of claim and counter-claim', and so, if our freedom allows it, draws from us the ability to receive from God what is unearned by us, and to offer to each other what cannot be claimed.

Which brings us to the topic of women in, more especially, *the Church*. The marginalisation of Christology in much feminist theology mirrors its unwillingness to find a positive role for the male gender in female flourishing. The delusion which would take innocent womankind as the healing and transfiguring agent of the historical process ruined by men finds its heretical ecclesial equivalent in the notion that it is the victimhood of women that redeems the world. (The possibility of a female co-victimhood, in dependence on the role of Christ, and so of a co-redemptrix is, however, one to which I shall, at the end of this chapter, return.) But the salvation in which, for Catholic doctrine, God sees to the fulfilment of his creative work has its own medium in a covenant between the Word incarnate and the Church which is itself nuptially – maritally – ordered, and where accordingly the gender-differentiated roles of a 'man' (Christ) and a 'woman' (the Church, his Bride) are of vital significance.

This nuptial dimension of the covenant of salvation not only makes it the case, negatively, that women cannot be ministerial priests. Positively, it shows the basis of feminine ecclesial authority – that is, the capacity of the Church's women to be life-giving sources (in the original sense of the word 'authors') of the Church's life. Though women do not stand sacramentally, as men may do, in the place of Christ, they are nonetheless a true source of life that completes the full meaning of male authority – since the latter is found only within the unity of the 'one flesh', that mystery of unity-in-differentiation whereby the Letter to the Ephesians treats the sacrament of marriage as an echo of the relation of Christ and his Church.

Women are authoritative for the Church in the intimate ingenious-ness of their creative responsiveness to the Saviour and his sacramental representatives of male gender. Thus Monica Migliorino Miller can write:

> The prime example of feminine authority is Mary, the Mother of God. Her life-giving 'yes' began a new creation and by it, she is rendered Queen of Heaven, Queen of Saints, Queen of Apostles. Feminine authority also can be seen residing in one like St. Monica, who exercised authority in calling her son, St. Augustine, to truth and holiness. It is found in early Church martyrs like Ss. Perpetua and Agatha who are actually the protagonists in a contest of wills against their oppressors. It is seen in the life of St. Margaret Clitherow, who, exemplifying the *ecclesia magistra*, preached the Catholic faith to her husband and defied civil authority by hiding priests in her own home. It is found in the life of St. Teresa of Avila, who, as a sign of the teaching and nourishing Church, reformed a corrupted religious order. It is found in St. Catherine of Siena, who, as a true voice of the *mater ecclesia*, called an exiled pope to courage and guided his return to Rome. Feminine ecclesial authority is seen in the lives of Dorothy Day, Joan Andrews Bell [heroine of the Catholic pro-life movement in the United States] and Mother Teresa of Calcutta. It is seen in the countless lives of

> Christian women who speak and live their feminine responsibility
> for the faith and who thus call all people, including husbands,
> priests, and bishops, to live a deeper life in Christ.[27]

Elisabeth Schüssler Fiorenza claims that at the heart of the gospel lies 'the discipleship of equals',[28] but the question is whether an undifferentiated concept of equality does not derive more from secular currents of Enlightenment and revolutionary thinking than from the tradition originated by the gospel – a tradition which speaks, rather, of multiform complementarity within a foundational brotherhood/sisterhood. The social anthropologist Adrian Edwards, a Holy Ghost Father, comments:

> The imposition of equality has often gone with the view of society
> as being composed of atomic individuals. But, as one of the
> characters of Malraux's *L'Espoir* remarks, the real opposite of
> oppression is not equality but fraternity. Life is enriched when it is
> experienced as the interplay of differences, rather than the
> juxtaposition of equivalences.[29]

Christian faith holds that God has given each human person the radical capacity for intelligence and freedom (whether or not they are able to exercise it at this or that time), and on this basis we posit a fundamental equality of all persons as images of the God of understanding and love. Such personal equality must not be confused, however, with that functional inequality whereby, in the Church, the non-anarchy (i.e. the *hierarchy*) of a manifold of co-ordinated offices serves a participatory communion where each makes their unique contribution to the common good.

We are dealing then with a complex, organic, dynamic kind of unity,[30] as St Paul's frequently cited teaching on the diversely membered body of Christ in 1 Corinthians (12.4–26) bears witness. Its just operation is not to be measured, accordingly, by the criteria of any secular model of political society. Rather, justice in the Church should be judged by 'how the church in its governance succeeds in bringing about full participation of all its members in the church's life and mission'.[31] And applying this to the question of the ordination of women, Benedict Ashley continues:

> Men alone are qualified for this particular function in the church
> not because they are superior as persons, but because they are
> qualified to be spiritual fathers and women to be not spiritual
> fathers, but spiritual mothers. The exclusion of women from
> priesthood, therefore, is not an injustice but a simple recognition
> of the woman's special gifts and special contribution to the church.
> In fact the church would be unjust to women if it were to call them

to a function inappropriate to their special gifts, just as it would be if it called men to an inappropriate role and ignored their special gifts as men.[32]

And Ashley concludes by drawing attention to the traditional 'ranking' of contemplative women in the Church above ministerial priesthood.[33] Their consummate activity anticipates the simultaneous completeness of acting yet rest of heaven, whereas the task of priests belongs with the struggle to sanctify the people of God on earth. That particularly 'hierarchical ordering' is sealed in the Blessed Virgin Mary – meditation on whose receptive ratifying in suffering and silence, petition and praise of the sacrifice that saved the world (she is, in a not altogether happy yet perhaps indispensable phrase, the 'co-redemptrix') has resumed in notable fashion in our time. Modern feminism, its excesses and distortions notwithstanding, may yet prove the 'question' which will stimulate the Church in 'answering' to a deeper grasp of women's co-involvement in divinely redemptive action.

## NOTES

1. O. Blanc, *Olympe de Gouges: une femme de liberté* (Paris, 1981²).

2. W. L. O'Neill, *The Woman Movement: Feminism in the United States and England* (London, 1969) .

3. S. de Beauvoir, *Le deuxième sexe* (Paris, 1949); B. Friedan, *The Feminine Mystique* (New York, 1963) ; K. Millet, *Sexual Politics* (New York, 1970).

4. N. Holmström, 'Do Women Have a Distinct Nature?', in M. Pearsall (ed.), *Women and Values. Readings in Recent Feminist Philosophy* (Belmont, Calif., 1986); A. Carr and E. Schüssler Fiorenza, *The Special Nature of Women?* (= *Concilium* 27.6, 1991).

5. See, for instance, G. P. di Nicola, *Ugualianza e differenza. La reciprocità uomo-donna* (Rome, 1988).

6. J. A. Riestra, 'Los movimientos feministas y su significación teológica: la mariologia feminista', *Estudios marianos* LXII (1996), p. 12.

7. P. Gaiotti de Biase, *Gli origini del movimento cattolico femminile* (Brescia, 1963).

8. M. Daly, *The Church and the Second Sex* (New York, 1968).

9. M. Daly, *Beyond God the Father. Toward a Philosophy of Woman's Liberation* (Boston, 1973).

10. M. Daly, *Gyn-Ecology. The Metaethics of Radical Feminism* (Boston, 1978).

11. J. J. Bachofen, *Mutterrecht und Urreligion* (Stuttgart, 1861; Basle, 1948³).

12. See for example, A. O'Hara Graff, 'The Struggle to Name Women's Experience: Assessment and Implications for a Theological Construction', *Horizons* 20 (1993), pp. 215–33. For the factors which function as necessary and sufficient conditions in calling any work an instance of 'Catholic theology', see my *The Shape of Catholic Theology* (Collegeville, Minn. and Edinburgh, 1991).

13. E. Schüssler Fiorenza, *In Memory of Her. A Feminist Theological Reconstruction of Christian Origins* (New York, 1983); R. Radford Ruether, 'Misogynism and Virginal Feminism in the Fathers of the Church' in idem (ed.), *Religion and Sexism. Images of Women in the Jewish and Christian Traditions* (New York, 1974), pp. 150–83.

14. A. West, *Deadly Innocence. Feminism and the Mythology of Sin* (London, 1995), p. xvi.

15. Ibid., p. 19.

16. Ibid., p. 112, drawing on – but modifying in more Augustinian direction, the judgements in P. Brown, 'Sexuality and Society: Augustine', in idem, *The Body and Society: Men, Women and Sexual Renunciation in Early Christianity* (London, 1988), pp. 387–427.

17. C. Walker Bynum, *Fragmentation and Redemption. Essays on Gender and the Human Body in Medieval Religion* (New York, 1991), p. 18.

18. Ibid., p. 57 and see Bynum, *Jesus as Mother. Studies in the Spirituality of the High Middle Ages* (Berkeley, Calif., 1982); and *Holy Feast and Holy Fast: the Religious Significance of Food to Medieval Women* (Berkeley, Calif., 1987).

19. Bynum, *Fragmentation and Redemption*, p. 59. Over against, e.g. C. P. Christ and J. Plaskow (eds.), *Womanspirit Rising: A Feminist Reader in Religion* (New York, 1979), and C. Spretnak (ed.), *The Politics of Women's Spirituality. Essays in the Rise of Spiritual Power within the Feminist Movement* (New York, 1982). See also B. J. MacHaffie, *Her Story. Women in the Christian Tradition* (Philadelphia, 1986).

20. Bynum, *Holy Feast and Holy Fast*.

21. Bynum, *Fragmentation and Redemption*, p. 74.

22. C. Lasch, *Women and the Common Life. Love, Marriage and Feminism*, ed. by E. Lasch-Quinn (New York, 1997).

23. 'The whole debate about political correctness is in reality an American domestic argument between old and new elites competing for status and power. It has little or nothing to do with the utter otherness of the mass of the world's oppressed', A. West, *Deadly Innocence*, op. cit., p. 165.

24. This does *not* licence exploitation by husbands: in the doctrine of Ephesians 5, the 'headship' of husbands is exercised, within the mutuality of love-relationship, by the greater sacrifice with which they serve wives. *Pace* modern critics, its is the *mode* of this headship, not the *fact* of it, which can be described as a cultural carapace. See B. Ashley, O.P., *Justice in the Church. Gender and Participation* (Washington, 1996), p. 101.

25. West, *Deadly Innocence*, p. 167.

26. Ibid., pp. 184–5.

27. M. Migliorino Miller, 'Adam and Eve – Women's Authority in the Church', *Crisis*, September 1995, p. 18. See also her *Sexuality and Authority in the Catholic Church* (Scranton, Penn., 1994).

28. Schüssler Fiorenza, *In Memory of Her*, p. 152.

29. A. Edwards, C.S.P., 'Gender and Sacrifice', *New Blackfriars* 67 (1986), p. 376.

30. Ashley, O.P., *Justice in the Church*, p. 17.

31. Ibid., p. 66.

32. Ibid., pp. 110–11. Ashley's argument turns on the twin postulate that 'the essential function of priesthood . . . is representational, iconic, symbolic, sacramental' (ibid., p. 88) and that Christ's maleness – as Son, Bridegroom, New Adam – is of considerable theological importance when seen against the backdrop of the *proper* (and not merely metaphorical) analogy in Scripture between God and the earthly father who gives us life and loves and cares for us – but does not, like an earthly mother, produce us (pantheistically) out of himself. As he writes 'of course women image [Christ] as he is human, but they are not well qualified to represent him precisely as he is the new Adam and the image of God as Father', ibid., p. 10.

33. Ibid., pp. 131–50.

# X

## *Remaking Religious Life*

THE concluding paragraph of the last chapter pointed to the profound importance in the Church of the Religious life – notably in its most fully 'bridal' form, that of contemplative women. Monastic vows are not a sacrament (unlike marriage vows) because, it may be suggested, they anticipate that life – this *heavenly* life – to which all sacraments mediate entry. Yet all is not well with the Religious life in the Church today.

The experience of Religious in the Western church over the last thirty-five or so years strongly suggests the truth of the old adage that it is easier to found a Religious institute than to reform one. Most Orders, Congregations and communities riven, to a greater or lesser extent, by conflicting evaluations of their past, present and future have, since the Second Vatican Council, reached some kind of *modus vivendi* which allows their boats to chug along – but without the capacity to set sights for a long voyage and put in place the training ('asceticism' was the ancient word) needed to get the sailors fit for the journey. If, 'politically', the time is not always ripe for more vigorous captains at the helm (for, like Europe after the Revolutionary and Napoleonic Wars, the Religious life in the West, following a period of great ecclesial and cultural confusion, may need above all, in Metternich's term, *repose*), at least it should be possible to clarify the doctrine of the Religious life, and construct a richer theology of its place in the Church.

Many accounts of what Religious are meant to be seem semi-secularised in their adoption of either contestationist or therapeutic models drawn from politics and the caring professions, or their orchestration of themes from ecologism and feminism. Doubtless there are here elements of thought and sensibility which can be incorporated into a genuine theology – on the classic analogy of the use of philosophy in dogmatics – but the heartlands of any evangelical and Catholic doctrine of Religious life will have to be situated somewhat nearer than this to the midpoint of revelation: the Father, in his epiphany in Jesus Christ by the Spirit for the salvation of the world.

## A doctrine of Religious life

It should hardly need saying, in the first place, that the specifically Christian Religious life (we are not thinking here of its analogues in paganism – and, at one period, Judaism) only makes sense when considered as a special calling within the Church, itself the body of those called out from the nations for the Father's glory. Without the divine electing choice whereby the incarnate Son calls those whom the Father designates *in the way* the Father wills, and in his Ascension and sitting at the Father's right hand ever draws disciples to him by the outpouring of the Spirit, there would be no such thing as a consecrated life of poverty, chastity and obedience among Christians. Only because someone believes their life-role in the Church to correspond to a kind of ecclesial vocation whose character is disclosed in the Gospels and made viable as a form of living by the power of the Spirit in the apostolic Church does one, as a Catholic Christian, attempt to live at all in the fashion indicated by those fundamental promises or vows.

From this side of the English Channel where impulses from American Catholicism are, owing to the latter's vast numbers and the common tongue, generally preponderant in matters of Religious life 'renewal', there is much to be learned from an older generation of European writers whose profound rooting in the theological culture has enabled them to write with insight into these connections. Thus the French Dominican Pie Régamey, in a sympathetic study prompted by the teaching, on this subject, of Pope John Paul II in early letters and addresses of his pontificate, takes as his *point de départ* the Pope's notion that the greatest task of Religious in the *contemporary* world is to restore a sense of the reality of God precisely by recalling people to the true nature of freedom – which they (Religious) can do best. How so? In the way of life they have chosen, freedom's transcendent orientation as reawakened by Christ and the Spirit is at its most palpable.[1] Atheistic humanism in all its forms – pragmatist, neo-positivist, psycho-analytic, Existentialist, Marxist, Structuralist, Nietzschean – robs man of a constitutive dimension of his existence: search for the infinite God to whom natural desire draws him. Human genius creates instead surrogate infinities, false objects for desire, which recoil against man and render true flourishing impossible. If this is the high drama of human life today, then it is also where the real 'relevance' of Religious life is situated. Such relevance is not to be sought, accordingly, in assisting the goals of the secular city or advancing such causes as ecology or feminism – which is not to say, however, that rejoicing is out of place when an overlap is discovered between divine revelation on the one hand and the aspirations of contemporary culture on the other. Still, the primary pertinence of the monk or the nun, the Religious brother or sister, lies elsewhere, and Régamey cites in this connection some words of the present Pope at Rio de Janeiro in 1980: 'You are called to realize salvation as signs and instruments of the invisible world . . . Do not conform yourself to this world's opinions and tastes.'² If relevance is the watchword, then, prayer will precisely *not* be abandoned for the sake of action; vows will *not* be interpreted along the lines of a secularist mentality which stifles their religious motivation; the discipline of an observant life in common will *not* be lightly set aside; the silence that is the mother of contemplation will not be disprized; habits will *not* be replaced by secular clothes; socio-political analysis will *not* be regarded as the best or even only means whereby to identify the goal that the Religious life sets.

Religious men and women do not need professional status (though it may sometimes be useful to the Church's mission if they acquire it) because what they are to be is first and foremost experts in the Infinite. Régamey emphasises the way Religious are required to be more rooted than are other Christians in the eternal world which breaks in on this one through the *mirabilia Dei*, the mighty works of God attested in Scripture. And this is true not only of the contemplative Religious but also of the active – who should be *contemplativus in actione*, contemplative in the very way he (or she) acts. At a profound level, the Religious life should be an anticipation of God's intimate dwelling with his elect people at the end of time.

> Just as the sea finds in you its ample connivance, and the stars of a fine night have secret friendships in our own, as flowers, affectionate animals, streams people our interior paradise, so the marvels of God, of which he gives us certain knowledge, become naturalised within us.³

It is our supernatural destiny – the divine friendship, mediated by the missions in time of Son and Spirit – that is to become second nature to us, over and above, or within, the first nature by which we participate in the sacrality of the cosmos. We must resist the temptation, accordingly, to settle for the 'first gift': that is, the goods of creation. No anthropology that falls short of the supernatural will serve the turn of Religious life. It cannot do justice to the scope that is ours when we heed the call of God to love him with a love that is 'spousal', resembling that of married friends. (Whatever our gender, we are always as creatures more feminine than masculine, more recipients than agents, vis-à-vis the Lord.)

The Religious life is directed to the same goal as all Christian living, but animated by an effort to lead the common life of Christians in a way that is more consistent, more integral, in its response to God's self-gift. St Thomas Aquinas' great eucharistic hymn, the *Lauda Sion*, recommends us to 'dare as much as you can': *Quantum potes, tantum aude*. The Saviour asks us to love God with all our strength by our *heart* – what is most intimate about ourselves, with its power to gather together all the elements that constitute our personality; by our *soul* – a reference, for Régamey, to the theologically founded hope that all the tendencies of our psyche will come into play in this spiritual love; and by our *mind* – our understanding as it wakens to the supernatural mystery of the friendship-love God offers, and so gives direction to our own love in return. The gospel counsels of chastity, poverty, obedience, which the Word incarnate gave his disciples as the best ways to tend towards the Father's limitless perfection, are proposed to our freedom, to make of them what our conscience will. But, on the *Lauda Sion* principle, the Christian should always be wanting to give more. For Régamey, the counsels are best understood not negatively as strategies for escaping concupiscence – the disordered passions of lust, covetousness and wilful autonomy – but positively in the context of a mysticism of divine union. All require some sacrifice in the way we approach the people we love (chastity), the goods of creation we cherish (poverty), and the sociality we naturally enjoy on earth (obedience).

Though the documents of the Second Vatican Council have little to say about the Religious life, or the Christian life *tout court*, as 'holy warfare', the new situation of post-Conciliar secularism obliges us, Régamey thinks, to recover the Pauline and Johannine language of battling with this world. Through a falsely secularist interpretation of the intrinsic goodness of earthly realities the spirit of the world has entered the Church, and, as so often in Church history (only the labels on the concepts change), Religious are now required to be signs of rupture and contradiction against the skyline of the secular city. And this is an obligation laid upon them, not simply for their own sake but for the good of all the Church.

## Where the Religious take their stand

Can we put these convictions into a dogmatically and exegetically coherent form? In *Christlicher Stand*, his account of the two funda-mental 'states of life' in the Church (the life of the counsels, or Religious life; and the life of the precepts, the Christian life lived in the *saeculum*, the world), Balthasar proposes that for *both* lives the *spirit* of poverty, chastity and obedience must be present. We cannot imagine a genuine love of God which did not offer him all the worldly goods at one's disposal (compare poverty), or the good that is one's own body (compare chastity) or the good of one's spiritual powers (memory, understanding, will) in so far as these are at one's disposal (compare obedience). The question of the relative significance of life in the world and the Religious life then becomes a matter of the contrasting ways in which this spirit is embodied.[4]

To bring out what is involved in this comparison, Balthasar finds he has to go back to basics – to our original creation. Following him there will enable us to understand better the crucial point Régamey is making. In terms of the Adamic condition there was nothing that resembles the obligation now incumbent on every Christian to decide whether they are called to the life of the counsels or not. In the first Paradise, the distinction between Religious and people in the world could not be drawn: it belongs to a world that once fell and is now in process of redemption by Christ. And yet because Adamic humanity, that humanity with which our first parents were created, is foundational for the rest of God's plan for us, our *Urstand* – our original state – must have some relevance for our subject. The lives of distinction between the various kinds of Christian life must also be lines of convergence which run back towards Adam's state.

What Balthasar will argue is that Religious life and life in the world each mirror one aspect of the Adamic condition which itself simul-taneously embraced both. Since it never occurred to Adam and Eve, until the Fall, to do anything but God's will, they did not need to renounce their wills to do the will of God, as Religious now renounce their wills in obedience. Instead, they felt themselves to be sovereignly free in the world, just as seculars do now – except that the freedom inspired by the protoparents was in no way an illusion. In their case, unlike that of anyone since who has not made the renunciation of self-will, their wills in fact coincided absolutely with God's for them. Similarly, they were entirely chaste, as Religious are called to be, and the purity of their unfallen souls radiated out through their bodies. But like people in the world now, they gave physical expression to their love for each other and saw the offspring of that love in deeper communion (if not yet in children). However, unlike seculars today, and in a way no modern sexologist could imagine, the body was admitted 'only in the role of a servant, to their fruitful yet utterly innocent, essentially spiritual love'. And lastly, Adam and Eve inhabited a state which was at once 'perfect riches and perfect poverty'. Like some people in the world now they enjoyed an abundance of the things they needed, but like Religious (should be), they were utterly ungrasping, unacquisitive, in the way they regarded the gifts of God.

So the state of original righteousness in which Adam and Eve were created can now be found only in two partial, fragmentary alternative kinds of living. *Either* it is found in the Religious life which expresses the inner attitude or disposition of the inhabitants of the Garden, *or* it is found in the life of seculars which expresses the outer fulfilment of the life the first humans lived, but without its inner quality.

Now this may sound as though Balthasar is going to be completely even-handed in the praise he gives to both Religious life and life in the world. Not so. As we might expect, given his desire to maintain the Church's tradition that *in some sense* the consecrated life constitutes a *better way*, he writes that the person who 'attempts to harness the blessings of paradise – i.e. the richness and fullness of life in the garden, as enjoyed by Adam and Eve, without their inner disposition of poverty, chastity and obedience reaps only a curse'.[5] The message of the biblical revelation is that, by the grace of Christ, man is called to recover the blessings of Paradise but only via Christ's example – in other words, in a sacrificial fashion which cannot avoid going through the cross. In the new Paradise of the Kingdom, freedom will be reached only by obedience, manifest spiritual fecundity only by virginity, and the eternal sharing of all good things only by poverty – even if, in the case of the great majority of people, the spirit or ethos of such obedience, virginity and poverty must suffice.

The way that, within the single community of the Church, the two lives diverge is, for Balthasar, dramatically displayed in the differing ways Jesus called disciples to him in the Gospels.

In calling the Twelve, Jesus made a selective choice from among his disciples. So much is obvious, but whereas in Catholic theology generally it would be more usual to see this special choice as the beginnings of the apostolic ministry, the ministerial priesthood, for Balthasar its primary meaning is that Jesus made the Twelve the foundation of what would be the life of the counsels in the Church. Only when with his approaching death his mission became identified with his perfect self-offering did he entrust to his apostles his sacramental sacrifice and give them power over the native virtue of that sacrifice, the forgiveness of sins. Only subsequently (in other words) did Christ ordain the Twelve to a special priesthood.

How does Balthasar formulate the distinction between those disciples of Jesus whom he sees as archetypes of the Religious life and those whom he regards as archetypes, rather, of Christians in the world? He writes:

> By virtue of Jesus' 'Come!' his 'Come and see!', his 'Come, follow me!', the apostles were henceforth always with him. If he sends them away, it is only that they may return to report to him all they have done and taught (Mark 6:30). The people, on the other hand, approach the Lord from the world, which is their dwelling place. After their encounter with him, they return to that world. The two forms of encounter, the two modes of approach, are in sharp contrast. The people's way to the Lord is to search for him in their necessity; their dismissal is attended with healing and grace for their subsequent existence in the world. The sending of the apostles into the world occurs only by the Lord's commission and for his purposes; their return to him is a return to the place where they belong.[6]

Both of these 'movements' – from Christ into the world for its good, and from Christ so as to return to him – are genuine forms of personal discipleship. Neither need apologise for its existence, and the distinction between them argues nothing about greater or less where charity – and so perfection – is concerned. Nonetheless, we can hardly mistake the fact that the Gospels do present the renunciation to which the Twelve are called as the fullest kind of discipleship. Poverty, Balthasar notes, is always placed first in any account of how disciples are to receive a 'hundredfold'. It is, he remarks, the necessary entrance gate to this way of life. Virginity comes second, presented as it is (at this stage) more as a recommendation than a necessary command.

> The fact that poverty is assigned so unequivocally to first place while virginity is initially less significant in terms of the promise can be explained as follows. The Lord called his apostles from the Israel of the Old Testament, where marriage was itself a state of promise. He who came to fulfil the law, not to destroy it (Mt. 5:17), did not want to build his Church on men who had not lived in the true messianic tradition. In the beginning, therefore, celibacy had to be by way of exception, although it should be noted that, even in the beginning, so much emphasis was placed on this exception – in John the Baptist, in John the Evangelist, in Paul – that through their example it had already become the rule for the generations to

be born under the New Testament. Indeed, from the Lord's command to his apostles to be always at the service of the brethren, of which Paul gave the eleven apostles such an illustrious example, it is obvious that renunciation of a wife is no less required than renunciation of house and lands and familial ties.[7]

It is obedience, however, that is really central owing to the fact that the Lord's service will be the exclusive content of the apostles' lives. In this perspective, relinquishing possessions by poverty and letting go of dependence on others by chastity is a means to the end of 'perfect apostleship'. Though Balthasar speaks of obedience as the 'outer and inner freedom to follow Christ wherever he goes', he also makes it clear that this is not to be understood in separation from the canonical or charismatic obedience owed to spiritual fathers and mothers in the Church-approved structures of religious life. Christ's perfect obedience to the Father becomes incarnate in the Religious in the relation to [Rule and] superior carried out within the 'supernatural sociology of the evangelical state'.[8]

The way of life which results – what Balthasar calls the state of election, his Ignatius-influenced term for the life of the evangelical counsels – will be incomprehensible to an unbelieving world because its sole foundation is Christ himself. As Balthasar puts it, citing the words of Jesus in Matthew (8.20) about how the Son of Man had nowhere, no place, to lay his head, the Religious stands at a 'non-place', what the Letter to the Hebrews calls, speaking of the place of the Crucifixion (13.12–13), a 'place outside', which is, in the language of St John's Gospel, 'not of this world' (18.36). The Son of Man, who is also Son of God, took on poverty, virginity, obedience, so as to lead man across the chasm which had opened between our original state (now, after the Fall, no longer open to us) and our final state, our final destiny (from which sin had also cut us off). Jesus took on from within a fallen world the task of meeting God's original request for perfect love – and this he could only do by a love that manifested itself in renunciation, by a sacrifice no longer joined to fulfilment and joy but carried out in the abandonment, the dark night, of the cross. However, the hidden fruit of that sacrifice – and this is something shown forth in the resurrection – is in fact a new Paradise.

The new state created by the Lord [that is, the Christian state] and possible only on the basis of his own way of life, of the unity of the two natures in his divine person, is, in its turn, a synthesis of earthly and paradisal life. It means taking up one's stand by the Cross, which is the gateway to paradise, or taking one's stand in the paradise that has been restored to mankind in the form of the Cross. It is fullness despite renunciation, happiness despite suffering. It is heavenly fecundity through renunciation of earthly fecundity, heavenly freedom in the bonds of earthly obedience.[9]

The *spirit* of the counsels, accordingly, is necessary to perfection in a fallen world where redemption is now available. But whether, in the concrete, my personal redemption as a disciple requires that I accept the vowed life as the full embodiment of the counsels depends on the Lord's own electing choice. Balthasar follows the Baroque Scholastic Francisco Suarez in holding that while the actual vows and the renunciations they entail are so useful to disciples questing for perfection that they may be called 'relatively necessary' in a fallen world for perfect love's attaining, nonetheless they are not absolutely necessary unless God calls me by a special act of his grace.

Such a division of the Christian state of life into two distinct lives was the best way of establishing the redemptive order in the Church. Obviously, not every member of the Church could become a Religious without human generation in the community of Christ coming to an end, and to that extent the Church herself ending (i.e. other than via conversion from outside), which would be absurd. There is in any case a corporate duty laid on man at the first moment of the creation, a duty to guard and foster the order of nature. And this would go for nothing (in a Christian civilisation) were all the baptised now called to lead the consecrated life.

> A universal command that, for the sake of the kingdom of God, obliged man to sexual abstinence and the renunciation of earthly goods and free control over nature would be tantamount to a nullification of these initial commands. If he were to command such universal renunciation, the Son, who came to complete the works of the Father and to demonstrate and confirm their goodness, would succeed only in abolishing them and showing them to be superseded and even inwardly imperfect. The universalization of the evangelical state within the Church would lead to Marcionism: to separation of the Old from the New Testament, of the order of creation from that of redemption, of Yahweh from Christ. In its most radical form it would lead, eventually, to the extinction of the human race and the destruction of man's earthly economy. For that reason, the state of election must always exist by way of exception in this fallen world. Those who are called to it will always be in the minority, destined by their exceptional mission to bear witness to the existence of another world, of man's first and last states rather than to bring these states to pass in the present world.[10]

And Balthasar continues:

> because it is the prescriptive will of the Church's Founder that those called to the state of election should be a permanent minority in the world in contrast to those forming the general state of believers, it is likewise his prescriptive will that the many who are not called to the special state of life should remain in the general, secular state. By reason of this prescriptive will, we must, therefore, regard the secular state, not as just the negative side of the state of election, but rather as a true state in the realm of redemption and of the Church. Nevertheless, it would be incorrect to designate this will as a second vocation to the Lord's service of equal rank with the first. *Being placed in the secular state can be described only as a not-having-been-called to a qualitatively higher state.*[11]

The final, italicised sentence here is, evidently, crucial. The situation of Christians in the world is a difficult one as Ignatius had already pointed out in the *Directorium* from which Balthasar's teaching on this subject flows. It is difficult because more complex than the life of the consecrated Religious. There is a tension in the situation of the lay Christian (and indeed the secular priest) which is absent from that of the Religious. To adapt Paul's words in First Corinthians on virginity and marriage, the secular is 'divided' – for the Christian in the world must follow simultaneously two sets of imperatives. He or she must realise the original command – concerned with the order of nature – to cultivate the earth, which Balthasar interprets as a command to *take responsibility for earthly culture*. And he or she must combine this with the new direction – the supernatural direction – given with the new life, the life of the redeemed in Christ on their way to the heavenly Kingdom. Consequently, as Paul explains in the same letter, ordinary Christians must, if they are married, live as if they were not; if they are buying things, behave as though they were not going to possess them, and in general use the world as though not using it, because 'the form of this world is passing away' (1 Cor. 7.29–31).

As Balthasar sums up the difference between the consecrated life and the life in the world under this aspect, the consecrated life, by reason of God's special call 'allows us to anticipate the world to come even in this world' (through the happiness which poverty, chastity, obedience, when generously lived should bring), whereas the Christian life in its secular form merely 'embodies life in transition from this world to the world to come'.

The life of the Religious who is radiant with the resurrection joy that comes from the cross is accordingly a fuller picture – a more striking icon – of the life of the Kingdom than is the life of a lay Christian working to transform earthly realities, perhaps as a statesman or social worker, spouse or teacher. For no matter how hard Christians in the world work, their efforts are not going to produce heaven. At best they may gesture towards that blessed country.

> The Christian, when he seeks to fulfil the cultural task assigned him by God, performs works of longing rather than of fulfilment or, at most, those works of fulfilment that he achieves are designed to awaken in the receiver a longing for the heavenly abode of all beauty, goodness and truth.[12]

What the secular Christian must do, therefore, the better to approximate to the life of the Kingdom, is to let the spirit of the counsels affect more and more what they do and are. To live out fully the vow of baptism will mean for the layperson to let 'the spirit of the vows pervade his life with increasing clarity'. Through baptismal grace, that spirit of the vows will 'enable [the secular] to participate interiorly in the essence of the other state of life, in the spirit of undivided love in the forms of poverty, virginity and obedience.'[13] For, appealing to St Thomas' philosophy of matter and form, Balthasar sees the Christian life in the world as the 'matter' which, so far as is possible, should be taken up by the 'form' of the consecrated life and thus transformed. And, he asked, why not? Both lives should, after all, be thoroughly typified by the willingness to do whatever God wants of us. Balthasar is calling, plainly, for a certain spiritual monasticisation of the laity, something we find historically in such phenomena as oblateship to monasteries, the tertiaries of the Mendicant orders, the diffusion of Carmelite, Ignatian and other spiritualities among the laity, and the development, since the Second Vatican Council, of mixed communities with a strongly monastic ethos where, however, Religious and laypeople live side by side.[14] And for Religious to have this inspirational effect (on laypeople – and on the 'secular' priesthood), they themselves must be living that life of the counsels with the maximum integrity and fervour.

## Invasion by modernity

By 'adapting' to modernity, instead of critically examining it in the light of its own classical Christian tradition, those responsible for the 'modernisation' of the Religious life in the Western Church after the Second Vatican Council have risked, rather, eviscerating it of all real substance. Embracing a world which recognised no inherently abiding norms and principles, where – by contrast – human culture was increasingly seen as the projection on to reality of what had its origin in autonomous will, modernising 'prophets' in Religious life created a massive internal conflict with what ecclesial life in its most sheerly Kingdom-oriented and so other-worldly form was meant to be. Joseph Becker in his study of the effect in one influential Religious Order, the Jesuit Society, argues that a relaxation of asceticism in the 1960s (pushed through by means of the claim that the personal and corporate discipline it involved had caused an inappropriate monasticising of an apostolic Order) produced a revolution in the living and understanding of the life out of all proportion to what seemed at first minor changes in horary, dress, and demeanour.[15]

The resultant obfuscation of that sign of divine calling that is the Religious life was certainly unfortunate for a culture needing grounding more than ever before in revelation's transcendent permanence and its supporting philosophy. Many Religious appear to have let go of the supernatural (the gracious surprise of the Holy Trinity's sharing their life with us) and the eschatological (the perfection of that sharing as our ultimate intended destiny). Disastrously, the impression can therefore be given that they continue to use God-language and to quote the 'Scriptures, but on their lips such language often seems a mythic overlay, a symbolic vehicle for motivating people to become engaged in the more important tasks of social, economic and ecological reform'.[16]

The best documented study of the crumbling of Religious life before an invasive modernity, confined though it be to Religious of one gender in one (albeit trend-setting) country, is Anne Carey's *Sisters in Crisis*. Carey's study finds five root causes for the crisis among American nuns: first, an understandable reaction to the overwork, and lack of both consultation and appreciation that was their lot before the Second Vatican Council; second, the invitation to rewrite their rules at a time when secular culture was querying both the place of authority and the role of women within it, and in a situation, moreover, where few of those in leadership positions were capable of reformulating the recipe of Religious life without spilling cream; third, the lack of a stable canon law in the Latin Church between the Council and the promulgation in 1993 of its new Code; fourth, the inconsistencies and plodding pace of the Roman ecclesiastical bureaucracy when faced with the flood of new constitutions seeking confirmation (communities would eventually either assume papal acceptance of proposed reforms or argue that, through delay, they had been in vigour so long as to enjoy the force of custom); fifth – and not unconnected with the latter – the seeming bewilderment of the Holy See at the seething cauldron which, in so many places, Religious life had become.[17] Local bishops feared to intervene, dreading adverse publicity and the effect on the infrastructure of their dioceses should Sisters engaged in, especially, teaching and nursing, withdraw. Carey summarises the consequences towards the end of her lengthy analytic narrative. 'Change-oriented leaders', influenced by the early neofeminism and campus radicalism of the 1960s, as well as by theological dissent, acquired positions of influence not only in their own institutes but in the wider associations ('Conferences') of religious superiors. From that position of strength they (in Carey's euphemism) 're-ordered the emphasis' of Religious life – away from sanctification and the Church's service towards secular agendas of variously 'progressive' kinds.[18] That many of the more ardent supporters of 'excessive' change eventually abandoned Religious life altogether did little to appease turmoil in communities now internally divided, with apostolates abandoned and morale subverted.

One of the strangest features of the decline in Religious life in many areas of the Western Church – at least to those who are strangers to the study of social pathology – is the tendency of its representatives to deny that anything is wrong at all. The facts, however, speak for themselves in that those Orders and communities which actually flourish and recruit – in the United States, France and elsewhere – have taken precisely the opposite road from the kind of 'renewal' Carey describes. They are brotherhoods or sisterhoods (or in some cases double communities) where the heart of the Religious life is taken to be the invitation to love God with peculiar directness; where a classical identity based on the historic sources and norms of monastic and Religious life is explicitly and unembarrassedly maintained; where a strong community life pertains, complete with common ritual practice, and where consecration (simply *being* a Religious) is prized as well as mission (what a Religious does).[19] The lesson is plain: our task (I write here as myself a Religious) is to learn it.

## NOTES

1. P. R. Régamey, *La Vie religieuse selon Pape Jean Paul II* (Paris, 1983), p. 13. A decade earlier, Régamey had produced his trilogy *Redécouvrir la Vie religieuse* in the form of I. *L'Exigence de Dieu* (Paris, 1969); II. *La voix de Dieu dans les voix des temps* (Paris, 1971); III. *La rénovation dans l'Esprit* (Paris, 1974).

2. Cited in idem, *'La Vie religieuse selon Pape Jean Paul II*, p. 14, with an allusion to Romans 12.2.

3. Ibid., p. 36.

4. H. U. von Balthasar, *Christlicher Stand* (Einsiedeln, 1977); ET *The Christian State of Life* (San Francisco, 1986).

5. Balthasar, *The Christian State of Life*, p. 122.

6. Ibid., p. 146.

7. Ibid., p. 155.

8. Ibid., p. 157.

9. Ibid., p. 161.

10. Ibid., p. 167.

11. Ibid., p. 168.

12. Ibid., p. 171.

13. Ibid.

14. A number of the latter are described in F. Lenoir, *Les Communautés nouvelles* (Paris, 1988).

15. J. M. Becker, S.J., *The Reformed Jesuits. A History of Change in Jesuit Formation during the Decade 1965–1975* (San Francisco, 1992).

16. A. Di Ianni, S.M., *Religious Life as Adventure* (Staten Island, N.Y., 1994), p. 73.

17. A. Carey, *Sisters in Crisis. The Tragic Unravelling of Women's Religious Communities* (Huntingdon, Ind., 1997), p. 132.

18. Ibid., p. 313.

19. Here one could usefully compare the rich and solid doctrine of Pope John Paul II's Post-Synodal Exhortation *Vita Consecrata* (1996), helpfully summarised by Fr Richard Moth in the 'documentation and information service for [British] religious', *Signum*, with the, alas, vacuous *trendiness* of contemporary 'progressive' discourse about Religious life in the subsequent issue of that journal. See R. Moth, 'A Summary of the Post-Synodal Exhortation *Vita Consecrata*', *Signum* 26.1 (1988), pp. 4–15; D. O'Murchu, M.S.C., 'What Are Religious Talking About These Days?', ibid., 26.2. (1988), pp. 5–12.

# XI

# Rescuing the Holy Innocents

THE issue of abortion is greeted by many Catholics with a resigned sigh – *resigned* because there seems little that can be done to shift attitudes, whether in the legislature or without, on an issue where 'pro-choice' rather than 'pro-life' attitudes have conquered majoritarian status, and a *sigh* because the reiteration of the moral point from the pulpit or elsewhere seems so predictable as to be banal. What such people need is the reawakening of their Christian imaginations to the implications of the topic.

I would like to approach the matter somewhat unconventionally, therefore, in the hope of returning freshness to this (if the scales would only fall from our eyes) life-and-death subject. The method will be to juxtapose the testimonies of a poet and a *spirituelle*.

## A poem

Charles Péguy is universally acknowledged as one of the four literary prophets of the French Catholic revival of the early twentieth century (the remaining members of the quartet being Léon Bloy, Paul Claudel, and Georges Bernanos). Péguy was born at Orléans, the city of Joan of Arc, in 1873, the son of a cabinet-maker in that town. His maternal ancestry mattered more to him, chiefly owing to his father's premature death (his health ruined in the Franco-Prussian War, when the little Charles was less than a year old). His mother's people were woodcutters and vinetenders in the Bourbonnais, that province of deep France between the Cher and the Loire whose best known centre is the ill-fated Vichy. His mother worked thriftily at the mending and making of cane chairs, a cottage industry she practised in a home which was rudimentary yet dignified: Péguy would later think of this as being 'of the people' at a time when there still *was* a 'people'.[1] He grew up an extremely serious boy. After his recovery of Catholicism, and the stream of poetry this set flowing, he would write in his 'Presentation' of the Beauce (the fertile plain spread out between Orléans on the Loire and the basin of the Seine) to Our Lady of Chartres:

> We were born on the border of your level Beauce
>> And longtime we have known, from earliest days,
>> The entrance to the farm, the peasants' stubborn gaze,
> The spade and trench and village with its close . . .
>
> We were born on the border of your level Beauce
>> And longtime we have known, from our earliest regrets,
>> Whene'er a sun before a scarlet curtain sets
> How much despair it hides and secret loss . . .[2]

Péguy's intellectual quality was soon recognised by his teachers and after military service he completed his education at the Ecole Normale and the Sorbonne, where he came under the philosophical influence of Henri Bergson whose notions of deep time (*la durée*), moral intuition and *élan vital* (over against empiricism, ethical calculus, and mechanistic theories of historical determinism) can be sensed in his later work. Péguy became a bookseller and editor of a journal – the *Revue de la Quinzaine* – which was strongly Socialist in its politics but in a deliberately anti-party spirit. The series *Cahiers de la Quinzaine*, from 1900 onwards, introduced many young writers to the French public – not least himself. In 1907–8 Péguy recovered his Catholicism; he disliked talk of 'conversion' as excessively individualistic, preferring to say he had ceased to renounce his faith. His *Mystères* and *Tapisseries*, long meandering poems, where speech given to God marvellously avoids both false sublimity and mateyness, witness to this spiritual revolution. Péguy completely avoided the narrow sociological sectarianism to which a century and more of anti-clericalism and indeed hostility to Christianity at large had often driven French Catholics. What unifies his mature poetic output is, in the words of Père Pie Duployé, a presentation of the world as the 'intelligibility of the Christian mystery' – such that a Christian understands the gospel only if he simultaneously hears all the world's 'great voices' – Jewish, pagan, and those of the 'utopian humanitarianisms' as well.[3] Here we are concerned with his lengthy poetic meditation – almost 150 pages in the Pléiade[4] edition – on the Holy Innocents, the Bethlehem children of two years and less put to death on Herod the Great's orders in the course of his scotching rumours of a messianic child: thus the infancy gospel narrative in Matthew 2.16–18.

Péguy's various *Mystères* are not, as Alick Dru explains, mystery plays – though Péguy had that genre of the mediaeval Church's popular literature in mind when he chose the title. Rather, they are: '*Mysteries* because they are variations on a single theme, the mysteries of the faith, hope and charity, the life of grace'.[5] How does the 'mystery' which concerns us here – the *Mystery of the Holy Innocents* – proceed? The poem – the great bulk of which is placed on the lips of the divine Father – opens with an encomium of the theological virtue of *hope*. Faith and charity are the great sisters in the trio of those divinely gifted dispositions which bond us directly to God himself: 'faith holds fast through century upon centuries'; charity 'gives herself through centuries of centuries'. In their august company hope is easily overlooked since she does not have the stature of the guardians of truth (faith) and love (charity). Yet the indispensability of this very little girl is indicated in the statement that 'it is my little hope/Who gets up every morning'.[6] Hope is for Péguy the virtue of ever fresh beginnings: 'that little promise of a bud which shows itself at the very beginning of April'. The buds of some vast and many-branched tree appear to be parasites or at any rate the tree's issue and an unimpressive one at that. But from the bud the tree comes: 'Every life springs from tenderness.' Unlike the trunk and bark, which are made for resistance and roughness, the bud is

> only made for being born and is only
>     commissioned to bring to birth.
> (And to make things last).
> (And to make itself loved).

> And I tell you, God says, without that burgeoning at the end of
>     April, without those thousands, without that unique little
>     burgeoning of hope, which obviously everybody can break,
>     without that tender downy bud, which the first comer can
>     nip off with his nail, all my creation would be nothing but
>     dead wood.
> And dead wood will be thrown in the fire.[7]

The Father's gaze now turns to the crucified Son who on Calvary came to resemble, in the cracking of his torn skin, the rough tree, yet had been a 'tender milk child' for he was born to regenerate by a new childhood the race of man. Christ had been 'a childhood, a burgeoning, a promise, an engagement; an attempt; an origin; a beginning of a Redeemer; a hope of salvation; a hope of redemption'. There then follows an extraordinary encomium to the night of the Crucified's entombment. First, the night brings to an end the day of sin inflicted and suffering undergone, suggesting that 'my Paradise / Will be nothing but a great clear night which will fall on the sins of the world'. But second this 'great shining night' is honoured and glorified by the Father since it (sometimes) obtains 'the most difficult thing in the world / The surrender of man . . .'.[8] The resistance that disables man from relaxing into the hands of God, from practising *abandon*, that key term of the French mystical tradition, is also what prevents him from practising the virtue of hope which expects all from God (it is *espérance*, the *theological* virtue), not from men (it is not *espoir*, the human trait). The Father's 'daughter of the silver cloak' can occasionally elicit from man that surrender into the divine hands which his human creature's scrupulous moralising and religiosity (and not just, then, sheer straightforward sinfulness) so easily prevent. Constant retrospective self-examination is no more in place in the Father's house than would be a guest who, having wiped his muddied feet at the threshold, insisted on going back time and again to repeat the performance. Péguy ascribes to God a 'cunning' (the original is stronger – *la malice*), at the antipodes from vengeful cruelty for it is 'the feints and ruses of my Grace, which so often plays with the sinner for his salvation'.

And in any case the appeal to the Father's paternal quality which the Son bade his disciples make their own in the *Pater noster* unmans (so to speak) the Father, so that the righteous anger our sins arouse in the divine justice cannot prevail. The opening words of the *Our Father* conquer the just wrath of God.

> Those words which go before every prayer as the hands of a
>     supplicant before his face.
> As the two hands of a supplicant advance joined together before
>     his face and the tears on his face.
> Those three or four words which conquer me, me the unconquer-
>     able,
> And which they send in front of their misery like two invincible
>     hands joined together.
> Those three or four words which advance like a strong prow in
>     front of a weak ship,
> And which cleave the wave of my anger.
> And when the prow has passed, the ship passes and all the fleet
>     behind it.
> Nowadays, God says, that is how I see them;
> And during my eternity, eternally, God says,
> By the contrivance of my Son, it is thus that I must eternally see
>     them.[9]

The metaphor of the ship of Christ, the 'ship that is my own son, loaded with all the aims of the world', turning the Father's guard and drawing triumphantly in its wake the 'immense fleet of prayers and penitence' of innumerable souls, such that all pleading and intercession rises to the Father concealed behind the pointed prow of the Son, forms the Christological climax of *The Mystery of the Holy Innocents*.

It gathers up what has been said in the poem so far. For when the Son first spoke the *Pater* that utterance was

> . . . a birth of prayer. A hope.
> A birth of hope.
> A branch and a germ and a bud and a leaf and a flower and a fruit
>     of speech.
> A seed, a birth of prayer.

The small beginnings which Péguy has until now associated with the virtue of hope become here a mighty battering-ram. In a highly condensed play on words 'in the point [the purpose] of the point [what Christ uttered], in that point itself there was a point [a weapon against the exclusive rule of divine justice]'. Elaborated in the two hundred or so lines that follow, the metaphor also opens up Mariological and ecclesiological vistas from the Christological centre. Behind the first 'fleet' as it enters the Father's horizon, comes also a second, consisting of prayer to the Virgin ('white caravels, humbly lying under their sails on the surface of the water'), and a third, of all other prayers made in the Church to God, at the Mass and Office and Benediction by monk at midnight and peasants before 'a good steaming bowl of soup' at dinner. But it is the 'fourth fleet' to which I would draw especial attention: here the poet looks forward (though without naming them) to the Holy Innocents themselves confessing Christ wordlessly, un-knowingly, whose mystery is the poem's subject. The 'fourth fleet' consisted of

> . . . all the prayers which are not even said, the words which are
>     not uttered.
> But I hear them. Those obscure impulses of the heart, the obscure
>     good impulses, the secret good movements,
> Which unconsciously spring up and come forth and unconsciously
>     rise toward me.
> Whoever is the source of them does not even perceive them.
> He knows nothing about them and is truly only the source,
> But as for me I gather them up, God says, and I count them and I
>     weight them.
> Because I am the hidden Judge.[10]

The person who truly prays the *Pater* can at last abandon himself to sleep – and the chief sense to be given 'truly' here is 'freely'. God does not need to prove his power by exacting love from man. ('My power blazes forth clearly enough in every substance and in every event.')

> ... All the submissions, all the lamentations in the world
> Are not worth one beautiful prayer from those free men kneeling
>    very upright. All the submissions in the world
> Are not worth the springing forth
> The beautiful straight thrust of a single invocation
> Of a free love. When Saint Louis loves me, God says, I am safe,
> I know what you are talking about. He is a free man, he is a free
>    baron of the Ile de France.[11]

In the course of the panegyric on St Louis (the French King Louis IX) which follows, Péguy drops another clue that points to the slain infants of Bethlehem. The firm yet gentle words whereby Louis chided the Sire de Joinville for saying he would rather have committed thirty mortal sins than be a leper Péguy's God the Father calls 'not unworthy of' the 'grandest word of Jesus in the Gospels' – indeed, resonant with their tone, adding:

> As in imitation and in honour of Jesus
> It has been granted to the Martyrs to undergo a death
> Not unworthy of the death of Jesus.

It might be thought enough that on the sacrifices of the martyrs, as on the scars of all the walking wounded who ever lived on earth, God would let fall his healing darkness, putting 'on the open mouths / Of the martyrs' wounds / . . . balm and oblivion and night'. But 'little hope' expects more from God, and so

> . . . from the relics of Judgment Day and from the ruins and the
>    rubble of Time
> She alone will bring forth new eternity.[12]

Péguy recounts the history of a youngest son, sold into slavery (the patriarch Joseph) and the Gospel story of the prodigal son as, precisely, images of hope (he very likely derived the combination, as Jean Daniélou showed, from the Lenten Liturgy of the old Roman rites).[13] The Old Testament hope was for a 'government', 'command, and 'kingdom' of this world – but in such a way that it could serve as the faithful figure of the New Testament hope for a version of those things that is *not* of this world and where they are in fact inverted in their normal meaning. That is why Jesus, who holds together the two covenants, being himself 'carnal, spiritual / Temporal, eternal / . . . Man /

God', set a little child in their midst as the ostensive definition of the grace which alone will win the Kingdom of heaven. The 'experience' boasted of by the worldly-wise the Father judges 'a pretentious wasting, / The diminution, the decrease, the loss of innocence. / And a perpetual degradation.'[14] A little child falling asleep saying (*jumbling*) its prayers God sees as the finest thing in creation though he has seen 'those plains and valleys of France / Which are more beautiful than anything / [and] the dark, deep sea, and the dark, deep forest, and the dark deep heart of man'. Indeed, the sight of that child is finer (and this, again, may be significant for the innocents theme) than the prospect of

> . . . martyrs inspired by faith
> holding firm as a rock on the torturer's frame
> Between the iron teeth
> . . .
> . . . martyrs flaming like torches
> earning palms forever green . . .[15]

The predilection of God for the child in its innocence and trustfulness urges the Father to promise salvation to dead infants: here Péguy makes use of the Office of the Dead for the Burial of a Child in the Roman Breviary.

> *Sinite parvulos venire ad me.*
> *Talium est enim regnum coelorum* are the words of my Son.
> But they are not only the words of my Son. They are my words.
> What a pledge, and the Church, my daughter the Church makes
>     me repeat them
> And makes me say them (and I shall never disavow a liturgy,
> A prayer, an address of my daughter the Church).
> Through the Church, through the ministry of the Priest I have
>     repeated the pledge, I have repeated the words of my Son:
> *Suffer the little ones to come unto me.*
> *For such is the Kingdom of Heaven.*
> Thus is my Roman liturgy entwined with my central and cardinal
>     teaching
> And with my Jewish prophecies.
> And the chain is Jewish and Roman, passing through a hinge, an
>     articulation,
> Through a central origin.
> Everything is foretold in my Jewish prophecies.
> At the centre, at the heart, everything is realized, everything is
>     consummated by my Son.
> Everything is consummated, everything is celebrated by my
>     Roman liturgy.

The Jewish prophet foretells it.
My Son tells it.
And I retell it.

And it is retold for me.[16]

The Holy Innocents – to come now directly with Péguy to the supreme subject of his poem – enjoy special significance because they are precisely martyred *infants*. Out of 'so many saints and of so many martyrs', they are surely the only ones who will be 'really white / really pure', having 'received from life no wound / Except that wound which gave them entry into the kingdom of heaven'. For Péguy they fulfil in pre-eminent fashion the condition outlined in the vision of the hundred and forty-four thousand who, in the Johannine Apocalypse (14.1–5), surround the Lamb on Mount Zion. They were 'redeemed from the earth' (in the Revised Standard Version's translation, but Péguy says 'taken away', *enlevés*, following the *empti* of the Vulgate), before they could become 'earthy'. They are certainly 'first-fruits of God and the Lamb' in the saving Incarnation: and above all, since they 'did nothing in existence / Except receive a good sabre cut / . . . struck at the right moment', it is undoubtedly true that 'in their mouth no lie was found'. And citing the Roman Office's acclamation of the Innocents as *flores martyrum*, 'the flowers of the martyrs', Péguy proposes that this trope must be understood to mean that these (alone, in Christ) are the flowers of which *all other martyrs are the fruit.*

Stretched on the rack, tied to the rack like fruit tied to espaliers
The other martyrs, twenty centuries of martyrs
Centuries and centuries of martyrs
Are literally fruits in season,
In every season spread on espaliers
And chiefly fruits of autumn
And my Son even was gathered
In his thirty-third season. But they, those simple innocents
They are even before the fruit, they are the promise of fruit.
*Salvete flores Martyrum*; those children of less than two years old
        are the flowers of the other Martyrs.
That is, the flowers which produce the other martyrs.
At the very beginning of April they are the pink flowers of the
        peach-tree.
In the middle of April, at the very beginning of May they are the
        white flowers of the pear-tree.
In the middle of May they are the red flowers of the apple-tree.
White and red.
They are the flower itself and the bud of the flower and the down
        on the bud.

> They are the burgeoning of the branch and the burgeoning of the
>     flower.
> They are the glory of April and they are sweet hope.
> They are the glory of the woods and of the months.
> They are early childhood.[17]

Péguy's God the Father gives seven reasons for the excelling glory of
the Innocents. The first three are easily disposed of: the infants are
exalted because God loves them; because they please God and because
it pleases him so to do. The fourth by this stage in the poem is
predictable: their very lack of experience enables redeeming grace to
find them with 'no lines [of "disappointment and of bitterness"] at the
corners of their mouths'. The fifth consideration, however, entails an
extraordinary exploitation of the themes of atonement theology: for
the Innocents represented, were substituted for, counted as, and took
the place of the incarnate Son to whose redemptive act in dying, in its
relation to humankind at large, those verbs are normally applied. The
Innocents are like the Son in the vicarious, representatively
substitutionary nature of their deaths.

> . . . because they were found to resemble my Son at the exact
>     moment of that massacre,
> That is why at present they are found to resemble the Lamb in his
>     eternal glory.[18]

Sixthly, since 'one of the greatest mysteries of Grace is the share of
chance', why should it not commend them to God that they were 'of
the same age as my Son, born at the same time, of the same race, / At
the same date'? And seventhly and lastly, in their softness, newness,
and unknownness, they are also like the child Jesus:

> . . . of all the imitations of Jesus Christ
> Theirs is the first and it is the freshest; and it is the only one
> Which is not in any degree
> Which is not even a fraction
> Of an imitation of some brand and some bruise and some wound
>     in the heart of Jesus.[19]

Hans Urs von Balthasar wrote of how Péguy's contribution to the
Church's spiritual and doctrinal tradition appears to be in the nature
of a preparation for the future.

> The regions that Péguy opens up to Christian devotion and to the
> Christian sense of the world and of existence are of a richness and
> a fruitfulness that has not yet been explored. The spring that has
> started to flow here pours from the eternal mystery of the childhood

of God through the eternal mystery of the childhood of Christ into
the eternal childhood which is given to men: eternal hope . . . Faith
and love pour out as hope, hope flowers in faith and love; all three
are eternal, circling life, happily sealed in innocence and in the
untouchable, unconscious quality of a child.[20]

## An inspiration

One possible way in which Péguy's insights into the Scriptures and
Liturgy of the Church in this particular poem have been (all un-
consciously) taken further is in the movement to 'claim' aborted children
as 'companions of the Holy Innocents' associated with the English-
woman Patricia de Menezes (née Adamson, 1940– ). In my account of
the spiritual content of her 'inspiration' (as she herself calls it) I do not
enter into the question of the provenance of the theme in her mystical
theology. I merely note two things. First, the Catholic Church regards
the devotion of the faithful as sometimes productive of fresh insights
into the content of public revelation, whether this be (a) in the humble
mode of actual graces which, at moments of a person's life, help them
to gain firmer hold on true intuitions; (b) through the more exalted
way of those Gifts of the Holy Spirit, and notably the Gift of Wisdom,
by which a person living in notable docility to that Spirit, is brought to
share the divine judgement on some matter; or (c) by way of a charism
of prophecy (whether or not in conjunction with visions or auditions)
where, in St Thomas Aquinas' phrase, by *gratiae gratia datae* – 'gifts
freely given', i.e. irrespective of personal holiness – some member of
the faithful receives a message, concerning for the most part an occluded
truth in faith and morals, aimed not so much at their own sanctification
as at its wider communication for the sake of the common good of the
rest of the Church. Secondly, such devotion-carried insights of the
faithful may in Catholic teaching form part of that process whereby
what is implicit or tacit in divine revelation, and in the interrelation of
its various aspects, becomes – through the work of theologians, and,
ultimately, the judgement of the magisterium, explicitly recognised –
and hence part and parcel of the defined doctrine of the Church. In the
words of *Dei Verbum*, the Dogmatic Constitution on divine revelation
of the Second Vatican Council:

> [The] tradition which comes from the apostles develops in the
> Church with the help of the Holy Spirit. For there is a growth in
> the understanding of the realities and the word which have been
> handed down. This happens through the contemplation and study
> made by believers, who treasure these things in their hearts (cf:

Luke 2.19, 51), through the intimate understanding of spiritual things they experience, and through the preaching of those who have received through Episcopal succession the sure gift of truth. For, as the centuries succeed one another, the Church constantly moves forward toward the fullness of divine truth until the words of God reach their complete fulfilment in her.[21]

Patricia de Menezes was born in Bristol, the youngest of six children from parents whose only religious affiliation was via the Salvation Army. These were the War years, and the family home was destroyed by bombing of the Port of Bristol in 1940. Evacuated to the Fylde Coast of Lancashire, she was educated at Tylesley Church of England Girls' School, but owing to her father's poor health was obliged to leave school to become a wage-earner when she was sixteen. In the late 1950s she, her parents and a brother emigrated to Canada; in 1961 she began studying fashion design at New York where her husband-to-be, a Goanese Catholic, was a student at New York University. They settled in England on their marriage (at Our Lady of Victories, Kensington); after the birth of their son, Subash, Patricia became a Catholic but by her own account a very poorly instructed one. Though two more children David Ashok and Maria Luiza would be born, Patricia managed to combine motherhood with the resumption of fashion and jewellery design, which she later taught for the Goldsmiths' Company in the City of London.

As is well known, the Salvation Army does not acknowledge the sacrament of baptism. Patricia experienced a great drawing to the baptismal waters, but her understanding of the rest of the sacramental life, and of Catholic doctrine at large was, after her reception, minimal. But then something happened. In her own words:

> During this time she was riding her bicycle to work through the countryside. As she was riding beside a field of ripe corn blowing in the wind she heard a loud and clear voice say, 'I AM THE BREAD OF LIFE'. She knew that the voice was God and she felt a great desire to find this Bread of Life and eat it but she had no idea where it could be found.[22]

A priest whom she approached helped her to make a general confession and sensing, presumably, some *attrait* towards Marian devotion, suggested she might profit from taking part in a group where the Rosary was prayed corporately. Placing oneself under the mantle of Mary by an act of consecration to her was, he added, a helpful spiritual practice.

It appears to have been this action which released the flood of imaginative visions (amounting to a 'vivid visual Catechism'[23] – doctrine in pictures) and interior locutions of Christ and his Mother in which the theme of 'crucified innocence' soon became prominent. In the writings of Patricia de Menezes our Lady bears the title 'Mother of the Hidden and Mystical Wounds'. This does not only indicate the Virgin's own 'dolours'. (Devotion to the Seven Sorrows of Mary, symbolised in the sword which, in the Canticle of Simeon [Luke 2.35], is said to pierce her through, was established in the thirteenth century through the Florentine mendicant Order called the 'Servites'.) The title is also meant to draw attention to the hidden wounds of Mary's children – the members of the Church, embracing *potentially* the whole human race – which the Blessed Virgin in her spiritual motherhood aims to tend and heal.

The themes of the writing generated by Patricia de Menezes' spiritual experience appear to be threefold. First, she rehearses the grand narrative shared by the Church's mystical theologians at large – purification and transformation by the divine Love leading to union with God – but with an emphasis on the humility, sense of dependence, and silence which alone can permit the soul to sing the divine 'Song of Love'. These exchanges with Christ (Mary plays only a limited role here) draw their language from Scripture, the Liturgy and Church doctrine but recast in a simple affective imagery – comparison with Thérèse of Lisieux comes to mind – of the little bird learning a new song. (Other symbols for the soul – donkey, eagle, peacock, flute, child – also appear.) Secondly, there is an expansion of the theological idea of the Holy Family in such a way that the writings present the adoptive entry of Christians into that Family by a kind of 'novitiate' as a divinely willed response to the (combined) social and spiritual evils of our time. But thirdly, and here is the pertinence of this particular Christian witness to the theme of the present chapter, Patricia de Menezes' 'inspiration' focuses on the salvific status of aborted children who constitute in some sense 'companions' of the original Holy Innocents of the Gospel.

Addressing the mothers of aborted children, Pope John Paul II, in his Encyclical letter *Evangelium Vitae*, predicted of their repentance 'You will come to understand that nothing is definitively lost and you will also be able to ask forgiveness from your child who is now living in the Lord'.[24] If this comment can be regarded as indicating the direction in which magisterial tradition in the Catholic Church is likely to develop (no *single* remark by a Pope can, however, constitute such a trend), then the question clearly arises: In what sense *are* aborted children 'living in the Lord'? It might be thought that, since they have never encountered the order of supernatural salvation, this could only be in the sense of a natural ordination to God, their Beginning and their End.

Here Christ's redemption would reach them simply as the *repair*, not elevation, of their nature. On this view, at the moment of their deaths, the Redeemer who entered common humanity to heal its sores would give them victory over the ethical disorder that springs from Adam's sin, and entry into that world of felicity sometimes called 'limbo' – and then, at the general resurrection, the reintegration, on the basis of his own resurrection, of body and soul. Or does 'living in the Lord' go further? These 'shewings' (to borrow a term from Julian of Norwich) of divine innocence lead Patricia de Menezes to conclude that children wilfully deprived of life by abortion have been washed in the Blood of Christ, have received the baptism of blood which the ancient Church ascribed to catechumens who died for the faith before they could receive ritual baptism, and both may and should be acclaimed as martyrs to the truth of revelation about the dignity and destiny of the human person from the first moment of his or her conception.

Now the classical theology of the Church has found no difficulty in the notion that children slain through hatred of Christ or of the Christian religion, even if they have received neither baptism nor its anticipatory surrogate, circumcision, *can* be regarded as martyrs.

> If enquiry into the circumstances of their deaths engenders the certitude that they were killed in hatred for Christ, the Church could canonize and celebrate them, as she celebrates, on the 28th December, the martyrdom of the Holy Innocents.[25]

May one say, that, in a time when the Church has taught with ever greater insistence and clarity the sacredness of the *conceptus*, and when liberal and radical forces at work in society have vastly extended the legal possibilities of abortion and the pressure to abort, that there is, in the entire 'pro-choice' movement, a definite *odium fidei*? Anecdotal evidence suggests that clinics and surgeons *do* sometimes find particular satisfaction in performing abortions on Catholic mothers.

There is more. The 'crucified innocence' of these children (evidently, they have no *personal* sins to bear) renders them peculiarly conformed to the divine-human Innocent One of the Cross (here the mind thinks back irresistibly to Péguy's poem). The present writer's (modest) experience of Catholic participation in the 'Pro-Life' movement in England, and notably its 'Pro-Life Action' wing with its abortion-clinic street vigils enables him to say that the more-than-averagely devout and committed Catholics (and other Christians) who participate in such activities bear out by their language – without knowing the fact – this claim. For to speak of aborturaries as 'new Calvaries' is in these circles quite a regular thing.[26] If this be an emergent *sensus fidelium* speaking, then the implication is that aborted children not only can be called members of the Church but are actually pre-eminent ones, peculiarly close to the Church's Saviour and Lord.

Publicly to call on these 'crucified innocents' as martyrs would require, however, not only theological clarification of their standing in relation to salvation in Christ. It would also mean a solemn act of acclamation – comparable to canonisation – on the part of the hierarchical Church. That is indeed crucial to Patricia's spiritual message which seeks a 'claiming' of the children by Mother Church through her accredited hierarchical representatives – not as though the validation of a new proposal about the revealed deposit were an end in itself but so that streams of fresh graces can pour forth on the world. In a typical utterance stimulated by the Divine Office reading from St Proclus of Constantinople for the Saturday Memoria of the blessed Virgin Mary, these words are given to the Mother of Jesus:

> Exercise your faith, Abraham's children, in the all-saving power of the Blood of Jesus, so that these innocents can be like millions of stars resplendent in the heavens, their innocence triumphant in his Divine innocence, witnesses to the Word.

On which Patricia de Menezes comments

> Our Lord wants the millions of aborted children to be numbered with the Saints; in some way considered martyrs to the Truth, the teachings of the Church and the divine Word. The Word of God had been disobeyed; this caused their death. Abraham is the Father of our faith. If the whole Church is united in a real act of Faith in the all-saving power of the Precious Blood of Jesus, these souls who have been slain for the Word and wait under the altar of the Catholic Church, can be raised to the altar and be like millions of stars lighting up the heavens. A great defeat of Satan and the forces of evil will take place. He will win no victory over these helpless, innocent children.

And more briefly, on a reading from Guerric of Igny where Mary's womb is said to be ever fruitful in bearing new children through her motherly compassion: 'the Mother of the Hidden and Mystical Wounds is trying to give birth to these children through Christ's Passion and Death in the Maternal Church.'[27] Or again, prompted by a Paschaltide Gospel-reading (John 5.17–30) on the Son's giving life to anyone he chooses:

> I AM the Son of God! My judgment is just. I judge the millions of aborted children not guilty of any personal sin. In My Love and Compassion I wash them, in My own Blood, of the sin of Adam

and Eve. As the New Adam I raise them up to bear witness to the truth to the whole world. I restore them to their Mother, the New Eve, who has pleaded for them, that they may be given voice and life in My Church, so that all may honour the Son as they honour the Father. Whoever refuses honour to the Son refuses honour to the Father who sent Him.[28]

The texts of Patricia de Menezes' 'inspiration' recognise their own audacity: what is spoken of is 'an unprecedented mercy [for] an unprecedented evil'[29] – abortion, namely, on a mass scale. Nevertheless what is proposed is not without support in that traditional reading of Scripture on which the Church's magisterium must rely in judging the evangelical compatibility of innovative writing. For Catholicism, of set purpose, has access to Scripture through the Tradition which created it and has carried it down the ages, according to the Church's living teaching and with the Liturgy as the primary organ of that 'traditioning'. Fr Francis Frost, sometime professor at the theology faculty of Lille and now at the Grand Séminaire of Ars, has pointed out, in an analysis of the de Menezes material, the suggestiveness of the liturgical texts for the feast of the Holy Innocents (28 December) in this regard. The three 'proper' prayers of the Mass – the Collect, the *oratio super oblata* and the prayer after communion 'all make it absolutely clear that the martyrdom which unites the Holy Innocents to the Lamb was a pure gift which required no conscious act of intelligence (knowledge) or will (love) . . . [Their] martyrdom is a pure gift'.[30] And Fr Frost notes not only the cardinal position of this feast prescribed for celebration as it is during the Octave of Christmas, the second most important season of the Church's year, but also the perhaps providential circumstance that the Pauline Calendar and Missal (promulgated by Pope Paul VI in the wake of the Second Vatican Council) modified the celebration of Holy Innocents Day to bring it more unambiguously into line with the feasts of martyrs: the priest, going to the altar-board, wears the red vestments of the Blood of Christ and martyrs' triumph, not, as formerly, the purple ones of mourning. The question is, however, whether in the absence of any sacramental sign of aggregation to the redeemed people (such as circumcision, an efficacious type of baptism), a *full* theological confirmation of the aborted *generally* to these little Jews who died for Christ's sake is feasible. But at the very least we have in the debate opened by Patricia de Menezes' inspiration a potent style of spiritual discourse about the affront of abortion to the Creator and Redeemer God. It is an investigation of the relevant themes of Scripture and Tradition well calculated to dispel that heedlessness of the evil of voluntary abortion which afflicts many Catholic Christians today.

## A professorial comment

The need to show the dogmatic and not simply the ethical under-pinnings of opposition to the abortion holocaust was clearly recognised in the address of Professor J. J. Scarisbrick, National Chairman of LIFE, to the Conference of Catholic Bioethicists held at Queens' College, Cambridge in the summer of 1998. Linking abortion to the related pro-life issues of euthanasia, contraception and artificial procreation, Professor Scarisbrick had this to say:

> Every abortion is an affront to God our Father who lovingly shapes and knits together, as the Psalmist (and the prophet Job) tells us, every human being in the secrecy and safety of the womb. Every act of euthanasia is an affront to God the Creator. Every contracep-ting act and every generation of a human being outside the human body is an abuse of the power of procreation generously bestowed by God on His creatures. Every one of those acts is also an affront to the second person of the Trinity who, by deigning to take on and thereby to elevate our human nature radically united Himself with the human race. Every human body has been ransomed by Him at a great price. Whatever we do or allow to be done to the least of His brothers and sisters we do or allow to be done to Him. And every one of these destructive acts is also an affront to the Holy Spirit, since the divine plan is that every human body shall become His temple. And since for nine months Mary's womb was the sanctuary of the Word Incarnate, a sacred vessel, Temple and Ark of the Covenant, the womb – every woman's womb – has been sanctified. Every violation of the womb is therefore a sacrilege, a profanation.[31]

It is also true, however, that – as the Lord who as Source not only of extraordinary graces for the good of the Church but also of our ordinary mental capacities for the direct good of the world surely desires – we must make use of all prudent natural strategies as well. Today, thanks to the development of techniques in such fields as endocrinology, biotechnology, immunology and pharmacology, the emphasis in (falsely so-called) 'reproductive rights' is shifting from the abortion of foetuses whom photography can display with fully formed toes, hands, eyes to the destruction of 'pre-embryos' by abortifacient drugs – far more cost-effective for health care providers as these are. By killing the pre-embryo outright or blocking uterine implantation (which leads to its death), such drugs achieve the desired result without troubling so many tender consciences as do foetal surgical abortions. Abortion casualty numbers will in all probability increase while negative emotional response to the destruction of life in the womb will decrease. The Church's trumpet must not give an uncertain sound as to when life begins (at the moment of conception): hitherto that has been a largely theoretical argument. Henceforth it will have the direst practical consequences. There will be a need to educate the public on the linkage between contraception and abortion – a linkage not only, with such drugs, technical in nature but also, and more widely, psychological as well. It was contraception that helped formulate the concept that babies are burdensome, and to the 'problem' thus stated, abortion – this holocaust of, currently, four hundred babies a day in Britain – became the final solution.

## NOTES

1. M. Villiers, *Charles Péguy. A Study in Integrity* (London, 1965), p. 27.

2. C. Péguy, *The Mystery of the Holy Innocents and Other Poems* translated by P. Pakenham with an Introduction by A. Dru (London, 1956), pp. 23–4.

3. P. Duployé, O.P., 'La Religion de Péguy', in *Péguy. Actes du Colloque internationale d'Orléans, 7, 8, 9, septembre 1964* (Paris, 1966, = *Cahiers de 1'Amitié Charles Péguy* 19), p. 179.

4. *Charles Péguy. Oeuvres poétiques complètes* (Paris, 1975$^2$), pp. 677–823.

5. A. Dru, *Péguy* (London, 1957), p. 78.

6. Péguy, *The Mystery of the Holy Innocents*, p. 69.

7. Ibid., p. 73.

8. Ibid., p. 76.

9. Ibid., p. 87.

10. Ibid., pp. 95–6.

11. Ibid., p. 102. Translation slightly altered.

12. Ibid., p. 116.

13. J. Daniélou, 'Péguy et les Pères', in *Recueil d'études en honneur de Bernard Guyon* (Paris, 1977), pp. 173–9.

14. Péguy, *The Mystery of the Holy Innocents*, p. 138.

15. Ibid., p. 140. Given Péguy's emphasis on the chain of consequences wrought by original sin, it is plausible to say with Georges Izard, 'he speaks less of the child than of childhood and of baptized childhood taken in all the purity and integrity of its type', E. Mounier, M. Péguy, G. Izard, *La Pensée de Charles Péguy* (Paris, 1931), p. 332.

16. Ibid., p. 144. André Robinet has suggested that Péguy was (also) influenced here by the arguments of Pius X's decree *Quam singulari* of 1910 calling for the admission of small children to Holy Communion that they might taste the Holy Mysteries before tasting vice. Thus A. Robinet, *Péguy entre Jaurès, Bergson et l'Eglise* (Paris, 1968), pp. 269–71.

17. Ibid., p. 163.

18. Ibid., p. 157.

19. Ibid., pp. 160–1.

20. H. U. von Balthasar, *Man in History* (ET London, 1967), p. 250.

21. *Dei Verbum* 8.

22. P. de Menezes, *The Song of Love* (n.p., 1994), p. xii.

23. Ibid.

24. John Paul II, *Evangelium Vitae*, 99.

25. C. Journet, *La volonté salvifique de Dieu sur les petits enfants* (Bruges, 1958), p. 79. I am grateful to Fr Hugh Barbour, O. Praem, of St Michael's Abbey, Orange County, for drawing my attention to this study by a leading Thomist theologian of the twentieth century.

26. For a comparison between being present at Calvary and outside an abortuary, see, e.g. J. Gallagher, *Maurice Lewis. Child of Mary, Defender of the Weakest* (London, 1998), p. 32.

27. Texts of 27 November 1993 in *Claiming of Children Killed in Abortion as Companions of the First Holy Innocents*, n.p., n.d; cf. Proclus of Constantinople, *Homilies on the Nativity* 1–2; Guerric of Igny, *Sermons* 47, 2–4.

28. Text from Eastertide 1996 in *Requests to the Church*, n.p., n.d.

29. Text from 4 December 1993 in *Scriptural References. Material Relevant to the Proposed Claiming of Aborted Children as Companion Martyr Saints of the First Holy Innocents*, n.p, n.d.

30. F. Frost, *Presentation of the Doctrine contained in the Messages about Divine Innocence*, n.p., n.d., pp. 14–15.

31. J. J. Scarisbrick, 'Contributing to Public Policy Debates on Bio-Ethical Issues: the Catholic Experience in England': I am grateful to Professor Scarisbrick for permitting me to cite his paper prior to its publication in the proceedings of the Conference. He himself acknowledges a debt to John Saward's *Redeemer in the Womb* (San Francisco, 1993). He also refers to Donal O'Mathuna, 'Abortion and the "Image of God"', in J. Kilner, N. M. de S. Cameron and D. Schiedermayer (eds.), *Bioethics and the Future of Medicine* (Carlisle/Grand Rapids, 1995), esp. pp. 206–9, as revealing 'the richness of the Hebrew words translated as "weave" in Psalm 139.13, "knit" in Job 10.11 and "in secret" in Psalm 139.15 – the latter carrying strong overtones of the child being hidden in the safety of the womb (as in a lair) by a protecting God'.

# XII

# *Reclaiming the Bible*

THIS book's Trinitarian and Christological, mysteric and sacramental presentation of Christian themes, explored by reference to a metaphysic of analogy and 'participation', is hardly compatible with a reductive reading of the Bible's content. Yet much of the contemporary approach to Scripture in the academy – treating the corpus either as a collection of Near Eastern texts to be quarried for the light they throw on the historical genesis and religious creativity of an ancient society, or, in the postmodern manner, as a concatenation of literary fragments to serve as illustration for the analytic techniques of deconstructing semiologists, champions of those endlessly 'deferring' signs – falls short of a truly *ecclesial* reading of the Bible in the spirit (the *Holy* Spirit) in which it was written. Hence the call today for a 'post-critical' exegesis: 'a truly Catholic reading of the Scriptures in the Church, in the light of her Tradition, in the spirit of her Fathers, guided by her Magisterium.'[1]

## Five principles of ecclesial exegesis

Those words of the English theologian John Saward introduce an account of the biblical interpretation practised by Paul Claudel who, despite his sometimes intemperate attacks on a scholarship with which (it must be said) he had small acquaintance, nonetheless furnishes five principles that are decidedly to the point.

First, Scripture is read in the Church, not outside her. The sensibility and intelligence needed for its appropriation are not *primarily* those of the critical toolbox of modern biblical studies but what Claudel called 'those which the whole Church majestically unfolds for us in her teaching and in her liturgy.'[2] The whole idea that the proper way to read the New Testament is by laying aside the witness of the Church to the Scriptures she in one sense originated, ignoring the subsequent tradition which is their unfolding, and substituting for the role of these a changing toolbox of methods, whose contents depends on the intellectual fashion of each age – this implies a profoundly unCatholic attitude to the Bible. To make a discerning subordinate use of those tools is fine – for the Logos is active in all sound natural reason. But the Church cannot make these tools her principal instrument in the appropriation of her own Scriptures. To use the contemporary jargon, the kind of 'hermeneutic' or interpretative standpoint we need is *not* a 'hermeneutic of suspicion' where the base line is that whatever Church orthodoxy has found in these texts is the one interpretation we will *a priori* suspect as false, but what I like to call a 'hermeneutic of recognition', where our basic stance is precisely the expectation that we will find in the texts signs and pointers to the developed Catholic Christian theory and practice. Only within such a hermeneutic can the specifically modern tools find their due place in ecclesial exegesis.

If we are to see what a genuinely catholic – holistic – reading of the Scriptures would look like, we must turn, secondly, to the Fathers and mediaeval doctors. They it was who built on the foundation of biblical typology (and in dependence on typology, allegory) the imposing tradition of spiritual exegesis which enables each text of Scripture to resonate within the widest possible chamber – not just the space of a biblical book or even the Canon as a whole but that of the Christian vision of the universe, a vision generated by the Church's reception of the biblical Word. Saward mentions in this connection a scene in *L'Annonce faite à Marie*, Claudel's drama set in the thirteenth-century French countryside – and the interweaving there of Scripture, Fathers and the Church's vision is worth a fuller glance.

On Christmas Eve in the forest of Chevoche, Mara Vercors seeks out, dead baby in her arms, her leprous sister Violaine whose fiancé she has conspired to take for herself. Violaine asks Mara to read for her (she has lost her eyes) the first lesson of each of the nocturns of Matins. And so the Isaian prophecy of light for those 'living in the land of darkness' and the beginning of St Luke's nativity gospel are con-textualised by the sermon of Pope Leo the Great about a day when all joy is born, to no one's exclusion. In a scene of supernatural intensity, the frozen corpse of the child suddenly becomes warm, as trumpets announce the passing by of the *dauphin* (it is the time of the Hundred Years' War) who is finally reaching Rheims for his sacring, and the long silent bells of Monsanvierge, its cloistered community thought extinct, ring out again – three wonders corresponding to the Latin Church's threefold celebration of Mass on Christmas Day, the topic of the other patristic text Mara reads from Gregory the Great's homilies. These patristic commentators enable Claudel to bring out the universal significance of the rebirth of humankind in the Child of Bethlehem, a rebirth imaged in the three confoundings of (hopeless) human expectation.[3]

But then thirdly, the spiritual sense discerned by an ecclesial eye with the enlightening grace of the Holy Spirit is not to be invoked *over against* the Bible's literal meaning – the sense entertained more immediately by the biblical author, especially as this affects 'historicity', the question of what, factually, happened. For what actually happened in events divinely originated for the sake of human salvation must not be supposed to pass blithely over the heads of any entities so mundane as mere facts. Salvifically *relevant* actual happenings take up matter and history and hence entail *factual* happenings. Claudel termed it 'literalist prejudice' to suppose that where there is symbolic meaning there cannot also be sober historical truth. 'The error of the whole mythical school . . . is to suppose that, because a fact is rich in teaching and meaning, it is a fictional product of the human mind.'[4]

And fourthly, the Canon of Scripture must not become the plaything of theological or ideological preference. The Church is nourished on the Word of God precisely because she digests Scripture *as a whole*. She does not go in for 'pick and mix' selectivity as to which portions of the biblical corpus she will consider genuinely inspired. It is heavily ironic that some Catholic writers are 'distancing' themselves from the full Canon (notably on feminist grounds) at a time when the world of historical scholarship is increasingly inclined to admit Catholicism's view of the contents of the Canon – and even to concede a special role to the church of Rome in its formation. Thus, for instance, Albert Sundberg, an American Lutheran expert on the history of the Canon of Scripture, considers it 'evident that both in content and doctrine, Protestantism, in its view of the Old Testament canon, has broken away from its historical heritage'. It is mistaken to suppose, Sundberg argued, that the Jewish canon, emerging officially in the later first century, was, as Reformation divines supposed, 'the defined Scriptures of Jesus and the apostle and of the early Church'.[5] Either some fresh argument for maintaining the restrictive Protestant canon (minus the 'Apocrypha') needs to be forthcoming, or the Protestant churches must revert, with whatever doctrinal inconvenience for themselves, to the Canon of traditional Christendom. Moreover, touching what concerns the heart of the Canon – the Gospels – the Anglican scholar T. C. Skeat has, between 1983 and 1997, built up a case for regarding the 'Four Gospel Canon' and the 'Four Gospel Codex' as interlinked – via the see of

Rome. In the early second century, so Skeat believes, the Great Church achieved a common mind on the Four Gospels (no more and no less), adopting the codex form in place of the earlier scroll (or roll) precisely to combine the four in a single volume of set length, as distinct from the indefinitely expansible bundles of rolls in use hitherto.

> Why no record of the decision has survived may perhaps be due to its instant and total success . . . That Rome played a leading part is suggested by the decision to use the codex, a Roman invention, and the involvement of Rome is perhaps confirmed by the inclusion of Mark, which at that time had seemed to be heading for oblivion.[6]

Is this the earliest known instance of magisterial intervention by the Petrine see?

Be this as it may, not only the integrity of the Canon but its essential unity of content is crucial to a truly ecclesial exegesis. Why despite the best efforts of the 'canon critics', led by Brevard Childs,[7] is it rather the internal differences and mutual tensions (and, so, radical critics would maintain, outright contradictions) of the Canon that are now most stressed? That emphasis chimes with a peculiarly modern intellectual prejudice in favour of seeing and having pluralism everywhere.

The desire to see and celebrate difference wherever possible, including in the New Testament Canon, is not something self-evidently right and proper, either in itself or as a way of tuning in to the Scriptures. It is not so much a gift of the New Testament churches to the contemporary Church as a gift – or perhaps we should say a poisoned chalice! – handed to the Church from contemporary culture. The privileging of difference over identity as a philosophical theme is peculiarly modern and indeed 'postmodern'. It is a favoured motif of the philosophy and literary theory which followed the collapse of cultural Modernism, the last great movement of secular humanism in the West, as cultural Modernism went down before the combined non-humanist forces of Freudianism, Marxism and Structuralism in the later 1960s. No doubt difference often is as important as identity. E. M. Forster remarked that a novelist's 'business lies with individuals, not with classifications'[8] – and we are all novelists when our interest in our fellow men and women is engaged. But identity also has its rights. What reader of *Where Angels Fear to Tread* would think it irrelevant to understanding Gino Castella and Mrs Herriton that both exemplify in different ways the *same* human nature?

The insistence that the New Testament writings were destined for utterly discrete groups and communities whose understandings of the gospel were not only different but also reciprocally unaffected and so quite possibly at variance one with another also paints its portrait of Scripture against an ideological backcloth.

This attempt to see difference everywhere and accord it sole value follows – since *groups and communities* are the issue – from the Romanticism of the early nineteenth century. In its opposition to the French Revolution of 1789 with its claim to the allegiance of peoples everywhere since it alone proclaimed the universal human rights to be enjoyed by all, that Romanticism stressed the incomparability of local cultures, insisting that people have the right to be in all senses different.

And just as the postmodern celebration of ontological difference, when unqualified by the complementary truth of identity, leads us into philosophical incoherence, so the Romantic celebration of communal difference, when uncomplemented by emphasis on our solidarity in the same human nature, renders us unable not only to criticise some other group but even to enrich it – a fate which a fashion in biblical scholarship would wish retrospectively on the New Testament Church. It is encouraging to see a reaction against the assumption of the truth in this *Tendenz*, a recovery of sanity exemplified in the essay collection *The Gospels for All Christians*, edited by Professor Richard Bauckham of the University of St Andrews.[9]

Finally, to revert once more to the quintet of Claudelian principles in exegesis, where the Bible is functioning as truly the *Bible of the Church*, it will be understood in a *Christocentric* fashion. 'No way through the Bible is there other than Jesus Christ, and to find it you have to have wings and rise above the vast ranges which to the pedestrian explorer appear confused and disconcerting.'[10] Though we cannot pick and choose as to what in the Canon *we shall have*, nonetheless *the Canon itself has* a centre. Here as everywhere in revelation, Christ is the centre. It is because Scripture is not its own centre that the many inner-biblical theologies can co-exist without detriment to its coherence, and the even more numerous extra-biblical theologies come to be, in the service of ecclesial thought, without jeopardising its originality. In the words of Balthasar:

> This is possible only because the fullness of the Bible crystallises concentrically around a human and divine centre, a centre which is indeed expressed in Scripture and everywhere flooded by its light but which essentially transcends Scripture and rests within itself as a sovereign reality. This centre which transcends Scripture, both as image and as force, has the power to organise the millennial history of thought and to effect within this history an *évolution homogène*.[11]

## The centre in question: the identity of Jesus

It is on what directly touches the figure of the Saviour that the expro-priation of Scripture from the Church to the academy – or to the proclivities of writers for the mass market – raises perhaps the gravest issues. Of course there can be no objection to the serious, disciplined, academic study of the Judaeo-Christian Scriptures in general and the Gospels in particular – though even here awareness of the role of these texts in a major world faith would, one supposes, naturally suggest a respect and delicacy in discussing them similar to that accorded the Koran – or even the Vedanta. The trouble is that in the confusion of competing methodologies for approaching the Gospels, the lack of agreed criteria for judging these materials – notably in the matter of the authenticity of the image of Jesus they project – is not merely a scholarly inconvenience. Worse, it opens the door to every kind of maverick interpreter – especially when, in a media climate largely hostile to Christianity, the resultant hypotheses are sufficiently startling to be commercially attractive.

The problem is not simply that the academic study of the Gospels is now, by ill-chance, situated in an environment of public debate which seeks sensation and rewards distortion. The estrangement of that academic scholarship from the Church which gave the Gospels birth undermines its practitioners' judgement by neutralising their feeling for what the texts are actually about. As a recent critic of some recent tendencies in the 'guild' of scholars has commented:

> The ways in which the historical-critical method has run amok are not disconnected from the ways in which biblical scholarship has become detached from communities for whom the writings of the Old and New Testaments have existential and normative importance.[12]

Contrary to the principles of *Wirkungsgeschichte* (the way impact and influence give clues to what some event *was*) laid down by the weightier students of interpretation theory this century, many such scholars delight in the maximum possible distance from the Church. And this is because – quite a-prioristically – they wish to offer the public a different Jesus from that of the Gospel portrait. Thus, for example, the 'Jesus Seminar' co-chaired by Professor Robert Funk and Professor John Dominic Crossan claims to be the ultimate in historical objectivity, complete with (colour-coded) voting on the authenticity or otherwise of sayings in the Gospels ascribed to the Lord. Yet Funk has recorded his commitment to producing a 'fiction' (a construct or projection) which will counter the fictions of traditional Christianity by the resolutely un-eschatological and non-'mythical' quality of its picture of Jesus – a missionary (or anti-missionary) aim scarcely compatible with the elaborate show of judicial nicety the Jesus Seminar maintains.[13]

Ancient historians are frequently shocked by the apparent arbitrariness of much present-day New Testament scholarship on questions of, precisely, historicity. Such dicta as that one cannot occupy simultaneously a written and an oral culture, or that only the shortest sayings can be remembered aright in the latter, are far from self-evidently true. The hectoring insistence on the 'counter-culturality' of Jesus sounds suspiciously late twentieth century, and can hardly avoid the charge of special pleading. Even such criteria as those of 'dissimilarity' and 'embarrassment' characteristic of a staider Gospel criticism, are at least faintly peculiar. If the 'dissimilarity' in question takes the form of a seeming disparity between a saying of Jesus and the preaching of the Church, it is equivalent to the criterion of causing 'embarrassment' to that Church and presumes a rupture or even an antagonism between the message of Jesus and that of the apostolic community. If it lies, rather, in a difference from the Judaism contemporary with Jesus it supposes that the faith of the patriarchs, of Moses, and the prophets was not integral to Jesus' message – that the Old Testament revelation was left unintegrated by the Revealer of the New. It may be replied that such critics are concerned only with identifying a hard core of historically defensible claims about Jesus' words (and by extension, deeds). But in that case they should not present it as a portrait. And moreover, it is sometimes forgotten that a core is so little nourishing to the eater that just that part of the fruit is thrown away.

It has always been part and parcel of Incarnation faith that there was 'more to' the Word incarnate than could be grasped or communicated by the earliest (or indeed, any) witnesses: the mystery of Christ, if he really be the infinite expressed in finite form, is necessarily beyond complete capture in any age short of the meta-time of heaven. But this is not, alas, what some contemporary writers mean by the 'hidden' Jesus. Misplaced ingenuity is frequently fuelled by the desire to find a Christ as unlike that of Holy Mother Church as possible, the better to show up that old beldame as, like the emperor, without any clothes. That the theses involved are so ludicrously contradictory one of another does not seem to lead to any slackening in the pursuit of this pastime. Thus we have Geza Vermeš' 'charismatic chasid' (but of the obscure rabbis on whom this Jesus is modelled almost nothing at all is known); Barbara Thiering's 'wicked priest' as otherwise found in the Qumran writings (but to arrive at the identification of that anonymous figure with Jesus there is needed a code as convoluted as any ever cracked at Bletchley Park); Marcus Borg's counter-cultural prophet (but his non-judgemental all-inclusiveness uncannily anticipates the political correctness of avant-garde late modern American élites); John Dominic Crossan's 'peasant Jewish cynic' (but no cynic philosopher is known ever to have reached Palestine).[14]

As Luke Timothy Johnson points out, whatever *frisson* the media may derive from these publishing events, students on these teachers' courses are usually unmoved by them. The reason is that scholars whose mode of self-presentation is antagonism to a traditional 'reading' of the Jesus of the Gospels presuppose a knowledge of that tradition by their students: and in much mainline Protestantism *and Catholicism*, that knowledge, after a generation of doctrinal and catechetical breakdown, is simply no longer there.

> The current debate concerning the historical Jesus takes place across lines of cultural institutions that have for much of their history been intertwined, and are now in considerable disarray and confusion. Just as the church must face hard questions concerning its response to modernity and its ways of mediating the tradition for succeeding generations, so does biblical scholarship within the academy face serious issues concerning its methods and purposes. The crisis has little to do with constraints imposed on scholars from the outside. It has much more to do with the emptiness of biblical scholarship apart from communities for whom these ancient texts have real-life significance, and the inadequacy of the historical critical method to meet the questions of significance posed by our culture today.[15]

Moreover, what the texts of the New Testament (including the Gospels) are primarily *evidence for* is not only unitary (over against the unending fragmentation of the sources by a hyper-critical method). It is also remarkably congruent with the Christological faith of the Church. In Professor Johnson's words (and the importance of this point warrants the length of the citation):

> When the witness of the New Testament is taken as a whole, a deep consistency can be detected beneath its surface diversity. The 'real Jesus' is first of all the powerful, resurrected Lord whose transforming Spirit is active in the community. But following Jesus is not a matter of the sort of power that dominates others, nor of 'already ruling' in the kingdom of God (1 Cor. 4:8). It is instead a matter of transformation according to the pattern of the Messiah. The 'real Jesus' is therefore also the one who through the Spirit

replicates in the lives of believers faithful obedience to God and loving service to others. Everywhere in these writings the image of Jesus involves the tension-filled paradox of death and resurrection, suffering and glory. Within the New Testament, no other pattern joins the story of Jesus and that of his followers. Discipleship does not consist in a countercultural critique of society. Discipleship does not consist in working overwhelming miracles. These elements of the Jesus tradition are not made normative in the way that the pattern of obedient suffering and loving service is. In short, abandoning the frame of meaning given to the story of Jesus by the four canonical Gospels is to abandon the frame of meaning given to the story of Jesus and of Christian discipleship by the rest of the New Testament. In the light of these simple observations, the question must be asked, Is what is claimed to be a pursuit of the historical Jesus not in truth a kind of flight from the image of Jesus and of discipleship inexorably ingrained in these texts? For our present age, in which the 'wisdom of the world' is expressed in individualism, narcissism, preoccupation with private rights, and competition, the 'wisdom of the cross' is the most profoundly countercultural message of all. Instead of an effort to rectify the distorting effect of the Gospel narratives, the effort to reconstruct Jesus according to some other pattern appears increasingly as an attempt to flee the scandal of the gospel.[16]

## The Babylonian captivity of Scripture

The Anglican Evangelical theologian Alister McGrath has spoken of Scripture as currently banished to Babylon thanks to the combined efforts, on the one hand, of those more-or-less secular students who have dragged it off to the academy, there to be submitted to an interrogation which from the nature of the case cannot yield up its sovereign fullness, and, on the other, those within the Church community who would impose on it an alien hermeneutic, whether, say, that of Liberationism in its Marxian forms or of radical feminism.

> We criticise the German Christians for obeying Hitler, conveniently choosing to overlook that they were simply submitting themselves to the prevailing cultural norms. We are doing the same today by allowing ourselves and our churches to follow societal norms and values, irrespective of their origins and goals. To allow our ideas and values to become controlled by anything or anyone other than the self-revelation of God in Scripture is to adopt an ideology rather than a theology; it is to become controlled by ideas and values whose origins lie outside the Christian tradition – and potentially to become enslaved to them.[17]

As McGrath points out, the 'paradox underlying the entire liberal enter-prise' is that for 'everyone for whom the gospel is made "relevant", there is someone else for whom it is made "irrelevant"'.[18] Just as for Hegel those who marry the spirit of the age soon find themselves widowers, so for McGrath those who exalt the needs of some hitherto underrepresented group to the status of sole criterion of meaning and utility for Scripture soon find themselves the object of rancour of some other (then or now) underrepresented constituency. It is a tell-tale sign of the limitations of such approaches that they cannot – without the most grotesque wrenching of texts from contexts – support preaching for much of the liturgical cycle and its lectionaries, and that they are practically useless to the pastoral clergy engaged in such tasks as visiting the sick and comforting the grieving.

As I have written elsewhere:

> The Scriptures are the word of life for the today of the Church only if they serve other salvific realities of a more fundamental kind: Christ, as Word Incarnate; the divine life brought about by the grace of the Holy Spirit; the sacraments of faith; the life and teaching of the Church, considered as drawing us to the Father. Whereas Scripture has, in permanence, a unique place as the normative and immediately accessible word of God thanks to its written character (*littera scripta manet*), this privileged rôle is exercised at the level of the Church *taken as a whole*, rather than on that of the individual faithful, whether he or she be scholar or illiterate. For the individual believer, pride of place must go, not to the written text but to the word of God as interpreted and actualised by the living community, the body of Christ of which he forms part.[19]

And how *does* the Church read Scripture? The answer is:

> in the Spirit as a canonically and narrationally unified whole centred on Jesus Christ and telling the story of the dealings of the Father with his people and the word in ways . . . that are typo-logically applicable to the present.[20]

In some wise words of a Lutheran thinker:

> The church's antecedent knowledge of Scripture's plot and *dramatis personae*, without which she could not read the Bible as a whole, is contained in what Irenaeus calls 'the rule of faith', the canon that the church propounds and teaches to her members regarding how to think and talk as Christians. There can be no churchly exegesis of the Bible that abstracts from this, that does not take the church's dogmas and ordinary teachings as playbill for the *biblical drama*.

Rarely do we appreciate the rather drastic point here. There can be no churchly reading of Scripture that is not activated and guided by the church's teaching. But there can be no reading of the Bible that is not churchly. Therefore there can be no reading of the unitary Bible that is not motivated and guided by the church's teaching. We will either read the Bible under the guidance of the church's established doctrine, or we will not read the Bible at all. When we attempt dogmatically rebellious or ignorant reading of Scripture, we will find only *dissecta membra* in our hands.[21]

## NOTES

1. J. Saward, 'Regaining Paradise: Paul Claudel and the Renewal of Exegesis', *Downside Review* 114, 395 (1996), p. 79.

2. P. Claudel, *J'aime la Bible* (= *Oeuvres complètes*, 21, Paris, 1963), p. 363.

3. P. Claudel, *L'Annonce faite à Marie, version définitive pour la scène* (Paris, 1940; 1989), pp. 153–84.

4. P. Claudel, F. Jammes, G. Frizeau, *Correspondance* (Paris, 1952), p. 58, cited J. Saward, 'Regaining Paradise', art. cit., p. 92.

5. A. C. Sundberg, Jr, 'The Protestant Old Testament Canon: Should It Be Re-examined?', *Catholic Biblical Quarterly* 28 (1966), pp. 203, 202; idem, *The Old Testament of the Early Church* (Harvard, Mass., 1964).

6. T. C. Skeat, 'The Origin of the Christian Codex', *Zeitschrift für Papyrologie und Epigraphik* 102 (1994), pp. 263–8. See also idem (with C. H. Roberts), *The Birth of the Codex* (Oxford, 1983); 'Irenaeus and the Four-Gospel Canon', *Novum Testamentum* XXIV. 2 (1992), pp. 194–9 ; 'The Oldest Manuscript of the Four Gospels?', *New Testament Studies* 43 (1997), pp. 1–34. I am grateful to Fr J. W. Hunwicke of Lancing College for calling these contributions to my attention.

7. B. Childs, *Introduction to the Old Testament as Scripture* (Philadelphia, 1979); *The New Testament as Canon: an Introduction* (Philadelphia, 1984).

8. E. M. Forster, 'Three Countries' (TS at King's College, Cambridge), cited in D. Stallybrass (ed.), *E. M. Forster. Where Angels Fear to Tread* (London, 1975), p. 8.

9. R. Bauckham (ed.), *The Gospels for All Christians* (Edinburgh, 1998). 'Diversity has now come to mean something like complete separation. The Gospels are studied in total isolation from the Pauline letters, as though there were no links at all among the earliest Christian communities. Not only Acts but also the evidence from Paul himself shows that such a compartmentalization is excessive and distorting': thus L. T. Johnson, *The Real Jesus. The Misguided Quest for the Historical Jesus and the Truth of the Traditional Gospels* (San Francisco, 1997), pp. 117–18.

10. P. Claudel, *Quelques principes d'exégèse*, p. 3, cited J. Saward, 'Regaining Paradise', p. 87.

11. H. U. von Balthasar, *The Glory of the Lord. A Theological Aesthetics I. Seeing the Form* (ET Edinburgh, 1982), p. 554. The words in italics refer to the classic Neo-Scholastic study of the idea of development, F. Marín-Sola, O.P., *L'Evolution homogène du dogme chrétien* (Fribourg, 1924). On Balthasar's account of Christ as centre of the Canon, see J. Riches, 'Von Balthasar as Biblical Theologian and Exegete', *New Blackfriars* 79, 923 (1998), pp. 38–45.

12. L. T. Johnson, *The Real Jesus*, p. ix.

13. Ibid., pp. 6–9.

14. G. Vermeš, *Jesus the Jew* (London, 1973); B. Thiering, *Jesus and the Riddle of the Dead Sea Scrolls: Unlocking the Secrets of His Life Story* (San Francisco, 1992); M. Borg, *Jesus, a New Version: Spirit, Culture and the Life of Discipleship* (San Francsico, 1987); idem, *Meeting Jesus Again for the First Time: the Historical Jesus and the Heart of Contemporary Faith* (San Francisco, 1994); J. D. Crossan, *The Historical Jesus, the Life of a Mediterranean Jewish Peasant* (San Francisco, 1991); idem, *Jesus. A Revolutionary Biography* (San Francisco, 1994).

15. L. T. Johnson, *The Real Jesus*, pp. 75–6.

16. Ibid., p. 166. I would, however, be more willing than Johnson to defend an attempt at creating a narrative of the life of Jesus (though *within the pattern* Johnson detects) – simply because all history writing implies *some* attempt at narrative construction. See my chapter, 'The Historian's Jesus', in A. Nichols, O.P., *Epiphany. A Theological Introduction to Catholicism* (Collegeville, Minn., 1966), pp. 65-105.

17. A . McGrath, 'Reclaiming our Roots and Vision: Scripture and the Stability of the Christian Church', in C. E. Braaten and R. W. Jenson (eds.), *Reclaiming the Bible for the Church* (Grand Rapids, Mich., 1995), p. 72. (The 'German Christians' were the party in German Protestantism under the Third Reich who accepted the need to review the content of the biblical revelation in the light of the National Socialist destiny of Germany.)

18. Ibid., p. 86.

19. A. Nichols, O.P., 'François Dreyfus on Scripture Read in Tradition', in idem., *Scribe of the Kingdom. Essays on Theology and Culture* (London, 1994), I, p. 55.

20. Nichols, *Epiphany*, p. 46.

21. R. W. Jenson, 'Hermeneutics and the Life of the Church', in Braaten and Jenson (eds.), *Reclaiming the Bible for the Church*, p. 98.

# XIII

# *Reconceiving Ecumenism*

THE Ecumenical Movement, as conceived from the launching of the 'Faith and Order' initiative of Anglicans, Protestants and the Orthodox in the 1920s and to which, on the eve of the Second Vatican Council, the Catholic Church was a late convert, has produced many great fruits – as well as a not few bitter ones. On the *credit* side it has generated a more charitable outlook toward Christians who follow some different rule of faith from one's own (though obduracies remain, especially, it must be said, among Orthodox and Evangelicals). It has led to fine scholars sitting down with experienced Churchmen and making from the theological and historical fragments of the Christian past some excellent position papers in which the doctrinal gaps between confession are if not closed then appreciably narrowed. On the *debit* side, it has also contributed to a general process of blurring ecclesial identities and muddying the waters of doctrinal conscious-ness on the supposition – among those who, assisted by news media, obtained no more than the general idea of what was going on – that allegiance to particular *credenda*, as opposed to general benevolence, is now distinctly *passé*.[1] It has also revealed, via the unwillingness of one side or the other (or both) in bilateral dialogue to press ahead with implementing even the most compendious and meticulously formulated theological agreements (the example of the twenty-five documents agreed between the Old Catholics and the Orthodox in the years 1973–87 is a case in point),[2] that other factors than the straight-forwardly doctrinal – questions of ecclesiastical prudence, of Church culture, and national and international politics – cannot be left out of these equations. And this is so however much professional ecumenists (to some extent a supra-ecclesiastical, international corporation) may deplore the fact.

The widespread perception that the wave of the twentieth-century Ecumenical Movement has crested is owed to more, then, than the simple fact of chronology – that the twentieth century is about to expire. There seems to be a case, accordingly, for a new agenda. I would like to see its construction in terms of three pillars: first, greater realism about the significance of ecumenical choices, and an enhanced candour about their why and wherefore; secondly, a positive determination on the part of all Christians who share in conscious fashion the central orthodox dogmas pronounced in the early centuries by the Great Church as well as the common patrimony of a classical Christian morality, to assist each other in the restabilisation of their Churches after decades of theological and ideological turbulence; thirdly, on the part of Catholics an increased readiness to sing the virtues of the unjustly stigmatised term 'Uniatism' – the reconciliation of diverse traditions around the figure of Peter.

## Ecumenical realism

How might 'greater realism' about the significance of ecumenical choices and 'enhanced candour' be applied? We can look at the cases of Constantinople and Canterbury, the two most important bilateral discussions from the standpoint of respectively Rome and Westminster: the Catholic Church universally, and that same Church in its English incarnation. Let us take 'Anglicans and Catholics' first.

### (1) Anglicans and Catholics

There are various ways in which the topic of 'Anglicans and Catholics' might be approached. One could, for instance, attempt a historical overview of the actual interrelations – or at any rate contacts – between the Anglican and Catholic communions since the English Reformation, for it would be quite wrong to suppose that such contacts were only initiated by the modern Ecumenical Movement, as Bernard and Margaret Pawley's study *Rome and Canterbury through Four Centuries* makes plain, not least in its title.[3] Again, one might come at the subject by way of the bilateral dialogue initiated by Pope Paul VI and Archbishop Michael Ramsey in the wake of the Second Vatican Council, giving as that Council did a mighty impulse to Catholic participation in the second phase of the Ecumenical Movement – the doctrinally serious 'Faith and Order' phase which succeeded to (without by any means supplanting) the more practically oriented and sentimental, or affective, first stage, 'Work and Life', whose deliberate abstention from issues of doctrine and Church order the Roman see had found so uncongenial. The Agreed Statements of the Anglican Roman Catholic International Commission ('ARCIC'), Mark I, on Eucharist, Ministry and Authority[4] (crucial foundations of Church life), and those of ARCIC II on justification[5] (*the* issue *par excellence* of the sixteenth-century controversies), and the foundations of morality,[6] constitute, clearly enough, an important set of documents which help define both the degree of consensus between the two Churches and, perhaps not less importantly, the limits of that consensus. This is especially apparent when these texts are taken together with the official response of the two Communions, appreciative but qualified as these were, and in the latter respect especially (at first at any rate) on the Catholic side.

Each of these approaches, that of the professional historian and that of the professional ecumenist, has its advantages and its disadvantages. Take first the historian's. Hegel, reportedly, when told that his theory of the historical self-manifestation of spirit did not agree with the facts, replied *Zu schlimm für die Tatsachen* ('Too bad for the facts!'). For those of us who do not wish to echo this remark, to know how in historical reality the Anglican and Catholic Churches have defined their own interplay can only be highly germane to any account of the interrelation of 'Anglicans and Catholics' today. On the other hand, such are the vagaries of historical actors (and actresses!), such the mixture of their motives, the idiosyncrasies of their personalities, the complexity of the conjunctures in which they found themselves, that the theological significance of their words and actions cannot be read off from them in any simple fashion, like an expression from a face. And in any case we could not rightly judge that theological significance without situating it in the entire context of Christian thinking as a whole.

The second approach, that of the ecumenist, by contrast, is theological through and through, consisting as it does in employing the historical theologian's informational knowledge and the systematic theologian's argumentative skills to produce essays in doctrine broadly acceptable to the two Communions concerned. The trouble with this approach is that it resembles too much the building of a house of paper – or at any rate cardboard. We simply do not know how solidly grounded, say, the ARCIC I document on the Eucharist is in terms of actual Anglican and Catholic attitudes: whether, in other words, a religious sociologist would consider that such agreement – which, essentially, marries a high doctrine of the Eucharist presence to a low doctrine of the Eucharist sacrifice, with the reduction of the extra-liturgical veneration of the reserved Elements to a footnote – can be made to 'stick' among the two constituencies involved.

There remains a third possibility which may be called the 'diagnostic' approach, because it attempts a diagnosis of the situation in the light of both empirical (or historical) and theoretical (or theological) considerations, all with a view to ascertaining whether a given Communion is well-advised to regard another as among its ecumenical partners of preference. This seems to be the method adopted by the Yale systematician George Lindbeck, a Lutheran, in an assessment of the relations between the Lutheran and Reformed traditions which could well serve as a model for how to evaluate Anglican-Catholic relations today.[7]

Lindbeck points out that the *prima facie* case for a union of the Lutheran and Reformed communities appears on the face of it quite overwhelming. Not only do these two families of Churches share the same hermeneutical formula for interpreting biblical revelation, a summation of the three Reformation 'solas' – *solus Christus, sola fides* (including *sola gratia*) and *sola Scriptura* – in the principle that all Scripture testifies to Christ and to justification by faith in him. Also, all possess, on the foundation of that same formula, a common recipe for identifying the Church – which is, so it transpires, that community where the gospel of faith *alone* by justification by grace *alone* in Christ *alone* is communicated in Word and sacrament. Moreover, since the mid-sixteenth century when their ways diverged, certain more particular disputed questions in theological doctrine and liturgical practice have largely evaporated under the pressure of academic theological scholarship and liturgical renewal. The contrasts of Lutheran antinomianism and Calvinist legalism, denial, or affirmation of the subjective certainty of final salvation, the heated debate over whether the flesh and blood of the risen and ascended Lord are 'capable of the infinite' and thus of omnipresence, not least in the Eucharist (Lutherans saying yea, Calvinists nay), are virtually past history. And as to the specifically contemporary development, Lindbeck writes:

> In our day, ecumenically inclined Reformed Christians are no longer iconoclastically and dogmatically low church, and it is this change in attitude and doctrine which more than anything else, it seems to me, has made the theological differences non-divisive. Opposition to everything Roman has lessened, historical research has taught us that the New Testament is neither high church nor low church (or, perhaps better, it is from our perspective a strange mixture of both), and the Reformed have stopped equating high church ceremonies with idolatry or superstition (the objection nowadays is much more likely to be to unmanly, high-brow aestheticism, but cocktail-drinking Anglicans are more often the butt of this accusation than are beer-swilling Lutherans).[8]

In fact, it seems the most natural thing in the world (or at least in the Church!) that these two traditions should accept the positive recommendations of their own bilateral dialogue and instate full communion without further ado.

Yet it is the case that among Lutherans of Professor Lindbeck's kind – strongly sacramental Lutherans who take doctrinal subscription seriously – there is absolutely no enthusiasm for union with the Reform; rather the opposite. Why? The reasons have to do with a diagnosis of the current ills of Lutheran church life, and a prognosis of the effect on those diseases of amalgamation with the Reformed. Such resistance to the establishment of full fellowship in pulpit and at altar turns on the belief that, within Lutheranism itself, a battle is being waged against sacramental minimalism on the one hand and the dilution of confessional standards on the other. Thus many Lutherans find themselves opposed to, first, any lowering – in the name of ecumenical eirenicism – of the ritual level of their liturgical life since, anthropologically speaking, this could only further subvert the estimation in which sacraments are held. Then second, there is the issue of doctrinal consciousness, for a number of Lutherans consider that confessional authority has eroded even more startlingly among the Reformed churches than in their own. Speaking frankly, Lindbeck makes his own the view of those Lutheran church leaders who, while favouring the unification of ecclesial communities, see 'no point to it when what makes it possible is the weakening of all definite commitments and convictions'.[9] He justifies thereby his own decision for the Roman Catholic Church as the preferred ecumenical partner of Lutheranism, on the ground that this dialogue – unlike that with the worldwide Reformed Alliance – will not have the effect of further eviscerating confessional and sacramental substance.

It would not be difficult to show that Lindbeck's account of the relations between the Reformed and Lutheranism is analogically true of those between Anglicanism and Catholicism. In that latter relationship likewise we have the example of a considerable shared patrimony, on the one hand, and, on the other, a modern process whereby through the same combination of academic theological scholarship and liturgical revision many of the differences in theological doctrine and liturgical practice which once set at loggerheads Rome and Canterbury are now mitigated in force. At the same time, however, we also find a marked Catholic reluctance to draw the 'obvious' conclusion.

When we think of that common patrimony, we can compose quite a formidable list: the acceptance of the first of the General Councils and the witness of patrology as a guide to the meaning of Scripture; the retention of the threefold ministry of bishops, priests and deacons (at least in their outward forms); the presence of much of the liturgical inheritance of the historic Western Church in the Prayer Book offices; and the continuance of a recognisably Latin-mediaeval institutional life in the canonical tradition of the Anglican Church. Should we then add those factors which, in the course of the last hundred years, have effected further *rapprochement*, we would need to name: the employment of similar methods of using Scripture theologically, through the (broad) acceptance of nineteenth- and twentieth-century critical exegesis; the development of a vernacular liturgy in the Church of Rome, with hymnographic borrowings from Anglicanism, to complement the ritual borrowings from Catholicism in the post-Tractarian Church of England; the convergence of Eucharist forms in Anglicanism and the Western-rite Catholic Church, owning to the fuller deployment of early patristic models of worship; and the emergence of distinguished Anglican students of the specifically mediaeval Western theological tradition, largely – though by no means wholly – spurned by early Anglicans, something matched by the tendency of twentieth-century Catholic theologians to go behind the mediaeval Scholastics (and their successors) to their patristic and biblical predecessors. Lastly, and on a different note, we have the similarity of accent of the two confessions in the intervention of their spokesmen in political and social (less so in moral) affairs.

But if this list can be regarded as consisting very largely of positive factors (and, clearly, question marks *could* be set against any easy assumption of the general beneficence of their operation – compare here my comments in Chapter III on the baleful aspect of liturgical reform), one can also call to mind – and here is where the medical, or indeed pathological, vocabulary of diagnosis becomes relevant – some more negative elements which have also become the common property, or common malaise, of the two bodies. Here one would have to mention first that theological liberalism, and indeed radicalism, which made Lindbeck pause in considering Lutheran-Reformed convergence. Such liberalism and radicalism, though now also present in Catholic theology and in the Anglo-Saxon cultural sphere even dominant there, have both deeper historic roots in Anglicanism and a relative wider extension – something owed to the greater integration of Anglican theology with largely secular universities as well as the debility of such instruments of doctrinal control as the Anglican episcopate can command. Secondly, we have the corrosive effects of the sexual revolution on classical Christian ethics which has made it impossible for Anglicanism and difficult for Catholicism to maintain the historic positions of Western Christendom on such major issues as abortion, divorce, genital homosexuality, contraception. (This second point might be regarded as the ethical self-manifestation of the first.) Thirdly, there is the phenomenon of Provincial autonomy in the Anglican Communion – a beast which, like Topsy, 'just growed', and has now become – as the handling of the issue of the ordination of women to the presbyterate and episcopate shows – a cause of major and endemic impairment to communion between Anglicans in different parts of the world. This same phenomenon of regionally dispersed authority has its Catholic counterpart in a Neo-Gallicanism which would 're-envisage' the Catholic Church as a federation of national churches whose relations are mediated by the chairmanship of Rome. A fourth factor increasingly common to both Churches is what one might term 'party spirit' – that is, in Anglicanism the longstanding 'networking' of like-minded Church people for collaboration at all levels over against other such networks of different temper, and in Catholicism the emergence of two opposed theological families – the *Concilium* and *Communio* connections – with their conflicting general programmes for the theological future, as well as, more widely, the tendency of individual diocesan and regional churches to take on a specific ecclesial character defined often by their enthusiasm or otherwise for papal policies.

So far as these four negative factors are concerned, they are, in the Catholic case, I take it, the effects for the most part of the intrusion of modern secular consciousness into the household of faith. Of course not everything that secular consciousness proposes or contains is necessarily to be shunned, for secular consciousness is nothing but the general human interpretation, possibly 'anonymously' affected by grace, of natural reality at large. It remains the case, however, that one could not imagine the Catholic Church as inhabited by theological liberalism and radicalism, a permissive sexual ethics, ecclesiastical nationalism and corporate partisanship in the forms in which we now know these, were it not for the challenge of secular modernity in different ways.

Unfortunately, the same four negative elements are not so much alien invasions of Anglicanism as actualisations of possibilities inherent in its structure and ethos. Thus, the rejection of the organic view of Church tradition and a magisterial role for the post-patristic episcopate in Council as well as papal authority opened the Anglican door as early as the mid-seventeenth century to forms of theological liberalism and radicalism. Only a much later age, admittedly, thought of extending such 'Latitudinarianism' from faith to morals. Again, the development of Provincial autonomy in the Anglican communion derives from the combined operation of two factors present from the first in the Church of England – the inhibition by the Tudor Crown of anything approximating to a patriarchal (super-metropolitical) authority for the Archbishop of Canterbury and the assumption that a Church is always or at least normally co-terminous with a nation. Finally, the inroads of party spirit were entirely predictable from the state of the Church of England as it left the hands of its makers. In my *The Panther and the Hind* I outline the unstable synthesis of theological ingredients which went into the making of Anglicanism and sufficiently explain its subsequent oscillations: there is no founding consensus, to which it can recur, no theological peace to which it can be recalled.[10] In a letter of 1836, some three years before he began to suspect that his rejection of Roman claims might not be valid, Newman told Hugh James Rose, a traditional high Churchman and first Professor of Divinity in the newly founded University of Durham,

> I do *not* love the 'Church of England' [so much as] the old Church of 1200 or 1600 years, the Church of the builders of our Cathedrals, the Church again of Andrewes, Laud, Hammond, Ken and Butler [all post-Reformation divines] (so far forth as they agree together and are lights shining in a dark place) . . . I love the Church too as embodying the good characteristics of the English ethos.[11]

But, he went on, he could not cherish the 'Church enslaved by the State', which had 'never been one reality, except as an Establishment'. 'Viewed *internally*, it is the battlefield of two opposite principles', (radical) Protestantism and Catholicism.[12]

My message is, I suppose, plain. Despite the considerable shared heritage of Anglicanism and Catholicism, and the many subsequently acquired positive characteristics they have in common – all of which of course justify and, more than justify, *demand* the exercise of Christian charity, good-neighbourliness, friendship, and common participation in much shared Christian work – for the Catholic Church to commit itself to organic union with the Anglican Communion must also be called, on a diagnostic analysis of the relations between the two, a self-destructive act.

Taking the largest possible view, it seems clear that only the Eastern Orthodox Church has a serious claim – in most respects, not all – to be treated as Catholicism's ecumenical partner of preference.

I come to this conclusion not with glee but with a decree of sadness. Like (I suspect) most English people who have moved from Anglicanism to Rome I look back with a *mélange* of nostalgia, irritation and a feeling of parricide. This cocktail of emotions is probably not shared by non-English converts – at any rate, not in the same way. For good or ill, as Newman pointed out in the letter I quoted, Anglicanism is bound up with being English. In Newman's lifetime only the Scottish Episcopal Church and the Protestant Episcopal Church of the United States of America existed as harbingers of the future global odyssey of Anglicanism. And yet, as the formularies of the various constituent Provinces of the Anglican Communion attest, the Church of England remains central to, and defining for, Anglicanism as a whole. For with the exception of the Scots (who doubtless have reasons of their own for downplaying the Englishness of Anglicanism), the constitutions of Anglican Provinces refer to the shared note of communion with the see of Canterbury as essential to Anglican faith and order, and in many cases specifically assert that they receive the universal faith as it is taught or explained by the Church of England in its historic formularies. Philip Thomas, in his 'A Family Affair: the Pattern of Constitutional Authority in the Anglican Communion', a contribution to the *Festschrift* for Bishop John Howe, the first Secretary General of the Anglican Consultative Council, puts the question, 'How does the Church of England relate to this pattern?' And his first answer is: 'It is the faith and history and line of ministry of the English church in which the rest of the communion's life coheres.'[13] This is both the glory and the tragedy of Anglicanism. In *Let Dons Delight*, Ronald Knox's dream sequence of conversations overheard in Oxford Common Rooms from 1588 to 1938, Dr Greene, who represents the high and dry Tory Anglicans alarmed by their new-fangled Tractarian supporters, has this to say on the latter's talk of 'apostolick' origin for the English Church.

> Why, of course it has come down to us from the apostles; that is a matter of common observation. But it has come down to us in our history as a part of English life, as the religion of a nation, adapted to its temper and modelled by its history; it is from that that it derives its substance; it is the religion of Englishmen or it is nothing. You and your friends are pursuing, as it seems to me, the phantom or ideal of a Church, which has no substance in reality; it is neither fish, flesh, nor good red herring. We all know of the dog in Aesop, who dropped his bone while he jumped after what was only a reflection in the water. So it is with you gentlemen; you neglect to preserve the Church of England as it is in fact, while you are running after an ideal church which is not there.[14]

That indeed is the conclusion to which some Anglo-Catholics, and also others of wider Churchmanship, have come in the last few years.

## (2) Catholics and Orthodox

Here I attempt an overview in four parts. First, I shall discuss why Catholics should not only show some ecumenical concern for Orthodoxy but also treat the Orthodox as their privileged or primary ecumenical partner. Secondly, I shall ask why the schism between the Catholic and Orthodox churches occurred, focusing as it finally, did on four historic 'dividing issues'. Thirdly, I shall evaluate the present state of Catholic-Orthodox relations, with particular reference to the problem of the 'Uniate' or Eastern Catholic churches. Fourthly and finally having been highly sympathetic and complimentary to the Orthodox throughout, I shall end by saying what, in my judgement, is wrong with the Orthodox Church and why it needs Catholicism for (humanly speaking) its own salvation.

First, then, why should Catholics take the Orthodox as not only *an* ecumenical partner but *the* ecumenical partner *par excellence*? There are three kinds of reasons: historical, theological and practical – of which in most discussion only the historical and theological are mentioned since the third sort – what I term the 'practical' – take us into areas of potential controversy among Western Catholics themselves.

The historical reasons for giving preference to Orthodoxy over all other separated communions turn on the fact that the schism between the Roman church and the ancient Chalcedonian churches of the East is the most tragic and burdensome of the splits in historic Christendom if we take up a universal rather than merely regional perspective. Though segments of the Church of the Fathers were lost to the Great Church through the departure from Catholic unity of the Assyrian (Nestorian) and Oriental Orthodox (Monophysite) churches after the Councils of Ephesus (431) and Chalcedon (451) respectively, Christians representing the two principal cultures of the Mediterranean basin where the gospel had its greatest flowering – the Greek and the Latin – lived in peace and unity with each other, despite occasional stirrings and some local difficulties, right up until the end of the patristic epoch. That epoch came to its climax with the Seventh Ecumenical Council, Nicaea II, in 787, the last Council Catholics and Orthodox have in common and the Council which, in its teaching on the icon and notably on the icon of Christ, brought to a triumphant close the series of conciliar clarifications of the Christological faith of the Church which had opened with Nicaea I in 325. The iconography, liturgical life, creeds and dogmatic believing of the ancient Church come down to us in forms at once Eastern and Western; and it was this rich unity of patristic culture, expressing as it did the faith of the apostolic community, which was shattered by the schism between Catholics and Orthodox, never (so far) to be repaired. And let me say at this point that Church history provides exceedingly few examples of historic schisms overcome, so if history is to be our teacher we have no grounds for confidence or optimism that this most catastrophic of all schisms will be undone. 'Catastrophic' because, historically, as Pope John Paul II has pointed out, taking up a metaphor suggested by a French ecclesiologist, the late Cardinal Yves Congar, each Church, West and East, henceforth could only breathe with one lung. No Church could now lay claim to the total cultural patrimony of both Eastern and Western Chalcedonianism – that is, the Christologically and therefore triadologically and soteriologically correct understanding of the gospel. The result of the consequent rivalry and conflict was the creation of an invisible line down the middle of Europe. And what the historic consequences of *that* were we know well enough from the situation of the former Yugoslavia today.

After the historical, the theological. The second reason for giving priority to ecumenical relations with the Orthodox is theological. If the main point of ecumenism, or work for the restoration of the Church's full unity, were simply to redress historic wrongs and defuse historically generated causes of conflict, then we might suppose that we should be equally – or perhaps even more – interested in addressing the Catholic-Protestant divide. After all, there have been no actual wars of religion, simply as such, between Catholics and Orthodox, unlike those between Catholics and Protestants in sixteenth-century France or the seventeenth-century Holy Roman Empire. But theologically there cannot be any doubt that the Catholic Church must accord greater importance to dialogue with the Orthodox than to conversations with any Protestant body. For the Orthodox Churches are Churches in the apostolic succession; they are bearers of the apostolic Tradition, witnesses to apostolic faith, worship and order – even though they are also, and at the same time, unhappily sundered from the *prima sedes*, the first see. Their Fathers and other ecclesiastical writers, their liturgical texts and practices, their iconographic tradition, these remain *loci theologici* – authoritative sources – to which the Catholic theologian can and must turn in his or her intellectual construal of *Catholic* Christianity. And that cannot possibly be said of the monuments of Anglican, Lutheran, Reformed or any other kind of Protestantism. To put the same point another way: the separated Western communities have Christian traditions – in the plural, with a small 't' – which may well be worthy of the Catholic theologian's interest and respect. But only the Orthodox are, along with the Catholic Church, bearers of Holy Tradition

– in the singular, with a capital 'T', that is, of the gospel in its plenary organic transmission through the entirety of the life, credal, doxological, ethical, of Christ's Church. There is for Catholics, therefore, a theological imperative to restore unity with the Orthodox which is lacking in our attitude to Protestantism, though I should not be misinterpreted as saying that there is no theological basis for the impulse to Catholic-Protestant *rapprochement* for we have it in the prayer of our Lord himself at the Great Supper, 'that they all may be one'.

I am emphasising the greater priority we should give to relations with the Orthodox because I do not believe the optimistic statement of many professional ecumenists to the effect that all bilateral dialogues – all negotiations with individual separated communions – feed into each other in a positive and unproblematic way. It would be nice to think that a step towards one separated group of Christians never meant a step away from another one, but such a pious claim does not become more credible with the frequency of its repeating. The issue of the ordination of women, to take but one particularly clear example, is evidently a topic where to move closer to world Protestantism is to move further from global Orthodoxy – and vice versa.

This brings me to my third reason for advocating ecumenical rapport with Orthodoxy: its practical advantages. At the present time, the Catholic Church, in many parts of the world, is undergoing one of the most serious crises in its history, a crisis resulting from a disorienting encounter with secular culture and compounded by a failure of Christian discernment on the part of many people over the last quarter century from the highest office-holders to the ordinary faithful. This crisis touches many aspects of Church life but notably theology and catechesis, liturgy and spirituality, Religious life and Christian ethics at large. Orthodoxy is well placed to stabilise Catholicism in most if not all of these areas. Were we to ask in a simply phenomenological frame of mind just what the Orthodox Church is like, we could describe it as a dogmatic Church, a liturgical Church, a contemplative Church, and a monastic Church – and in all these respects it furnishes a helpful counter-balance to certain features of much Western Catholicism today.

First, then, Orthodoxy is a *dogmatic* Church. It lives from out of the fullness of the truth impressed by the Spirit on the minds of the apostles at the first Pentecost, a fullness which transformed their awareness and made possible that specifically Christian kind of thinking we call dogmatic thought. The Holy Trinity, the God-man, the Mother of God and the saints, the Church as the mystery of the Kingdom expressed in a common life on earth, the sacraments as means to humanity's deification – our participation in the uncreated life of God himself: these are the truths among which the Orthodox live, move and have their being. Orthodox theology in all its forms is a call to the renewal of our minds in Christ, something which finds its measure not in pure reason or secular culture but in the apostolic preaching attested to by the holy Fathers, in accord with the principal dogmata of faith as summed up in the Ecumenical Councils of the Church.[15]

Second, Orthodoxy is a *liturgical* Church. It is a Church for which the Liturgy provides a total ambience expressed in poetry, music and iconography, text and gesture, and where the touchstone of the liturgical life is not the capacity of liturgy to express contemporary concerns (legitimate though these may be in their own context), but, rather, the ability of the Liturgy to act as a vehicle of the Kingdom, our anticipated entry, even here and now, into the divine life.

Third, Orthodoxy is a *contemplative* Church. Though certainly not ignoring the calls of missionary activity and practical charity, essential to the gospel and the gospel community as these are, the Orthodox lay their primary emphasis on the life of prayer as the absolutely necessary condition of all Christianity worth the name. In the tradition of the desert Fathers, and of such great theologian-mystics as the Cappadocian Fathers, St Maximus and St Gregory Palamas, encapsulated as these contributions are in that anthology of Eastern Christian spirituality the *Philokalia*, Orthodoxy gives testimony to the primacy of what the Saviour himself called the first and greatest commandment, to love the Lord your God with your whole heart, soul, mind and strength, for it is by the light of this commandment – with its appeal for a God-centred process of personal conversion and sanctification – that all our efforts to live out its companion commandment (to love our neighbour as ourselves) must be guided.

And fourth, Orthodoxy is a *monastic* Church, a Church with a monastic heart where the monasteries provide the spiritual fathers of the bishops, the counsellors of the laity and the example of a Christian maximalism. A Church without a flourishing monasticism, without the lived 'martyrdom' of an asceticism inspired by the Paschal Mystery of the Lord's cross and resurrection, could hardly be a Church according to the mind of the Christ of the Gospels, for monasticism, of all Christian life ways, is (as we saw in Chapter X) the one which most clearly and publicly leaves all things behind for the sake of the Kingdom.

Practically speaking, then, the re-entry into Catholic unity of this dogmatic, liturgical, contemplative and monastic Church could only have the effect of steadying and strengthening those aspects of Western Catholicism which today are most under threat by the corrosives of secularism and theological liberalism.

I turn now to the actual genesis of the schism (a condition of understanding its possible resolution) from a Catholic standpoint, along with some account – necessarily summary and unadorned – of the four historic 'dividing issues': those disputed questions which historians can show to have most worried many Easterners when looking at developments in the Latin church, and which constituted the agenda of the reunion Councils, Lyons II in 1274 and Florence in 1439. This is of course an enormous subject which would require an account of most of Church history in the first millennium to do it justice. Here I can only give a brief indication and refer readers interested in more historical detail – and certainly there is no shortage of fascinating material available – to my *Rome and the Eastern Churches: A Study in Schism.*[16]

The development of the schism between Greek East and Latin West was owed essentially to three factors. The first of these is the increasing cultural distance, and so alienation, suspicion and eventually hostility, which counterposed, one against the other, the Byzantine and Latin halves of the Mediterranean basin, as also tracts of Europe further afield – especially Russia on the one hand, the Germanic world on the other, evangelised as these had been from, respectively, Greek and Roman mother-churches. As a common language, a common political framework, a common social structure, and a common theological universe became, in the late patristic and early mediaeval periods, a thing of the past, Eastern and Western Christians ceased to feel themselves parts of one commonwealth – something given especially brutal expression in the sack of Constantinople by the crusader host in 1204.

The second principal factor in the making of the schism was the rivalry between the Byzantine emperors and the Roman popes considered as officers of the Christian commonwealth responsible for its overall direction and for the adjustment of organisational problems or clashes within it. Constantine the Great not only inherited the imperial ideology of the supreme rulers of the Roman *res publica*, but also permitted – perhaps encouraged – the transformation of this ideology into a fully-fledged imperial theology by such figures as Eusebius of Caesarea.[17] The Christian emperor, though pretending to no power to determine doctrine, did claim an overall right of supervision for the public, external life of the churches. But this was exactly the position which those in the West who supported the developing theology of the unique 'Petrine' ministry of the Roman bishop wished to give the pope. In the first millennium there was no generally agreed ecclesiology of the Roman primacy. There are Latins who took a minimalist view of it, Greeks who took a maximalist. But in general of course Westerners came to favour a high theology of the Roman church and bishop, Easterners to regard such a theological doctrine with foreboding as a departure from the ethos of the Pentarchy, the idea of the necessary concord of the five patriarchs Rome, Constantinople, Alexandria, Antioch and Jerusalem – which by the eighth century at least must count as the normal Byzantine picture of what specifically episcopal leadership entailed.

The third and last factor in the turning of tensions into an actual break was the emergence of the four disputed questions which served as lenses concentrating the heat given off in these chronic or structural tensions until it became explosive. In order of their historic emergence, these questions or topics are: the *Filioque*, the nature of the Roman primacy, the use of azymes or unleavened bread in the Western Mass, and the doctrine of Purgatory, and especially the symbolisation of the intermediate state as a purifying fire. On all these points, even that of azymes which might be thought an issue singularly unprofitable or at least peripheral to Christian thought, theological ideas of great interest were brought forward on both sides, though probably only the *Filioque* and the primacy question would be regarded as 'dividing' issues today. As regards the *Filioque* – the procession of the Holy Spirit, according to the amended Latin version of the Creed of Nicaea-Constantinople, not only from the Father but from the Son as well, I believe that, could we count on a modicum of good will, we might well be able, without damage to the doctrinal integrity of our two communions, to resolve this technical issue in Trinitarian theology: technical, yet also crucial for how we see the Spirit in relation to the Son, and so their respective economies in their interaction in our lives. The matter of the Roman primacy is less easily disposed of, and I will return to it at the end of my presentation.

So much – very schematically, and inadequately – on the historic genesis of the schism and its quartet of doctrinal conflagration points. The operation of the three factors – the mutual cultural estrangement, the conflicting expectations for the roles of emperor and pope, and the specifically theological issues – meant that by the 1450s the Byzantine church, in rejecting the Florentine union of 1439, had definitely broken communion with the Roman see. This situation was gradually extended in a rather uneven way to the rest of the Orthodox world in the course of the sixteenth and seventeenth centuries, there being some examples of *communicatio in sacris* – for instance of the use of Latin clergy, chiefly Jesuits, to preach and hear the confessions of the Greek Orthodox faithful – even as late as the first half of the eighteenth century in some places.

I come now to the question of the present state of Catholic-Orthodox relations. After a preparatory phase of initial contacts known as the 'dialogue of charity', the Catholic-Orthodox theological dialogue was officially established in 1979, with the 'common declaration' made by the Ecumenical Patriarch Dimitrios I and Pope John Paul II at the conclusion of the latter's visit to the Phanar, the patriarchal seat in Istanbul, in November of that year. At that juncture the situation between Orthodox and Catholics was from one point of view more hopeful than at, say, the time of the Council of Florence, but from another viewpoint it was less hopeful. It was more hopeful in that the participation of the Orthodox in the Ecumenical Movement from the 1920s onwards had accustomed them to the idea of work for Christian unity – though a strong and vociferous minority have always expressed reservations about this policy as likely to confirm what Catholics would call 'indifferentism'. If at its origins the Ecumenical Movement was largely a pan-Protestant conception, the entry of the Orthodox into its ranks pressed that Movement, nonetheless, in a direction which made it possible for the Catholic Church to join it, nearly forty years later, on the eve of the Second Vatican Council. The Orthodox had this salutary effect in that their voices – combined with those of neo-patristically minded Anglicans (a species more common then than now) – succeeded in dispelling the sense that ecumenism was basically a movement preparing a purely moral and sentimental, rather than doctrinal and sacramental, union of Christians. Along these broad lines, then, the Orthodox churches had functioned highly consecutively within the Ecumenical Movement up to the 1980s, though whether they can continue to do so in the context of the World Council of Churches in the future – given the capture of the latter by a largely secular agenda – remains to be seen.

To this glowing account of Orthodox ecumenism one important caveat must be appended. It is possible to overrate the theological component of the role of Orthodoxy in the twentieth-century Ecumenical Movement by overlooking the fact that the desire of many Orthodox for greater contact with Western communions was in part a pragmatic and even political one. With the collapse of the Russian Tsardom in 1917, that mighty protector of the Orthodox churches was no more, and Orthodox communities in hostile States like Bolshevik Russia or Kemalist Turkey, or in comparatively weak confessionally Orthodox states such as Bulgaria and Greece, needed the support of a still surviving Christian political conscience in such great Powers of the first half of this century as Britain and the United States. This realistic caution about the motives of some Orthodox ecumenism brings me to the *less* hopeful features of the situation which surrounded the opening of official dialogue at the beginning of the 1980s.

In the more than 500 years since the collapse of the Florentine Union, Orthodox and Catholics had had time to practice yet more polemics against each other, to coarsen their images of each other, and also to add (especially from the Orthodox side) new bones of doctrinal contention, though in one case – the definition in 1870 of the universal jurisdiction and doctrinal infallibility of the Roman bishop – the dismay of the Orthodox was of course entirely predictable, as was pointed out by several Oriental Catholic bishops at the First Vatican Council. We find for instance such influential Orthodox thinkers as the Greek theologian John Romanides attacking the Western doctrine of original sin as heretical, thus rendering the Latin Marian dogma of the Immaculate Conception – Mary's original righteousness – superfluous if not nonsensical. Or again, and this would be a point that exercised those responsible for the official dialogue of the last fifteen years, some Orthodox now wished to regard the pastoral practice whereby many local churches in the Latin West delay the confirmation (or chrismation) of children till after their first Holy Communion as based on a gravely erroneous misjudgement in sacramental doctrine.

None of this, however, prevented the Joint International Commission for Theological Dialogue between the Roman Catholic Church and the Orthodox Church – to give it its mouthful of a title – from producing three very useful documents on the shared understanding (in the Great Church of which Orthodoxy and Catholicism are the two expressions) of the mystery of the Church herself, in her sacramental and especially eucharistic structure, seen in relation to the mystery of the triune God, the foundation reality of our faith. These statements are known by their place and date of origin: Munich 1982, Bari 1987, and Valamo (Finland) 1988.[18]

The shadow cast more recently was in 1979 only a cloud on the horizon, a cloud, as in Elijah's dealings with Ahab in the First Book of Kings, no bigger than a man's hand. And this is the threat posed to the dialogue by the reinvigoration of hitherto Communist-suppressed Uniate or Eastern Catholic churches, notably those of the Ukraine and Transylvania, in the course of the later 1980s and 1990s. The existence of Byzantine-rite communities in union with the Holy See was already a major irritant to the Orthodox, even though some of these communities, for instance in Southern Italy and Sicily, had enjoyed an unbroken existence and were in no sense the result of prosyletism or political chicanery. What the Orthodox quite naturally and rightly object to is Uniatism as a method of detaching Orthodox dioceses and parishes from their mother churches on a principle of *divide et impera*. Not all partial unions with the Byzantine Orthodox can be brought historically under this heading, for some, such as that with a portion of the Antiochene patriarchate which produced the present Melkite church, are principally the result of Eastern, not Western, initiative. But that the Pope (John Paul II) who presided over the beginnings of Catholic-Orthodox dialogue should also be a pope who played a major role in the destruction of Communism has certainly proved to be one of the ironies of Church history. The passing of Marxist-Leninist hegemony, the internal disintegration of the Soviet Union, the copycat rebellions against a Nationalist Communist *nomenklatura* in such countries as Romania, made possible the re-emergence of Oriental Catholic churches once forcibly reunited with the Orthodox by Stalin's Comintern in the aftermath of the Second World War. The process has been sufficient to place in jeopardy the project of Catholic-Orthodox reunion which is the one goal of ecclesiastical as distinct from merely public policy most dear to the heart of this extraordinary Slav bishop of Rome. Thus in June 1990 at the plenary meeting of the Commission at Freising in Bavaria, the Orthodox refused to continue with the official agenda in discussing 'Conciliarity and Authority: the Ecclesiological and Canonical Consequences of the Sacramental Structure of the Church' until a document could be agreed on the Byzantine-rite Catholic churches, a document actually produced at Balamand in the Lebanon in 1993 and which has, regrettably, failed to satisfy many Orthodox whilst angering many Oriental Catholics.[19]

This brings me to the fourth and concluding section of my 'overview' where, as mentioned at the outset, I will single out for, I hope, charitable and eirenic comment one negative aspect of Orthodoxy where, in my opinion, the Orthodox need Catholic communion just as – for quite different reasons already outlined – Catholics need (at this time in history above all) the Orthodox Church.

The animosity, indeed the barely contained fury, with which many Orthodox react to the issue of Uniatism is hardly explicable except in terms of a widespread and not readily defensible Orthodox feeling about the relation between the *nation* and the Church. There must be, after all, some factor of social psychology or corporate ideology which complicates this issue. Bear in mind that the Orthodox have felt no difficulty this century in creating forms of Western-rite Orthodoxy, for example in France under the aegis of the Romanian patriarchate or more recently in the United States under the jurisdiction of an exarch of the patriarch of Antioch. And what are these entities if not Orthodox Uniatism – to which the Catholic Church has, however, made no objection. Nor do such non-Chalcedonian churches as the Assyrians (in Iraq and Iran), the Jacobites (in Syria) or the Syro-Malabar Christians of South India react in this way to the notion that some of their communities may be in peace and communion with the elder Rome. A partial – and significant – exception among such non-Chalcedonian Orthodox churches is the Copts of Egypt – precisely because of the notion that the Coptic patriarch is father of the whole Coptic nation. In other words, what we may call a political factor – giving the word 'political' its broadest possible meaning – has entered in.

It is the close link between Church and national consciousness, patriotic consciousness, which renders Uniatism so totally unacceptable in such countries as Greece and Romania, and it is this phenomenon of Orthodox nationalism which I find the least attractive feature of Orthodoxy today. An extreme example is the widespread philosophy in the Church of Serbia which goes by the name of the mediaeval royal Serbian saint Sava – hence *Svetosavlje*, 'Saint-Sava-ism'. The creation of the influential bishop Nikolay Velimirovich, who died in 1956, it argues that the Serbian people are, by their history of martyrdom, an elect nation, even among the Orthodox, a unique bearer of salvific suffering, an incomparably holy people, and counterposes them in particular to their Western neighbours who are merely pseudo-Christians, believers in humanity without divinity.[20] And if the origins of such Orthodox attitudes lie in the attempts of nineteenth-century nationalists to mobilise the political potential of Orthodox pleasantries against both Islamic and Catholic rulers, these forces, which I would not hesitate to call profoundly unChristian, can turn even against the interests of Orthodoxy itself – as we are seeing today in the embarrassing campaign on the Holy Mountain Athos to dislodge non-Greek monks and discourage non-Greek pilgrims, quite against the genius of the Athonite monastic republic which, historically, is a living testimony to Orthodox inter-ethnicity, Orthodox internationalism.

To a Catholic mind, the Church of Pentecost is a Church of all nations in the sense of *ecclesia ex gentibus*, a Church taken from all nations, gathering them – with, to be sure, their own human and spiritual gifts – into a universal community in the image of the divine Trinity where the difference between Father, Son and Spirit only subserves their relations of communion. The Church of Pentecost is not an *ecclesia in gentibus*, a Church distributed among the nations in the sense of *parcelled out* among them, accommodating herself completely to their structures and leaving their sense of autonomous identity undisturbed.

Speaking as someone brought up in a national Church, the Church of England, though I am happy to consider myself perfectly English (and shall have something positive to say about the theological significance of nationhood in my closing Chapter), I also regard it as a blessing of catholicity to be freed from particularism into the more spacious life of a Church raised up to be an ensign for all nations, a Church where those of every race, colour and culture can feel at home, in the Father's house.

It is in this final perspective that one should consider the role of the Roman bishop as a 'universal primate' in the service of the global communion of the churches. One of the most loved titles of the Western Middle Ages for the Roman bishop was *universalis papa*, and while one would not wish to retrieve all aspects of Latin ecclesiology in the high mediaeval period, to a Catholic Christian the universal communion of the local churches in their multiple variety *does* need a father in the pope, just as much as the local church itself, with its varied congregations, ministries and activities, needs a father in the person of the bishop. It is often said that such an ecclesiology of the papal office is irredeemably Western and Latin, and incapable of translation into Oriental terms. I believe this statement to be unjustified. Just as a patriarch, as regional primate, is responsible for the due functioning of the local churches of his region under their episcopal heads, so a universal primate is responsible for the operation of the entire episcopal *taxis* or order, and so for all the churches on a worldwide scale. Needless to say, this office is meant for the upbuilding, not the destruction, of that episcopal order, founded ultimately as the latter is on the will of the Redeemer in establishing the apostolic mission, and further refined by Tradition in the institution of patriarchal and other primacies in this or that portion of the ecclesial whole. But at the same time, if the ministry of a first bishop is truly to meet the needs of the universal Church it will sometimes have to take decisions that are hard on some local community and unpopular with it.

Were the Orthodox and Catholic Churches to become one, some reform of the structure of the Roman primacy would nonetheless be necessary, especially at the level of the *curia romana*. The Congregation for the Oriental Churches would become a secretariat at the service of the permanent apocrisaries (envoys) of the patriarchs and other primates. The great majority of the other dicasteries would be redefined as organs of the Western patriarch, rather than the supreme Pontiff. And yet no universal primacy that merely rubber-stamped the decisions of local or regional churches would be worth having; it would be appearance without reality. Thus the pope as universal primate would need to retain: first, a doctrinal organ for the co-ordination of Church teaching, and secondly, some kind of 'apostolic secretaryship', replacing the present ill-named 'Secretariat of State', for the harmonisation of principles of pastoral care. To these could be added, thirdly, whichever of the 'new curial' bodies dealing with those *outside* the household of faith might be deemed to have proved their usefulness, and finally, a continuing 'Council for the Public Affairs of the Church', for the defence of the freedom of the churches (and of human rights) vis-à-vis State power. The utility of the fourth of these to the Orthodox is obvious. As to the rest (of which only the first two are crucial in importance) they should function only on the rarest occasions of 'crisis-management' as instruments of papal action in the Eastern churches. Normally, they should act, rather, as channels whereby impulses from the Eastern churches – impulses dogmatic, liturgical, contemplative, monastic in tenor – could reach via the pope the wider Church and world. For this purpose the apocrisaries of the patriarchs, along with the prefects of the Western dicasteries, would need to constitute their governing committees, under papal presidency. It should go without saying that Oriental churches would naturally enjoy full parity with the Latin church throughout the world, and not simply in their homelands – the current Catholic practice.[21]

The Orthodox must ask themselves (as of course they do!) whether such instruments of universal communion (at once limiting and liberating) may not be worth the price. Or must the pleasures of particularity come first?

## Mere Christianity

I will deal (much) more briefly with my remaining two 'pillars' for a new ecumenical agenda: first, an appeal for mutual assistance for the sake of what C. S. Lewis called 'mere Christianity' and secondly, an attempted rehabilitation (shorn of proselytism) of the 'Uniate idea'.

Fortunately, there exist in a whole host of denominations Christians open to the total mystery whose contours were defined by the oecumenical Councils of the first millennium and concerned to practise the classical Christian morality (not an ecclesially dividing factor) of all the ages. C. S. Lewis – critic, philosopher, imaginative writer and weaver of myths but above all lay theologian – is surely their patron. The phrase 'mere Christianity' is his and he meant it to denote no insipid interdenominational transparency, but something positive, self-consistent, and inexhaustible.[22] It takes a peculiar combination of breadth and narrowness – of generosity of temper and focusedness of mind – to see its point. It is not meant to indicate that *all* the verities of faith and order that Jesus Christ instructed his apostles to preserve and disseminate until the world's end are comprised within these central beliefs and moral suasions. Evangelicals, Anglo-Catholics, conservative Lutherans, as well as Catholics and Orthodox, have issues of substance to debate even when they remain firmly committed to the basic truths of the revelation in action of the Father through the incarnated Son and outpoured Spirit for the world's salvation – and to the moral practice which belongs with the life of the Kingdom won by Christ's atoning work. But, steadied by just these commitments, they have a doctrinal and moral seriousness which renders them ecumenical in the best sense of the word. They stand on the mountain which alone gives sight of further realms, beyond these dogmatic and ethical heart-lands, though as yet they are not agreed on the shape of that country beyond, where mists obscure contours and proportions. There is no other vantage-point from which separated Christians may view the prospect of a single Church, with unity of doctrine, and a common sacramental life in that canonical structure which the apostles handed down. Here humanistic benevolence or a general desire for 'reunion all round' could only be false guides. The American Evangelical theologian S. M. Hutchens has written:

> The mere Christian thinks the world a wonderful creation, but darkened and fallen by the actions of men and evil spirits, and he allows the darkness to weigh upon him. To such a man the coming of God Incarnate into the world is an advent of such truth, beauty, and light so welcome to his soul that he seeks it out as willingly as a starving man seeks bread. All that is connected to Christ, in particular the teachings through which he is borne to us, are thus also of inestimable value to him. He loves to hear them, even when they cause him pain (since he is a sinner), and he will not stand to hear them slighted, abridged, or effaced. These are to him sacraments, holy mysteries, the body and soul of Christ. He is coming to know Christ by accepting them as a whole, and this wholeness includes the testimony of the wisdom of the ages as defined by the Person of Christ whom he knows, yet seeks. He has found in his pilgrimage others of the same mind, who, despite differences of understanding of the outworkings of the mystery of Christ, have seen the same vision and are animated by the same love. The first sign of this fellowship is the 'dogmatic' one, but doctrinal consensus is not enough – one must have the same love. Belief in the central teachings of the faith and concern for their preservation are not merely 'tests,' but signs of recognition, the common language, and 'ecumenical orthodoxy' is a way of describing the unity we have in the diversity we tolerate. As a practical matter, those closest to the center of this fellowship are people who have pressed against

'the world' of St. John, found it hostile, and are at war with it. This explains much of their 'ecumenical' attitude. It is far easier to view other Christians as allies and to subordinate disagreements to the common agreement once one has a clear view of the common enemy. There is a shared mistrust among us of Christians who appear to be motivated by the desire to accommodate. I have come to believe this is the principal difference between 'our kind' of ecumenism and ecumenism as it is more commonly known: ours is the fellowship of comrades in arms. Nothing could be more different than our ecumenism and that of the secularizing Christian.[23]

It is a quality of Christian *obedience* to the Gospel for which we should be looking out – a far cry from the prudential ingenuity with which, for instance, the 1995 Porvoo Agreement between British and Irish Anglicans and Baltic Lutherans cites as grounds for the desirability of Church unity such factors as: growing European union; the spiritual vacuum in Europe; the duty of working for peace, justice and human rights; ecological problems; and the need for mutual understanding across national boundaries. This rainbow combination of themes was underpinned, we may speculate, by a more hard-nosed managerial rationality, disclosed, indeed, when archbishop George Carey of Canterbury welcomed the agreement as tending to create 'the biggest Christian confessional body in northern Europe'. But the only conglomerate unity known to the New Testament is unity in the mission of the Messiah, around Peter.

## Union around Peter

Catholic ecclesiology locates the fullness of the Church's being on earth in the maximal convergence of those Christian traditions authentically expressive of Tradition around the figure of Peter. It is for this reason that 'Uniatism' – an understanding and practice of Church unity with two key features, legitimate distinctiveness and orientation to the rest via the Petrine office-holder – *cannot* be for Catholics a dirty word.

What then of the Balamand Statement, which I had occasion to mention in referring to the doldrums into which Catholic-Orthodox relations have recently fallen? The applying of illegitimate methods and pressures to wean away Christians from one ecclesial allegiance to another is always that – illegitimate, and the Balamand document can hardly be faulted on that score. Extreme animus on the part of the Orthodox (and the non-Chalcedonian Orientals) to the notion that a number of Eastern Christians might live *both* in full possession of the traditions of the East *and* in peace and communion with the see of Rome is, as I indicated above, clearly linked to issues of ethnicity and nationalism. Not for *all* separated Oriental Christians is the Uniate idea anathema. And the irony is that this document was issued – in the Levant and with its eyes turned firmly Eastwards – at a time when the Uniate notion is beginning to acquire fresh pertinence and attractiveness to Christians in the separated ecclesial communities of the West (one thinks here first and foremost of Anglicans).

For the East especially there is also the threat of 'Latinisation'. A misplaced confidence in the superiority of the Latin rite and way of doing things has certainly soiled the term 'Uniate'. But then it needs purification, not excision from the language, on the well-known principle *abusus non tollit usum*. Petrinity properly means not Latinisation but Catholicisation – a very different thing.

What official ecumenism has not yet come to terms with is the possibility that, in so far as the reunion of Christendom may be further advanced by the Parousia, this could be neither through the entry into full unity of whole denominations nor simply through individual conversion to a mother-church but through the emergence of a new constellation, around the Petrine see, of bodies minoritarian when compared with their churches of origin yet representative of the elements of true catholicity in their parent traditions. This would be a far cry from the union of all Christians in a single ecumenical Church; a far cry but not a faint echo for such bodies, united yet unabsorbed, would be by their very existence 'prophetic' of, and 'sacramental' signs of, an ultimate reconciled diversity which belongs more with the consummation of history in the Kingdom than to its earthly course.

As things are, one must regretfully conclude the structures of official ecumenism – desirable though they are from other viewpoints (charity, scholarship) – impede rather than enable such a realistic yet ecclesiologically speaking supremely congruent goal.

## Conclusion: into the crystal ball

What of the future? As I have emphasised, the Catholic Church will have to determine whether her *principal* ecumenical partner is to be Orthodoxy, with the pre- and non-Chalcedonian Eastern churches as ancillary satellites, or the separated Western churches and communities deriving from the Reformation. The well-known problems of ethnicity and nationalism in the Orthodox world will inhibit the first option; but the decision will largely form itself on inner-ecclesial grounds, in dependence on whether the next pope maintains the defence of a classical doctrinal liturgical and ethical life with fervour or, alternatively, some embarrassment. The Orthodox will make further agreements with the non-Chalcedonian ('Monophysite') churches, but are unlikely to know what, organisationally, they could do with them. They will be unaffected by the move of the Assyrian ('Nestorian') church towards union with Rome, just as the 'Monophysites', on discovering the progress of such erstwhile Christological 'left-wingers' towards the centre of the patristic spectrum, will find this development less of a disincentive than one might suppose. As to those ecclesial bodies which originate in schismatic movements within the Western Church, these will not themselves be ecumenically stable. The Union of Utrecht, in which the Old Catholic churches are joined, may well dissolve over the issue of women's ordination,[24] whereupon the Polish National Church will look increasingly to Rome (with or without a Slav pope), and the Old Catholics of Germany, Austria, Switzerland and the Netherlands to a convergence of Protestant episcopal churches along the lines indicated by the recent 'Porvoo Declaration' of Anglicans and Scandinavian and Baltic Lutherans. For the reasons given by Lindbeck, some high dogmatic and sacramental Lutherans may prefer a form of Uniate arrangement with Rome – as may one or two of the numerous (roughly twenty) bodies constituting the so-called Traditional Anglican Movement. Though these occupy a diversity of positions on a continuum stretching from Anglo-Catholic to Evangelical-charismatic, they have come into existence, frequently at much personal cost to their members, by testimony to truths and values which the Catholic Church holds dear. Fissiparous they may be, but the Orthodox Church in America has rightly recognised their frequently substantial catholicity by its institution of formal dialogue with the Anglican Catholic Church in February 1997. The United States may well be a privileged locus for Catholic relations with Romeward-tending High Anglicans, since its episcopate lacks that anxiety at the notion of a continuing corporate identity for previously separated Christians which afflicts the leaders of the Catholic community (for a variety of reasons, some good, but more bad) in England and Wales.[25] The alliance of liberal Old Catholics and Anglicans with moderate Lutherans may eventually incorporate a Methodism already episcopally-ordered in many places. Some Anglican Provinces may prefer to enter national schemes for the unification of all non-Roman Western Christians, on the model of the Church of South India. Elsewhere their Evangelical minorities may be tempted into alliance with other Radical Protestants.

For the time being the principal fault-line of disagreement will continue to run through the communions as much as between them, while the inertial force exerted by the pull of staying where one is familiar will militate against too large-scale an exchange of ecclesial populations. Meanwhile in the confusion, the need for an organ of primacy will become clearer, not least among the Orthodox. In the babel, some well-known words may attain a new attractiveness.

> Tu es Petrus and super hanc petram aedificabo
> Ecclesiam meam.

Liberal Catholics will be among the last to see the point.

## NOTES

1. Even those who should know better are sometimes willing to sell a birth-right for a mess of pottage. For a repudiation of the present welcome revival in Catholic apologetics as 'an obstacle to ecumenism', see T. P. Rausch, S.J., 'The Third Stage of the Ecumenical Movement. Is the Catholic Church Ready?', *Ecumenical Trends* 26.10 (1977), pp. 1–7.

2. U. von Arx, 'Der orthodox-altkatholische Dialog. Anmerkungen zu einer schwierigen Rezeption', *Internationale Kirchliche Zeitschrift* 419 (1997), pp. 184–224. Dr von Arx mentions such factors as: the replacement of confessional goals, among the Old Catholics, by a more *trendif* ecumenism of ecology, feminism and interfaith dialogue; the conversion to Old Catholicism of progressive Roman Catholic clergy whose orientation is to Anglicans and Evangelicals rather than the Orthodox; and the 'political' impossibility of ending, at the Orthodox Church's behest, the arrangements for intercommunion made with Anglicans and, in Germany, Lutheran-Evangelicals.

3. B. and M. Pawley, *Rome and Canterbury through Four Centuries. A Study of the Relations between the Church of Rome and the Anglican Churches, 1530–1981* (London, 1981²).

4. These, together with the 1982 'Final Report', may be found in *Called to Full Unity. Documents on Anglican-Roman Catholic Relations* (Washington, 1986).

5. *Salvation and the Church* (London, 1987).

6. *Life in Christ. Morals, Communion and the Church* (London, 1992). ARCIC II also produced a general statement of the ecclesiology underlying ARCIC I: thus *Church as Communion* (London, 1990).

7. G. A. Lindbeck, 'The Reformation Heritage and Church Unity', *Lutheran Quarterly* 2.4 (1988), pp. 477–502.

8. Ibid., p. 492.

9. Ibid., p. 497.

10. *The Panther and the Hind. A Theological History of Anglicanism* (Edinburgh, 1993).

11. *The Letters and Diaries of John Henry Newman, Volume V*, edited by I. Ker, T. Gornall, G. Tracey (Oxford, Oxford University Press, 1994), pp. 301–3, cited S. Gilley, *Newman and his Age* (London, 1990), p. 152.

12. For a rebuttal of the later nineteenth-century claim that the Anglican Reformation, despite some excesses, had a fundamentally Catholic character, see D. MacCulloch, 'The Myth of the English Reformation', *Journal of British Studies* 30 (1991), pp. 1–19.

13. S. W. Sykes (ed.), *Authority in the Anglican Communion. Essays Presented to Bishop John Howe* (Toronto, 1987), pp. 119–43.

14. R. Knox, *Let Dons Delight. Being Variations on Themes in an Oxford Common Room* (London, 1939; 1973), p. 183.

15. Cf. A. Nichols, O.P., *Light from the East. Authors and Themes in Orthodox Theology* (London, 1995).

16. Edinburgh, 1992.

17. J. M. Sansterre, 'Eusèbe de Césarée et la naissance de la théorie "césaropapiste"', *Byzantion* 42 (1972), pp. 131–95, 532–94.

18. Conveniently gathered together in P. McPartlan (ed.), *One in 2000: Towards Catholic-Orthodox Unity* (Middlegreen, Slough, 1993).

19. A communiqué published in its English form in *One in Christ* XXX 1 (1994), pp. 74–82.

20. See T. Bremer, *Ekklesiale Struktur und Ekklesiologie in der Serbischen Orthodoxen Kirche im 19. und 20. Jahrhundert* (Würzburg, 1992).

21. A justifiable cause of anger among Oriental Catholics today; see T. E. Bird, 'The Vatican Decree on the Eastern Catholic Churches Thirty Years Later', *Sophia* 21.4 (1994), pp. 23–9.

22. C. S. Lewis, *Mere Christianity* (London, 1952; 1955).

23. S. M. Hutchens, 'The Editors On Line', *Touchstone. A Journal of Mere Christianity* 10.4 (1997), pp. 9–10.

24. U. von Arx, 'Internationale Altkatholische Bischofskonferenz in Wislikofen, Juli 1997', *Internationale Kirchliche Zeitschrift* 87.3 (1997), pp. 225–40.

25. For an account of these bodies, see G. Diefender, 'The Traditional Anglican Movement Today. An Update on the Continuing/Traditional Anglican Churches', *The Christian Challenge* XXXIII. 7 (1994), pp. 16–23.

# XIV

## *Resituating Modern Spirituality*

### Existence in a 'modern' world

Such phrases as 'modern man' and 'the modern world' can carry dubious implications. Has there been, through cultural change, a transformation of the character of the human species as such, with the result that whatever wisdom the human past might legitimately boast is now inapplicable? It is not self-evident that the patterns of human living in the twentieth century are to *that* degree different from what they have been in the past. It is not so clear that modern society is more different from all past societies generally than any one such society has been from any other. Yet this is what must be the case if talk of this special animal, 'modern man', is to be justified – at any rate in the strong sense I have ascribed to the phrase so far.

In the realm of spiritual theology, a hectoring stress on modernity usually takes the form of an insistence that man has 'come of age', when compared with the 'immature' attitude of dependence on God characteristic of past styles of praying. Petition, trust, awe, adoration, will then be 'out'; recognising God as our collaborator in the task of world-making will be 'in'. It seems strange that the philosophy of the Superman, for which human autonomy is the keystone of all value, and which worked itself out to its own terrifying conclusion in the gas chambers of the Third Reich, should live on in liberal Christianity over fifty years after its *dénouement* in political history.

And yet there must be some general factors which mark out the contemporary situation, and suggest to people such a phrase as 'the modern world'. And since praying always has a time and a place, a context, this must be of significance for prayer, and so for a theology of prayer today.

The planet Earth in the twentieth century has contained a number of touching, sometimes colliding, 'worlds' – using that term for cultural wholes, distinct realms of what can be counted on as understood, believed or assumed by different sets of people. Hampstead today is different from up-country Sarawak, and Hampstead in 1900 from the same urban village in 1999. Nevertheless, there is a unifying factor: the modern secular tradition of the West is, for better or worse, the outstanding influence in the world of this century. For better or worse, that tradition over the last hundred years has powerfully shaped – at varying rates, it is true, and to differing degrees – the worlds-within-the-world. The rise of the natural sciences to a position of predominance in human understanding; the civic emancipation of women, and the attempts to redefine the significance of gender distinction that constitute feminism; State Communism, liberal welfare capitalism, hyper-nationalism, in political life; the revolutions in transport and communications; biological engineering and its near antonym ecological consciousness; the prolonged collapse of metaphysics now issuing in the vacuities of postmodernism – a list such as that doubtless offers a more or less correct inventory of striking features of a common world. What can it all mean for prayer?

One thing is obvious. If we compare that list with a comparable catalogue of dominant features of Western mediaeval society – to take one great 'whole' informed by Christian faith – it is surely clear that the mediaeval Christian at prayer was supported culturally by a whole way of life. This is true no matter what the volume of practical deviation, in morals or believing, from the norms of that largely lost Christendom. By comparison, the contemporary Christian experiences an absence of God in the world today. Naturally, this cannot mean that God has actually withdrawn himself from creation: the very idea of creation as God's continuous sustaining of finite being, which otherwise would fall into nothingness, makes such a suggestion absurd. Nor can it be the case that God has withdrawn from involvement in human affairs. To affirm that would be to deny Jesus' teaching on the incessant character of the Father's saving activity (John 5.17a) and his own inauguration, through his cross and resurrection, of God's lordly reign. What is true is rather that our culture gives us few, if any, overt signals of God's presence. Conversing with God is not something we take in with the cultural air we breathe – as once it was for many in this country before the Western tradition took its secular turn, and, especially, perhaps, on the eve of the sixteenth-century Reform when a lay devotional culture saturated every aspect of life, both for the individual and for the group. Owing to the imaginative constraints created by secularisation, a large chunk of a culturally transmitted human basis for prayer and contemplation is lost to us, at least for the foreseeable future.

However, so far as the members of the Church, the faithful, are concerned, we are not speaking – by definition – of a loss of faith, but of the deprivation of what is in a Christian culture the humus or compost which nourishes faith in its normal development. We are thinking of obstacles in the way of the growth and blossoming of faith. But in the teaching of Jesus, such obstacles to faith are simply occasions when we renew relationship with him: 'Why are you fearful? You believe in God; have faith then in me' (John 14:1). So the modern Church which for these purposes I propose to define, for reasons that should become clear, as beginning in *1886*, has witnessed a whole harvest of distinctively contemporary masters and mistresses of prayer. Their prayer life appears to have arisen with a force and intensity unusual in the history of spirituality from out of a sense of what their very existence demanded. They could not take prayer for granted, and then, on that basis, have useful and illuminating things to say about it. They found out, rather, that for them existence was not bearable without prayer. Theirs was *existential praying*. There will be more to say about this phrase later; meanwhile, it will suffice to stake out the bald claim that this is, firstly, the feature detectable among modern masters of prayer which most justifies our seeing a family resemblance between them, and, secondly, that such an ethos of prayer has something valuable, or even *in*valuable, to offer those who, like them, have to find God concretely, personally, in the spiritual desert of modern society.

## From Notre Dame to Auschwitz

Christmas night 1886. If we want an hour of clock time by which to date the beginning of a notably contemporary experience of sanctity and prayer, we might do worse than to select this. It was at Vespers at Notre Dame de Paris on Christmas Day 1886 that Paul Claudel, the poet and dramatist, came to his sudden overwhelming realisation of God as a simplicity that could enter all the complexities of life and master them. He described this experience as 'a sudden, piercing sense of the innocence, of the eternal childhood, of God, a revelation quite beyond the power of words to express'.[1]

On the same night a little girl, brought up in the mould of a conventional middle-class piety, received (in her own words) the 'grace of full conversion . . . the grace to leave my childhood behind', so as to discover, in place of the enclosed and protected world of affluent and affectionate parents, the divine Childhood itself, with its inexhaustible yet, once again, simplifying demands.[2] It was the custom, in the Martin household, to put 'surprises' for the youngest, idolised daughter in a special pair of 'enchanted slippers' in the fireplace. That Christmas night, in dawning horror, Thérèse overheard her father, tired and irritable after Midnight Mass, saying in the drawing-room, 'Well, thank goodness it's the last year this is going to happen'.

> Céline [her sister], who knew how touchy I was, saw my eyes shining with tears and was ready to cry herself; in her loving sympathy, she knew exactly what I was feeling. 'Oh, Thérèse,' she said, 'don't go down just yet; it'll only make you miserable looking inside your slippers now!'

These may seem unpromising materials for a conversion experience, but this was how Thérèse of Lisieux came to understand this moment.

> She didn't know the Thérèse she was dealing with; our Lord had changed me into a different person. I dried my tears and went down at once; my heart was beating fast, but I managed to get hold of my slippers and put them down in front of Papa, and as I took out my presents you would have thought that I was as happy as a queen. Papa smiled, his good humour restored, and Celine thought she must be dreaming. But no, it was a sublime reality . . .[3]

Three years after this loss of natural childhood, Thérèse entered Carmel to devote herself to a life of prayer, regular observance and mortification. But when she tried to pray, her childhood piety shattered, all she could see was the God of fear and majesty, to be reached, if at all, only by a great ladder even whose lowest rung was above her reach. At best, this God was a God with two faces, one loving, the other severe and unsearchable. The offices and prayers she recited with her community were addressed to this Janus-God. The methods of meditation put before her seemed to her like step-ladders for the impossible task of reaching stars, and left her as far away as before from the God she sought.

Under the pressure of this experience, she discovered in the Scriptures what she called the 'little way of spiritual childhood', a spirituality which consisted in seeing God as loving father, and herself as a little child. She rediscovered the openness and serene loving trustfulness of her own childhood, but this time no longer as limited by her family circle or circumscribed by any finite context of support. It was now a childhood open to the infinite, to the God of the mysteries of creation and redemption, who asks of his children a love as wide as the world. She felt irresistibly drawn to a way of being that was at the same time a way also of loving and praying. Her prayer became simply the experience of response to the living God, whose love is more demanding than his wrath, a prayer in which the soul knows its own radical need of God, is aware that it is in the desert, yet rejoices to be there – for here is where the true God is to be found, and where channels of love can be scoured in the self that will unite her at the deepest level to others. As the *Autobiography* puts it:

> Even a little child can scatter flowers, to scent the throne-room with their fragrance; even a little child can sing, in its shrill treble, the great canticle of Love. That shall be my life, to scatter flowers – to miss no single opportunity of making some small sacrifice, here by a smiling look, there by a kindly word, always doing the tiniest things right, and doing it for love. I shall suffer all that I have to suffer – yes, and enjoy all my enjoyments too – in the spirit of love, so that I shall always be scattering flowers before your throne; nothing that comes my way but shall yield up its petals in your honour. And, as I scatter my flowers, I shall be singing; how could one be sad when occupied so pleasantly? I shall be singing, even when I have to pluck my flowers from a thorn-bush; never in better voice than when the thorns are longest and sharpest. I don't ask what use they will be to you, Jesus, these flowers, this music of mine; I know that you will take pleasure in this fragrant shower of worthless petals, in these songs of love in which a worthless heart like mine sings itself out.

And Thérèse goes on, in Ronald Knox's translation, to speak of how this 'floral tribute' of a prayed existence will be turned, in heavenly fashion, into a mediation for others of the grace of Christ.

> Because they give pleasure to you, the Church triumphant in heaven will smile upon them too; will take these flowers so bruised by love and pass them on into your divine hands. And so the Church in heaven, ready to take part in the childish game I am playing, will begin scattering these flowers, now hallowed by your touch beyond all recognition; will scatter them on the souls in Purgatory, to abate their sufferings, scatter them on the Church Militant, and give her the strength for fresh conquests.[4]

Thérèse's autobiography, stylistically too perfumed for English taste, though its (literally) flowery language belongs with what has been called an entire 'flower poetic' in nineteenth-century French literature, opens many of the doors to distinctively modern holiness.[5] First, there is candour in regard to one's anxiety at 'being a self', for selfhood becomes more of an agendum than a datum – more of a do-it-yourself job than something given – when the pattern defining human existence in a traditional society is stripped away, and the religious metaphysic undergirding the sense of reality cast aside. Secondly, we find as a consequence an interior experience of that desert which, historically, Christian monks have sought exteriorly, for now the desert is experienced as *existence itself*. A third hallmark of Thérèse's spiritual manifesto is the emphasis on the supreme simplicity of encounter with God, modelled as her presentation is on a small number of crucial biblical incidents and passages. Fourthly, she stands for a complete coincidence of life and prayer. And fifthly this text characterises the fundamental dynamism of prayer as love – a love that unites one simultaneously to God and to neighbour, by a movement whose direction is, therefore, neither 'vertical' nor 'horizontal' but *sui generis*, participating in the unique salvific mission of the incarnate Word, for whom obedience to the Father and the salvation of the world were one and the same, and whose disciples, accordingly, do not see the neighbour except in God, nor God apart from the Mystical Body of Christ.

Thérèse's doctrine, originating as it does with a cloistered nun who died of tuberculosis at the early age of 25, may strike us as simply naïve, unless we realise the crucial role played in the subversion of the Gospel, in the closing years of the last century, by attack on Jesus' teaching about the need to become 'as little children'. For Marxism, it is not *by receiving* but by my own act, my own labours that I become myself. With the Nietzsche of *Thus Spake Zarathustra*, the child is reinstated, but as a monstrous prodigy, a symbol of the hoped-for 'new man', beyond the 'death of God', a being self-created, or, in Nietzsche's own words, 'a game, a self-moving wheel, a first movement, a sacred affirmation'. Moreover, scepticism about the divine Child of Bethlehem and Nazareth was becoming a commonplace of an intellectually self-absorbed theological liberalism. In 1892, the very year of Thérèse's discovery of the way of spiritual childhood, the Lutheran historian of doctrine Adolf von Harnack, together with twenty-four other Liberal Protestant professors, published the 'Eisenach Declaration' which stated that 'no decisive significance for faith' could be ascribed to the narratives found in the opening chapters of the first and third Gospels. They thus deprived a spirituality of childhood of its Christological foundation, the assumption of childhood by the Son of God. For orthodoxy, by contrast, the divine Word anticipates his later adult teaching, 'Unless you turn and become like children . . .', by becoming a child himself. He comes to us in the humility and simplicity with which he wants us, through him, to go to the Father.[6]

But let us return through the six years to 1886, the symbolic date at which I place the beginning of spiritual modernity – that is, modern spirituality – in the Catholic Church of the West. It was in that same winter of 1886–7 that a young cavalry officer, Charles de Foucauld, made the first communion of his conversion at the Parisian *église saint Augustin* – the parish of a noted spiritual director, the abbé Henri Huvelin. De Foucauld, finding the somewhat vacuous existence of a man-about-town intolerable after his experience of fighting with the French army in the North African desert, had gone into the confessional of this formidable priest. He stayed standing, leaned forward toward the grille, and said, 'Monsieur l'Abbé, I haven't got the faith. I have come to ask you to instruct me'. To his surprise, the occupant of the box replied, 'Kneel down and make your confession to God. You will believe'. 'But I didn't come for that!' 'Make your confession' was the gruff reply from out of a sacerdotal confidence rarely met with now-adays.[7] Certain gestures allow certain attitudes to arise. The formulation comes from the dramatist Bertolt Brecht, but the underlying truth was known already to Pascal. The decision to act in a certain way, to take up a particular posture by something one does, can enable one to shift the vantage-point from which the world is seen. One can argue interminably about God's existence, but to receive it into the heart as a truth assented to at all levels of the personality, a truth held, in Newman's words, 'with real assent', requires an act of love, the kind of act in which the bonds of egocentrism are snapped so that one can step into the spacious world of being at large. Sometimes, choosing to act in a certain way, choosing a particular form of existence, is the only way through to a theoretical grasp of truth. This is, I take it, an important element in the meaning of the word 'existential', and it is well illustrated in this encounter between these two men, one of whom had already achieved, and the other of whom was about to embark upon, an impressively deep life of prayer.

It was Huvelin who gave to de Foucauld, and so to the Petits Frères (and Soeurs) who follow him, their spirituality of the heart of Christ as the matrix of prayer.[8] In this teaching, Christ's heart is seen as the source from which human beings can be rejuvenated, to the point of finding their own hearts alive with Christ's love, especially for the wretched, the sick, the poor. For de Foucauld, personal devotion to the heart of Christ is the central and irreplaceable focus of the life of prayer, and, so far from, as is sometimes alleged, leading to a self-indulgent and individualistic piety, it is the essential way in which to affirm the universal scope of the Incarnation. He wrote of the brotherhood he dreamed of but never lived to see:

They will not be missionaries exactly, but they will form a cloistered family, vowed to adore the Sacred Host exposed day and night. They will have no financial security but will live in poverty and work. They won't preach except by their silence, which is always more eloquent than words. They will be adorers bringing the Master to the Infidel. If just the very touch of the hem of Christ's Garment could heal a sick woman, think how much his presence in the Sahara could do.

And on the basis of this life centred on the Eucharist as the sacrament of charity, the fruit of the loving sacrifice of the Christ whose heart was broken on the cross, he wrote from his Saharan hermitage:

I want all the inhabitants [of this place], whether Christians, Moslems, Greeks, Jews or idolaters, to look upon me as their brother, the universal brother. They begin to call the house the 'fraternity' . . . I must embrace all men for God's sake in the same love and the same self-forgetfulness as Jesus.[9]

In 1909, he made his last visit to France. From then on, the desert would be his abiding home. In 1910 the abbé Huvelin died, on his lips the words *Nunquam satis amabo*, 'I shall never love enough'. In the same year, 1910, another French Catholic based in North Africa, the young Jesuit Pierre Teilhard de Chardin, left Cairo so as to begin fresh studies at Paris. He was to offer in his own spirituality, as interpreted by cardinal Henri de Lubac, a remarkable theological presentation of de Foucauld's fundamental intuition. If prayer, understood as loving devotion to God in Christ, is truly authentic, then the one who prays will become a channel for Christ's divinising presence, with unlimited ramifications. Prayer is to be at once more personal *and more cosmic*, more closely related to the entire work of God in creation and transfiguration.

According to de Lubac, it was in the context of prayer that Teilhard found his way to a sense of the God of Christian faith which would make sense in a world increasingly aware through scientific discovery of the immensity of the cosmos, and the power to master nature which technology places in human hands. For Teilhard, the inner dynamism of the cosmos, seen in the emergence of man in the evolutionary process, is 'personogenesis', the making of persons, but only the heart of Christ fully reveals and realises the personifying depth of the Creator's love. As he wrote: 'The true infinite is not an infinite of dispersion, but of concentration'. And de Lubac places next to this statement Claudel's *Magnificat*, which celebrates his conversion in that Christmas of 1886.

Lord, I have found you.
You have cast down the idols,
and now I see you as a person.[10]

In God, for Teilhard, lies the ultra-personal, and ultra-personalising centre. In prayer we place ourselves within this centre's radiance. Indeed prayer is existence in the ambience of this personalising centre of the world. He traced the conflict that was ravaging the world by 1940 mainly to 'the inner fact that men have despaired of this personality of God'. For Teilhard, the sacred heart of Jesus is the point from which the fire of God bursts into the cosmic milieu to set it ablaze with love. In prayer, we relocate ourselves in this divine source, and in contemplating him, contemplate at the same time the destiny of our world. Prayer, precisely through being Christocentric, has a cosmic significance.[11]

At the time when Teilhard was penning his analysis of the spiritual roots of the second great European war of this century as the product of a failure of the spirit of prayer, the result of despair about the possibility of abandoning oneself to the personalising centre of the universe, another Carmelite (but this time a woman as different as could be from Thérèse Martin), a sophisticated don in a German University, a Jewess, and convert in adult life to Catholicism, was entering the gas-chambers of Auschwitz. St Edith Stein has left a testimony of mastery in prayer no less remarkable than Thérèse's. Like hers, it stresses two characteristically modern notes that I have mentioned: the need for a self-abandonment to God deeper than customary in conventional piety, and the discovery of a way to new life in God through accepting the darkness, the felt absence of God, in a spirit of trust, and even of joy.[12] Edith Stein was herself someone whose conversion witnesses to the primacy of the existential. The stuff of a praying life – in her case that of Thérèse of Lisieux's own patron, the Mother of Carmel, Teresa of Avila, whose name Stein would take in religion – (Sister Teresa Benedicta of the Cross) – can open up a fresh perspective on reality. After reading that foundational autobiography of the Carmelites, Teresa's *Vida*, Edith remarked: *Das ist die Wahrheit*, 'This is the truth' – the truth, that is, simultaneously of Teresa and God, since if such a woman is real, then so too is God.[13] From out of her own praying years, and on the eve of the Nazi holocaust of Jewry in which she perished, Edith Stein wrote:

To be a child of God, that means: to be led by the Hand of God, to do the will of God, not one's own will, to place every care and every hope in the Hand of God and not to worry about oneself or one's future. On this rests the freedom and the joy of the child of God. But how few even of the truly pious, even of those ready for heroic sacrifices, possess this freedom! They all walk as if bent down by the heavy burden of their cares and duties.

Edith goes on to offer a way of understanding spiritually the apparent absence of God in the modern world.

God is there. But he is hidden and silent. Why is this so? We are speaking of the mysteries of God and these cannot be completely penetrated. But we may look into them a little . . . God has become Man in order once more to give us a share in his life . . . The suffering and death of Christ are continued in his mystical Body and in each of his members . . . And so a soul united to Christ will stand firm, unshaken even in the dark night of feeling estranged from and abandoned by God. Perhaps divine Providence uses her agony to deliver another, who is truly a prisoner cut off from God.[14]

Praying from out of spiritual darkness, in other words, bears a relation to the prayer of Christ in Gethsemane, on the cross, and in the descent into Hell – and so carries a redemptive charge for others. And this, to return in my end to my beginning, is how, on the scale of the entire Mystical Body, the novelist and dramatist Georges Bernanos understood the mission of (the 'little') St Thérèse. In his *Les grands cimitières sous la lune*, written under the impact of the Spanish Civil War and the coming pan-European conflagration, he wrote of her and of the influence of her 'little way' on modern Catholic spirituality:

It may, after all, have been among the intentions of this mysterious girl to allow our wretched world a moment of supreme respite, to give it a breathing space in the shade of its familiar mediocrity, since those little hands, innocent and terrible little hands, expert in cutting out paper flowers, though chapped to the bone by laundry chlorine, have sown a seed whose growth nothing can now stop.[15]

And in the same author's *Dialogues des Carmelites*, a play set in the French Revolution, understood as the archetype of the political upheavals of this century, and an initiation of Godlessness, the prioress carries an image of the Holy Child from cell to cell for the sisters to venerate on Christmas night. Soeur Blanche, whose fear of death occupies the centre of the drama, murmurs, 'How small he is, and how weak'. 'No', replies Mère Marie, 'How small he is *and how strong*.'[16]

# Conclusion

May we sum up then the main family resemblance of some masters and mistresses of prayer in the last hundred years? First, a childlike simplicity which is a true childhood in its dependence, openness and self-surrender, yet is a childhood in a new mode, the fruit of detachment, self-sacrifice and self-transcendence. Second, a prayer which is existential in the sense that it is prepared to allow itself to run on beyond what the analytic or calculating intelligence alone might make of it. A prayer which, in this sense, is willing to be taught by experience, since it is open to the mysterious depths of man (and woman) living with God. Third, a prayer which is at one and the same time intensely personal, indeed devotional, vis-à-vis the figure of Jesus Christ and yet also cosmic, aware of the vast dimensions of God's creative and transformative work, and can be both of these together since Jesus Christ himself is, as the pre-existent Logos, the Word through which the world was made, and, as the crucified and risen Lord, the foundation of the new world of the resurrection. Fourthly, and finally, this is a prayer especially at home in the desert, whether of the Sahara, of Auschwitz, or simply of the modern city, because it knows that, in accepting in a generous spirit our deprivation of many of the conventional props and assurances of a culturally transmitted religion we may be ushered with peculiar immediacy into the presence of the living God. One cannot but think here of David Walsh's powerful case that in the lonely struggles of such figures as Dostoevsky and Solzhenitsyn the crisis of modernity is already (proleptically, by anticipation) resolved.

> Theirs is an insight that has been achieved by living through the . . . spiritual and political crisis that has defined our era . . ., confronting the darkness at its core and surmounting it by means of the spiritual truth beyond it . . . Indeed, the degree to which they have won through to an order of existence beyond the ideological madness has made the depth of their understanding possible. Only someone who has broken out of the restricted horizon of ideology can see clearly what has been left behind. And only those who have fully contemplated the abyss can be sure of having attained the spiritual truth capable of overcoming it.[17]

## Some caveats

Is our age, then, in some sense an especially favoured age for spirituality? I think not, for reasons both *a priori* and *a posteriori*. *A priori*, it is part and parcel of the Lordship of the crucified and risen Christ over history that no age of the Church can better any other in so constitutive an aspect of mankind's sharing in the mystery of the Saviour. But also, *a posteriori*, the kind of prayer I have tried to describe, though it has undeniable greatnesses which I have tried to bring out, has also the vices of its virtues. I want in conclusion to mention three. First, such a simplified existential prayer, centred on the charity of the heart, is exposed to the danger of its own caricature, which is a sentimental subjectivism. Where such a spirituality becomes disengaged from the wider theological, historical, sacramental and moral structure found in the Church's doctrine, it rapidly degenerates into a vague mystical benevolence, as with *Teilhardisme* at its worst, or into the sentimental banalities of many modern prayer cards, with their kittens, butterflies and soporifically trivial uplifting thoughts. 'All you need is love' is both a truth and an untruth, or, rather, it has its properly evangelical truth only in the context of all the dogmas of the Church. It is, I think, instructive that one of the rare canonical interventions of Church authority in matters of iconography in modern Catholicism was precisely this: the forbidding of the making and venerating of images of Christ consisting in a heart alone. In this sense, an important corrective to the spiritualities I have been describing is found in the deliberately archaising spiritual theology of the Irish Benedictine, and later abbot of Maredsous, in Belgium, Columba Marmion.[18] Marmion, who began his monastic life in my crucial year, 1886, went back to the Fathers and the best of the mediaevals so as to produce a spirituality of participation in the mysteries of redemption, seen as historic events with everlasting significance, re-presented in the liturgical cycle and demanding from the worshipper the development of a range of relevant virtues. Without the aid of this wider structure, the modern Christian can easily fall victim to the false consciousness which a modern Anglican writer describes as follows:

> Religion is perceived to be the heaped-up accumulation of the agreeable; God is love, and therefore he is to be envisaged as the great guarantor of whatever in life makes for human satisfaction. In its sentimentalised representations contemporary Christianity has become an uncomplicated sanctifying of the pathetic human disposition to seek basic emotional companionship, and in its intellectualised manifestations it amounts to a variation of the common humanist preoccupation with the values of human moral consciousness.[19]

I will deal more briefly with my second and third *a posteriori* objections. The second caveat to enter concerns the lack of any developmental account of prayer in these spiritualities. It is true that the variety of human temperament and experience, as well as the diversity of God's gifts, rules out of court any fully *systematic* description of progress in contemplation. Indeed the attempt to impose one single phenomenology of prayer and mysticism (usually a conflation of the accounts given by the two sixteenth-century Carmelite doctors, John of the Cross and the great Teresa) has done harm in both theory and practice. Surely, however, there are some statements about stages in which the development of prayer and, hopefully, contemplation, can helpfully be made, not least because a large number of texts from the tradition of spiritual doctrine testify to them in various ways.

Thirdly and lastly, I am left with the uncomfortable impression that such an apparently simple and foundational approach to prayer as the existential one is only in fact possible – paradoxically – for élite souls. Those who would sacrifice religion to save faith may end up by losing both. To perform a feat of abstraction reducing to a state of sublime spiritual simplicity *both* the complexities of God's approach to us in revelation and its continuance in the Church's Tradition *and* the complexities of our response to him in our varied needs, situations and stages on life's way, is an achievement of which comparatively few people will ever be capable, this side of the beatific vision. In any widespread or popular form, mystical holiness will always be bound to a ramified and somewhat untidy devotional culture – hence the need for a re-creation of that 'Christendom', with a social ethos founded on transparency to revelation – whose passing, in the course of the nineteenth century, was the presupposition of my story.

## NOTES

1. Cited N. D. O'Donoghue, 'The Paradox of Prayer', *Doctrine and Life* 24.1 (January, 1974), pp. 26–37.

2. Ibid.

3. R. Knox (tr.), *Autobiography of a Saint. Thérèse of Lisieux* (London, 1958), pp. 127–8.

4. Ibid., pp. 237–8. Knox was able to use, for the first time in English, the full authentic text of Thérèse's *Histoire*. A complete edition of her writings, and material pertinent to her life and mission, was produced in the years 1971 to 1989 by the Parisian Editions du Centenaire under the general editorship of D. Delalande, O.C.D. For Thérèse's spirituality see especially P. Descouvement, 'Thérèse de l'Enfant Jésus', in *Dictionnaire de Spiritualité* 15 (Paris, 1991), cols. 576–611. An outstanding study is B. Bro, O.P., *La Gloire et le Mendiant* (Paris, 1974).

5. P. Knight, *Flower Poetics in Nineteenth Century France* (Oxford, 1986). Cf. also E. M. Forster's report of a literary culture far removed in space from the French: 'Pathos, they [Aziz and his friends] agreed, is the highest quality in art; a poem should touch the hearer with a sense of his own weakness, and should institute some comparison between mankind and flowers', *A Passage to India* (London, 1924; 1995), p. 130.

6. J. Saward, 'Faithful to the Child I Used to Be. Bernanos and the Spirit of Childhood', *Chesterton Review* XV 4/XVI. 1. pp. 465–86, who refers us to N. Hausman, *Frédéric Nietzsche. Thérèse de Lisieux. Deux poétiques de la modernité* (Paris, 1984) .

7. M. Trouncer, *Charles de Foucauld* (London, 1972).

8. Ibid., p. 64. See M. T. Louis-Lefebvre, *Abbé Huvelin, Apostle of Paris, 1839–1910* (ET Dublin and London, 1967), pp. 9–10. See also P. Lethellieux, *Un prêtre, l'abbé Huvelin 1838–1910. Avec de nouveaux documents* (Paris, 1957²).

9. Trouncer, *Charles de Foucauld*, p. 149. For de Foucauld's spirituality, see J. F. Six, *Itinéraire spirituel de Charles de Foucauld* (Paris, 1958); his correspondence with Huvelin was edited by Six (Tournai, 1957). For his own writings, published and unpublished, see P. Quesnel, *Charles de Foucauld: les etapes d'une recherche* (Paris, 1966).

10. Cited H. de Lubac, *La Prière du Teilhard de Chardin* (Paris, 1964); ET *The Faith of Teilhard de Chardin* (London, 1965), p. 14.

11. On Teilhard's attempt to marry the cultus of the Sacred Heart with a cosmic Christology, see ibid., pp. 46–8. *Pace* Teilhard's critics, while he by no means altogether escaped the temptation of pantheism, he tried to neutralise that temptation by stressing how the action of love – in this case, divine love – is both differentiating and communicative. Orthodox faith in Incarnation and Eucharist imply both the absolutely distinct reality of God and creature and their most intimate union.

12. See H. Graef, *The Scholar and the Cross: the Life and Work of Edith Stein* (London, 1955), who stresses, pp. 90, 130, Edith's teaching on silence, emptiness, and renunciation of self as things to be practised not only by Carmelites but by all the baptised.

13. R. Posselt (Teresia Renata a Spiritu Sancto, O.C.D.), *Edith Stein, Schwester Teresia Benedicta a Cruce. Philosophin und Karmeliten* (Freiburg, 1962), pp. 55–6; see also N. D. O'Donoghue, 'The Witness of St Theresa', *Doctrine and Life* 20 (1970), pp. 672–3: 'There is no explaining away that strong, delicate process of transformation by which she became what she became. "All that dower of lights and fires" which the poet [Crashaw] saw in her could only have come from above: it was indeed a dowry, something given by a loving father, enriching the bride for that high marriage of the spirit of which terrestrial marriage is but a faint reflection.'

14. Cited Graef, *The Scholar and the Cross*, pp. 139–40. One can compare with this the ideas of the Anglican lay theologian Charles Williams on the possible scope of 'coinherence', the applying of redemptive suffering to another. See G. Cavaliero, *Charles Williams. Poet of Theology* (London and Basingstoke, 1983), pp. 135–7

15. G. Bernanos, *Les grands cimitières sous la lune* (Paris, 1930), p. 242.

16. Bernanos, *Oeuvres romanesques* (Paris, 1961), p. 1656. I draw these citations from Saward, 'Faithful to the Child'.

17. D. Walsh, *After Ideology. Recovering the Spiritual Foundations of Freedom* (San Francisco, 1990), p. xii.

18. 'Perhaps the greatest spiritual master of the past century', declared the (no doubt biased!) editors of his English language correspondence. See G. Ghyssens, O.S.B., and T. Delforge, O.S.B. (eds), *The English Letters of Abbot Marmion, 1858–1923* (Dublin, 1962), p. 5. The most recent life, which uses manuscript sources uncovered in the course of preparing Marmion's Cause, is M. Tierney, O.S.B., *Dom Columba Marmion. A Biography* (Blackrock, Co. Dublin, 1994). See also Aidan Nichols, O.P., 'In the Catholic Tradition: Dom Columba Marmion (1858–1923)', *Priests and People* 11.7 (1997), pp. 283–8.

19. E. Norman, *Entering the Darkness. Christianity and its Modern Substitutes* (London, 1991), p. 33.

# XV

# *Recentring on the End*

THE 'horizontalism' of much contemporary Western culture, and its partial invasion of a Church inevitably subject to that culture's inroads through a policy of 'openness to the world', must necessarily affect our view of time. The time of history, on the Christian view, is essentially *apocalyptic*. History is a creative movement towards an incalculably great and yet by no means unknown issue. And in every moment of its time each human situation has a qualitative novelty about it. Both aspects of history as apocalypse – the unveiling of a End to the total process, and the unveiling of abiding meaning in each of its distinct moments – suggest a relation between the temporal and the eternal. Yet nothing is more characteristic of cultural immanentism – the confidence of a secular culture that human resources are or shall be sufficient unto themselves – than the suppression of interest in the relation between eternity and time. The notion that time is best symbolised as an arrow in flight, albeit to no known target, is, however, philosophically as well as theologically naïve. The issue merits underlining in a period when the Churches are celebrating the bimillennium of the Incarnation of the Logos, that unique rerelating of the Eternal with time.

## The Eternal in time

The crucial point to grasp is that time cannot simply be known *from within time*. Time moves in precipitate fashion from future into past (at every moment the future *becomes* past) and does so in a way which ineluctably involves ourselves. That is why the understanding of time we have from within that movement can only be highly relative. But if time, in its constant disappearance, raises the question of whatever it can be that grounds time's beginning, sustains time's course and achieves time's end – and in this sense presses time toward its own self-transcendence in the eternal, so for Christian faith the Eternal – the answer to the philosopher's question – is constantly entering into time by its presence and power. God and the world are not to be thought of as opposites. And so when we conceive them as respectively the Eternal and the temporal, we must say that eternity's transcending of time is creative. Eternity does not cancel time but redemptively reveals its true potential.

With the Russian Christian philosopher-theologian Evgeny Lampert we must take care not to fall into a kind of Monophysitism on these matters, supposing that the Eternal swallows up time, such that the goal of those who live in time must in every sense be non- or supratemporal – just as Monophysite Christologies so affirm the divinisation of the humanity assumed by the Word as to leave no continuing room for its creaturely integrity. Neither, following Lampert's other warning signal, must we go to the other extreme of the Christological spectrum and adopt a Nestorian manner of thinking through this interrelationship. It is not enough to have eternity and time side by side, juxtaposed. Rather, revelation's claim – and so the claim echoed by the orthodox – is to uncover time's hidden transcendent meaning.

> The deadly ambiguities of time cry out for an answer beyond its own limits: it aspires at each and every point towards a moment where it is coincidentally transcended and fulfilled. This moment is, as it were, a final point in time if seen from one angle and it is eternity if seen from another . . . Man's creatureliness, that is, his very relation to God and God's relation to him, is existence in time, and peace is given to man through the final leap into the beyond which does not annul time but fulfils it.[1]

The key, then, is the Incarnation, which reveals to us that the real subjects of history are God in relation to man, and man in relation to God. Thus personal initiative and personal creativity (whether divine in God himself, 'theandric' – divine-human – in Christ, or human in ourselves) are history's primary agencies. This saves us from dreadful errors about history: from the pessimism which views the historical process as a naturalistically predetermined evolution which we should just allow to happen since there is nothing very much we can do about it; from the complacency which declares that history has now 'come to an end', for we are all to be consumerist democrats now; from the optimism which (à la Hegel) treats history as the progressive self-expression of a corporate mind immanent in the world process and gradually eliminating what is negative from the contents of historical experience; from the militancy of racialist, nationalist or class-based aggression. Over against these dystopias or delusions, Christ was able to reveal time's true *telos*, its end and goal, through the Word's divine entry into time, his never to be abandoned assumption of it. After Jesus Christ, humankind continues to exist, true, in a *perpetuum mobile*, but the flux of events is no longer bewildering. Insight is now available into time's divine-human significance, into – accordingly – both time's tragedy and its promise. That is why the Christian conception of history is apocalyptic, that of an 'unveiling'. The fulfilment of history in the divine reign in Jesus Christ has been disclosed as already hiddenly present in history's course, and is nonetheless also still to come by an astounding vindication of the power of that hidden presence – that final 'show-down' with the disintegrative forces in the temporal process which the word 'apocalypse' more commonly conveys.

History is time in the process of acquiring meaning. Other animals live in time. Man alone, owing to his peculiar concern with meaning, lives in history – in a time which indicates relations with others, and with *the* Other, God. Though, manifestly, historical events are exposed to influence from geography, climate, physiology and a host of physical factors, they are lived out by a species which has assimilated its own environment and goes beyond that environment's limits. A civilisation will always be an act of creation.

But what is the task actually addressed to human freedom and creativity? Human capacity is undermined by the disintegrative temporality of our specific mode of existence. God calls on man to appropriate the End – time's *telos* – by uniting the world to the Father in the way that the Incarnation of the Son made possible and the outpouring of the Holy Spirit actually achieves. God in Christ has created in the fullness of time in his own incarnate, crucified and glorified person that centre from which all that lives in time must be approached, and not only approached, or understood, but transformed. History is now not only that from which God calls us into his Kingdom; it is also where in Jesus Christ he has come to be with us, entering within our limits and into our sufferings, to burst them from within. The poet Hopkins knew this:

> Not out of his bliss
>     Springs the stress felt
> Nor first from heaven (and few know this)
>     Swings the stroke dealt –
> Stroke and a stress that stars and storms deliver,
> That guilt is hushed by, hearts are flushed by and melt –

But it rides time like riding a river
(And here the faithful waver, the faithless fable and miss).

It dates from day
Of his going in Galilee
Warm-laid grave of a womb-life grey;
Manger, maiden's knee;
The dense and driven Passion, and frightful sweat:
Thence the discharge of it, there its swelling to be . . .[2]

Meaningful time – history – is, we may say, both 'vectorial' and 'punctual'. *Pace* the simplistic 'arrow of time' model typical of Neo-Positivism, it needs to be symbolised not only as a directed line receiving its orientation from its end (*vectorially*) but also (*punctually*) as a series of points whereby each historic moment on the directed line enjoys its own relation to God, unique, unrepeatable – a relation which may of course be negative, representing judgement, not positive, representing promise – and indeed the cross of Messiah Jesus is supremely both.

Jewish consciousness – the consciousness of Israel – is therefore historical consciousness *par excellence* just because it conceives history as *Providence*, a story of divine acts by which God gives meaning to the destiny of his people and, through them, to humankind as a whole, all in view of an ultimate End which will resolve the chronic or 'systemic' problems of life on earth – and notably those which the apocalyptic literature of the Bible itself addresses, evil (its virulence yet stimulus to heroic good), authority (its necessity yet oppressiveness) and time itself (its provision of opportunity, and yet limitations).[3]

Notice how Israel does not present as unilateral the purposive acting of God. Rather, in her perception, does God allow his own omnipotence to be conditioned by the freedom of human response – though this does not mean that God fails to exercise real power over all things leading them to their appointed End (else he would not be God). What it does mean is that God's determination of events is not mechanistic but personal – allowing for the factor of reciprocity. In no way does the New Testament depart from this picture, except of course by the dramatic breakthrough in which it registers God's new deed in Christ as the revelation of his sovereign will no longer just in message or in providential activity but *in the personal hypostasis of the Son*. The heart of the New Testament proclamation is that through the Son the Father is leading the whole created universe – cosmos and history – to the ultimate fulfilment of the Kingdom (cf. Eph. 1.9–10). Thus the Fathers of the Church could conceive Providence anew as a Christological 'economy' – a design of the Father to sum up all things in Christ.

## Cosmos and the End

Though the Christian hope is focused on persons – human persons, in their relation to divine – it is not without a care, then, for the wider cosmos in which human lives are set. It follows that the animal creation – in its setting in the vegetable and mineral! – comes likewise within its purview. In apocalyptic perspective, care for the environment and its animal occupants means the stewardship of an earth which must be handed back in its maximum richness of life for transfiguration by the Creator – now the Redeemer – God.

The American Lutheran theologian H. Paul Santmire has set out two rhetorical questions, the first of which expects a negative, the second an affirmative, reply.

> Is the final aim of God, in his governance of all things, to bring into being at the very end a glorified kingdom of spirits alone who, thus united with God, may contemplate him in perfect bliss, while as a precondition of their ecstasy all the other creatures of nature must be left by God to fall away into eternal oblivion?
>
> Or is the final aim of God, in his governance of all things, to communicate his life to another in a way which calls forth at the very end new heavens and a new earth in which righteousness dwells, a transfigured cosmos where peace is universally established between all creatures at last, in the midst of which is situated a glorious city of resurrected saints who dwell in justice, blessed with all the resplendent fullness of the earth, and who continually call upon all creatures to join with them in their joyful praise of the one who is all in all?[4]

Humankind is the pinnacle of creation, not its centre – only God can be that – and in a world where man is not the be-all-and-end-all of things, we can and should say that animals, and with them the organic and inorganic worlds without which their life is unthinkable, really matter. The importance, however, of locating ecological concern within the eschatological framework that Santmire indicates is that, deprived of this framework, it easily becomes a distraction from the 'centering on the End' – an *alternative* to sharing in the divine venture of bringing all things together under Christ and not a *form* of it.[5]

With the Parousia, for Augustine of Hippo, the whole biophysical realm – the material-vital world – will become transparent to the presence of God as the almighty creativity who originated it, sustained it, and, after its travail in the history of nature, grants its renewal.[6] For Francis of Assisi the eschatological consummation is anticipated, in a life of childlike simplicity, loving all the creatures of the earth (we note his solicitude for the less obviously attractive, like worms). Possibly the making of the Christmas crib (a devotion, so historians report, he did not initiate, yet fostered) commended itself precisely as a parable of the 'peaceable Kingdom', with men and beasts in company around the Christ.[7]

Many species of animal and plant are lost to nature's history (most, of course, before the appearance of *Homo sapiens* on earth, others without our less informed predecessors' knowledge – so this is not necessarily an indictment of man). Again, many delicate webs of interdependent life among species have been rudely ruptured by the invasive expansion of human populations who are now, in their new habitats, largely here to stay (and the making of cities is a precondition for that civilisation which makes possible nature's reworking in culture in its highest forms). Very often, then, spilt milk cannot be put back (by us) into bottles – and some of the milk was cream. But we can still perform significant *gestures* of stewarding care for animals and plants and the environment at large. And the knowledge – born of divine revelation – that such gestures are 'sacraments' of God's final restoration of the creation in a new Jerusalem where nature's vitality and luxuriance are enhanced (thus the vision of the biblical canon's last book) prevents such gestures from merely suggesting countryside or zoological 'theme-parks'. Hope that the losses of the history of nature (including man) will be redeemed can only be *super*natural.

Furthermore, it remains the case for many of those millions who do not live in the English Home Counties, or other analogues thereof, that raw nature (nature neither cultivated in horticulture, agriculture and the taming of beasts, nor fabricated in culture) remains as awesome and fearful as ever it was. There is still a struggle with nature, the earth and the animals, to survive, exercising all man's gifts of ingenuity and not always succeeding then. Here too, when the conflict is unequal in another direction the vision of the pacific kingdom of the End is an incentive to hope.

## Millennium and apocalypse

At any 'millennial' celebration of the first coming of the incarnate Lord in history, we think especially of the final Apocalypse, his definitive coming to consummate God's creative and redeeming purpose for time, at 'the End'. Throughout the history of the Church, Christians have scanned historical events and noted what appeared to be significant dates and anniversaries, just in case these might be 'signs' of the End. Given the view of early Christians that the 'fullness of time' in which the Incarnation had happened was in part defined by the providential diffusion of the *pax romana* throughout the Mediterranean basin of which Palestine formed a (peripheral) part, the sack of Rome by the Goths in 410 and various natural disasters that followed in the succeeding decade gave rise to speculation – whether anxious or hopeful – along these lines. In an interesting exchange of letters between bishop Hesychius of Salonae (the modern city of Split in Croatia) and St Augustine, Augustine's correspondent complained that too many people were treating the Lord's Parousia as a topic to be avoided, whereas in reality it was something to be 'loved and longed for'. Augustine agreed, but warned against all attempts to calculate or predict the consummation of historical time through the advent of the Kingdom. It is, he argued in letter 199,

> not the one who affirms that the Lord is near who 'loves his coming' any more than it is the one who affirms he is not near; but rather is it the one who waits for him, whether near or far away, with sincere faith, with unshakeable hope, and with ardent love.

As a Jesuit specialist in the 'eschatology' – the doctrine of the ultimate realities – in the Fathers has commented:

> The Christian always believes that the end is near, [Augustine] could assure Hesychius, because Christ is the end of our history and Christ is always near; yet to translate that sense of his nearness into precise temporal terms, to calculate the date and the manner of his final appearance and history's final transformation, would be to violate the mystery, the hiddenness of his Kingdom.[8]

Augustine's caveat did not prevent his fellow Catholics from doing what he advised them against – for instance the German hermit Bernard of Thuringia in the decades before the first millennium, the year 1000. But on the whole the sacramentalism of Catholic doctrine (the incarnate Lord is *already* present in history, communicating his holiness through the Church and her sacraments and redeeming, in the transfigured humanity of his saints, soul and body, the original creation) meant that Catholicism has been less hospitable to the more excited forms of apocalyptic speculation found in some kinds of Protestantism.

It would be a mistake to suppose, however, that Catholicism is not waiting for an apocalyptic End. For a true climax to history, a genuine consummation of all things, must necessarily involve a divine action which crowns the saving interplay of divine freedom and human freedom redeemed in Christ, that interplay which gives time its eternal significance along the line of its course. If for Augustine it is true *both* that 'the End is already here' (concealed, yet really present, in the power of Christ's Godmanhood) *and* that 'the End is coming', we must conclude that for him the 'way to the End is in the End itself'.[9] What we celebrate, at this bimillennium, in the Incarnation is precisely the coming of the One who is at the last to consummate all things. Eschatology is not so much about *ta eschata*, the 'final realities' in the neuter plural, as it is about *ho eschatos*, the 'ultimate one' in the personal singular, Jesus Christ. Time for us is moving, in the power of the Spirit of the Son, sent from the Father, to that goal, within time and yet beyond it, which is the final revelation of God's glory. Because we live *from* the Christ who is personally the End and therefore *in* the End, we should be perfectly familiar with the notion that he will declare himself for what he is at the end of time likewise. *At the moment* God's Kingdom, present sacramentally in the Church, in her preaching, in the holy signs of her worship, and in her saints, is hidden 'kenotically' – like the Christ of the Nativity, the ministry and the cross – in the ambiguities of time. But *then* the veil will be rent, and the hitherto invisible presence become plain. We already share in the transfigured cosmos whose nucleus is Christ's risen and ascended body and are activated by its energies. But then we shall *see* the glorified Saviour as the Lamb of the new temple, the new heavens and new earth where righteousness dwells so as never more to abandon the human (and cosmic) city. Because God is God he must come into his own. He cannot ultimately be defeated. And yet the divine plan for the world, made in the eternal counsels of the Holy Trinity, whose *first* act is exclusively divine (the creation), and whose *second* act (the redemption) is exclusively 'the work of God in the incarnate Lord' (though Catholics see a role for a representative woman in the consent thereto of the Blessed Virgin Mary), cannot be fully realised until by a *third and final* act all time, all history, is taken up into the Eternal through a final resolution of the drama of human freedom in its confrontation with the divine Creator of that freedom (the Trinity) and its divine-human Liberator (the Trinity in Jesus Christ). And as history enters the Kingdom, so, as we have seen, will nature likewise, for human beings are never intended to live without their bodies (*both* the soul *and* the body are the 'I') and so in separation from their material environment.

This is the truth which the inspired writer of the Book of Revelation, the last and climactic work of the New Testament canon, wished us to know. Reworking images and scenes from the prophetic books of the Old Testament – 'bright images from earlier prophetic works laid alongside powerful new icons of a sovereign God and his redeemed people',[10] St John presents the crucified and risen Christ as the centre of a 'New Jerusalem' in a universe refashioned, when the 'Lamb' –

who revealed, by enacting it, the Father's sacrificial love in his Incarnation and on the cross – will show himself victorious over evil by his glorious Parousia, and streams of living water flow from his throne for the healing of the nations.

## The Great Jubilee: what must be done

In considering the practical lessons we might usefully draw from contemplation of the redemptive Incarnation in its relation to the Parousia, the End of time, the present holy father – Pope John Paul II – invites us to work out a programme for the universal Church via the idea of *jubilee*. In the Old Testament, the jubilee year was an important example of the sanctification of time. Every fifty years, the Lordship of the God of Israel over his people, and over the Land he had given as their own possession, was acknowledged in a particularly striking way as the poor were (in principle at least) reinstated as sharers of the riches of Israel, and slaves and prisoners (once again, in principle) set free. And this was done – at any rate, it was *partly* done – for God's sake, in obedience to him and for his glory. When the Saviour, at the beginning of his ministry in Nazareth, according to Luke,[11] declares that an oracle of the prophet Isaiah which ascribes to the Messiah the proclamation of a unique jubilee, a 'year of the Lord's favour',[12] is now being fulfilled in his listeners' hearing, he sets the tone for his own forthcoming messianic activity. *All* the work of Christ will be 'jubilee'. Hence, to recall that work to her children the Church too, like the People of God of old, has, during history, celebrated jubilees of the Incarnation and the Atonement calling Christians to renewed rejoicing in salvation, as well as to deeper conversion, and, in particular, urging those in need of reconciliation with each other, in the name of Christ, to make peace.

In his encyclical letter *Tertio Millenio Adveniente* (1994) the Pope proposes that the 'Great Jubilee' of the year 2000 be used not to launch a 'new millenarianism', an expectation of the Parousia as now imminent (that would expose him to the criticisms voiced by St Augustine), but to achieving an 'increased sensitivity to all that the Spirit is saying to the Church and to the Churches, as well as to individuals through charisms meant to serve the whole community'. The purpose, so the Pope explains, is to 'emphasize what the Spirit is suggesting to the different communities, from the smallest ones, such as the family, to the largest ones, such as nations and international organizations, taking into account cultures, societies and sound traditions'.[13] In what ways are our communities open to the End made possible by the Incarnation, when Eternity threw open time to God? 'Despite appearances', the Pope remarks, referring presumably to the phenomenon of secularisation in Western and Western-influenced societies, 'humanity continues to await the revelation of the children of God, and lives by this hope'.[14]

What is involved, as the Pope spells out, is *confirming our faith* (we can call this the *intellectual* challenge of the Jubilee); *sustaining our eternal hope* (we can call this the *spiritual* challenge of the Jubilee); and *rekindling our charity* (we can call this the *moral* challenge of the Jubilee).[15] Meeting these challenges is possible in the Jubilee-time if that time arouses in Christians joyful confidence in grace founded, however, on a sober realism about their own past failures and present shortcomings – a joy, then, based on conversion, on the grace of the forgiveness of sins. The Pope calls on the members of the Church to repent of the 'counter-witness and scandal' they may have given. Of course, some 'scandal' – literally, a stumbling-block – is evangelically necessary, for, as the Theologian of the Pontifical Household, the Swiss Dominican Georges Cottier, has pointed out, the gospel of the cross necessarily 'scandalises' by not only revealing the depths of the love of the self-humiliating God but also requiring us to transcend the limitations of our own self-enclosed identities in return. But here we are talking of 'the scandal of sin, incitement or bad example [which] brings with it the fall of our brother'.[16] In fact, the Pope is thinking especially of crimes committed by the sons and daughters of the Church *in her name* – and notably any actions which may have precipitated or hardened schisms, and expressions of intolerance which have harmed rather than served the cause of truth. At the same time, the Pope is evidently aware that confessing vicariously the sins of other people , particularly if they are dead and cannot reply for themselves, becomes all too easily a recipe for self-congratulation, and so he speaks also in this connection of present-day failings of the Church's members, and notably the collusion they can practise with a false secularism and ethical relativism (thus generating indifference to religious and moral truth), the spiritual uncertainty into which they fall by (often culpable) ignorance of the Church's theological doctrine, and the injustices which they can support through neglect of her social doctrine on fundamental human rights. But since excessive dwelling on these negative features of the Church's life is hardly congruent with the joy of jubilee, the Pope rounds off his account by reminding his readers of the many Christians who have joyfully achieved heroic sanctity, or happily given up life itself as martyrs, for the sake of the bliss that lay ahead of them when their creation reaches its consummation at the End, in Jesus Christ.[17]

As the present millennium draws to its close, the burning issues facing the Church differ, at any rate in part, so the Pope explains, in diverse segments of the earth's surface. He speaks, for instance, of the realisation of the jubilee by a Synod for the Americas, whose principal concern was evangelisation and economic justice, the sharing of resources; by a Synod for Asia, which addressed the elements of truth in, yet basic soteriological insufficiency of, Buddhism and Hinduism; and a Synod for Oceania to reflect on the existence of peoples who 'in a unique way evoke aspects of human pre-history'.[18] These are themes which will retain their high pertinence to these global regions long after the present anniversary is past.

However, the faith which the gospel houses is ultimately one, as is the human race itself. And so, in explaining the three-year structure of the preparation for the Jubilee, John Paul II can explain things relevant to everyone. In the year of the Son, all Catholics were asked to deepen their understanding of the Saviour, the knowledge of Scripture which speaks of him, their appreciation of the grace of their baptism which gave them entry into his life and a basis for unity with other Christians. That year, 1997, was to be *par excellence* a year of *faith*. In the year of the Spirit, they were asked to renew their confidence in the Holy Spirit – in his power, notably through the grace of confirmation, to activate the members of the Church for mission, to empower a new evangelisation and vivify our expectation of history's wondrous End. That year, 1998, was to be *par excellence* a year of *hope*. In the year of the Father, Catholic Christians – and all Christians who heed this call – are asked to live their lives more fervently as a pilgrimage with their neighbours to the Father's house, to become more deeply converted through the sacrament of penance, and to recommit themselves to being the Christian soul in human civilisation, currently in crisis as this is through the lack of clear moral foundations. The year 1999 is to be, *par excellence*, a year of *charity*: that generous, hospitable charity which the eleventh-century German historian and geographer Adam of Bremen considered to be so marked a feature of a people newly converted to the gospel – in the case he was considering, Iceland.[19]

The Anglo-Welsh poet David Jones wrote of Christ: 'It is easy to miss Him / at the turn of a civilisation.'[20] What will become of the civilisation of the Western world is a disputed question, but the turn of a millennium is at any rate a good point at which to take stock of the cultural resources that may support the threefold – intellectual, spiritual, ethical – renewal of the Church. For though on the eve of a new millennium we are to look forward, it is characteristic of redeemed time that it abandons nothing of what is precious from the past but carries it forward towards eternity.

An example may help. The present portion of *Christendom Awake* was written originally to be spoken in Iceland. In that country one could think of those vital intuitions which the Gospel either confirmed or introduced in Icelandic culture: the *importance of law*, since just rules for acting convey something of the divine mind whose revealed law – the Torah – became incarnate in Jesus Christ. Not for nothing were 'lawspeakers' the regents of the Icelandic Commonwealth. One thinks too of the role of *merry-making and feasting* in the ancient Norse mythology. Perhaps assisted by the geographically dispersed character of Iceland's population, and the need for relief from a difficult climate, this theme gave a first glimpse of Christian eschatology, where the Kingdom is presented as a banquet, for the story of the world will turn out to be essentially a *commedia*: it has a happy ending. And finally there is the *motif of a story* itself: for the sagas which are Iceland's enduring contribution to the literature of the world are narratives, stories – and the Gospel confirms that the key to all reality is the story of one who was born of a virgin and suffered under Pontius Pilate, for the preconditions of that story are found in the Trinity, the only true God, and its consequences stream out through history ultimately to affect the order of the cosmos itself.

When in Snorri's *Edda*, Eilifr exchanges the worship of Thor for that of Christ, the latter is acclaimed as 'Rome's mighty king.'[21] May this initiative for the end of the millennium from the present bishop of Rome find a resonance in the Church, and among people not only in but also after the year 2000, wherever its rumour is taken.

## NOTES

1. E. Lampert, *The Apocalypse of History. Problems of Providence and Human Destiny* (London, 1948), p. 40.

2. G. M. Hopkins, 'The Wreck of the *Deutschland*' in N. H. Gardner and N. H. Mackenzie (eds.), *The Poems of Gerard Manley Hopkins* (Oxford, 1967), p. 53.

3. See S. D. O'Leary, *Arguing the Apocalypse. A Theory of Millennial Rhetoric* (New York, 1994).

4. H. P. Santmire, *The Travail of Nature. The Ambiguous Ecological Promise of Christian Theology* (Minneapolis, 1985), pp. 217–18. Cf., D. Burrell, C.S.C. and E. Malits, C.S.C., *Original Peace. Restoring God's Creation* (New York and Mahwah, N.J., 1997), pp. 80–94.

5. At its worst: 'instead of finding in Biblical tradition ample support for recognition of animal subjectivity, the careful tending of nature, and divine glory and sublimity as disclosed therein, [eco-theology] insists (after little historical reflection), on jettisoning orthodoxy, and constructing a more purely immanent, embodied, developing limited Godhead . . . [But] the Old Testament attitude which did not want to muzzle the ox too hard, that sought to embrace a particular symbiosis of humans, animals and plants within its notions of "cosmic order", was not in love with immanence and process, but rather with eternity and transcendence.' J. Milbank, *The Word Made Strange. Theology, Language, Culture* (Oxford, 1997), pp. 262, 261.

6. Augustine, *De civitate Dei* XXII. 29.

7. R. C. Petry, 'Mediaeval Eschatology and St. Francis of Assisi', *Church History* 9.1 (1940), pp. 54–69.

8. B. E. Daley, 'Judgment Day or Jubilee? Approaching the Millenium', *America* 176. 19 (1997), p. 10. Cf. idem, *The Hope of the Early Church. A Handbook of Patristic Eschatology* (Cambridge, 1991).

9. Lampert, *The Apocalypse of History*, p. 44.

10. Daley, 'Judgment Day or Jubilee,' p. 16.

11. Luke 4.16–30.

12. Isaiah 61.2.

13. John Paul II, *Tertio Millenio Adveniente*, 23, with an internal allusion to Revelation 2.7ff.

14. Ibid.

15. Ibid., 31.

16. G. Cottier, 'Counter-witness and Scandal', *Tertium Millenium* 1 (1996), pp. 102–5.

17. *Tertio Millenio Adveniente*, 37.

18. Ibid., 38.

19. Adam of Bremen, *Descriptio Insularum Aquilonis*, 35, cited in C. Dawson, *Religion and the Rise of Western Culture* (London, 1950), p. 114.

20. D. Jones, 'A, a, a, Domine Deus', in idem, *The Sleeping Lord and Other Fragments* (London, 1974) .

21. Cited in D. Strömback, *The Conversion of Iceland. A Survey* (London, 1975), p. 54.

# XVI

# *Epilogue: Renewing Priestly Mission*

MY suggestions for 're-energising the Church in culture' have been addressed to a general Church public, not especially to priests. And yet the future of the priesthood is pivotal to the life of the Church since that priesthood is the public representation of the difference which the divine reordering of the world makes in Jesus Christ.

## Mission and sacrifice

If we ask, what are the defining themes of the Catholic priesthood, we shall find few better answers than 'mission' and 'sacrifice'. We can tell that from the way those themes are intertwined in Christology, the priesthood's source. Like the royal priesthood of the faithful, the ministerial priesthood takes all its meaning from the priesthood of Christ in which it is a participation. A priest for ever after the style and fashion of Melchizedek, for whose origin Genesis gave no particulars (but this priest, the Logos, is *literally* without temporal beginning, the eternally begotten Son and Lord), Jesus Christ is by nature the priestly Mediator of men to the Father, since he is in his own person the 'God-man'. He is also priest by right of his atoning Sacrifice on the Tree. He is both the definitive priest, the *Omega* of human priesthood in salvation history and also what we can call the 'fontal' priest, the *Alpha* of the new priesthood for the last age in which we live now. But the Letter to the Hebrews, from which these notions are derived, does not separate Christ's priesthood from his mission – his apostolate. He is, in the words of the writer to the Hebrews (3.1), 'the apostle and high priest of our profession'. For Hebrews, Jesus' exercise of priesthood is located in his obedience to the will of the One who sent him. In offering himself, body and soul, by a priestly sacrifice he shows himself to be *the* apostle

233

*par excellence*, the One sent. 'Then I said, "Lo, I have come to do thy will, O God"' (10.9). In other words, priesthood is intimately connected with doing the will of the Father in mission. As Irenaeus of Lyons will put it in more consciously Trinitarian guise a century or so later: 'The Son performs the good pleasure of the Father. The Father sends, but the Son is sent and comes.'[1] These convictions of the author of Hebrews are echoed in the Johannine writings. For St John, Jesus is the One whom God has sent so that he might offer himself as the perfect expiation for our sins (cf. John 3.34; 1 John 2.2). In the Fourth Gospel, the High Priestly Prayer of Jesus for the Twelve is filled with language that is not only sacrificial but also sacerdotal, but this language is never found in isolation from that of mission. The Twelve are priests because they are like Jesus, apostles. They are chosen and consecrated for the sake of extending the mission of the Son. 'As thou didst send me into the world' (prays our Lord to his Father), 'so I have sent them into the world' (John 17.18). And just as being sent into the world of sin meant for Jesus a life of self-oblation consummated in sacrificial dying, so also the apostles, according to the Synoptic tradition, are called to take up their cross and follow Christ (cf. Matt. 10.39), and in the Gospel of John to be persecuted, indeed, as Christ was (John 15.18–16.4).

The apostles are the archetypes of the Church's ministerial priesthood. This they are, however, not simply as imitators and therefore exemplars of Christ's priesthood through their being sent forth – and sent forth, moreover, to be sacrificed. It is not just, or even mainly, *self-*sacrifice they are to practise. Rather is it the belief of the Church that those who bear the apostolic ministry are called actually to offer the sacrifice of Christ himself, and to find in that offering meaning and vigour for their own sacrificial lives. At the Last Supper when in the words of Aquinas' great Corpus Christi hymn, the *Lauda Sion*, the eternal High Priest 'gave himself with his own hand', he also made the Twelve co-offerers of his sacrifice and in this way revealed to them the sacerdotal character of their own apostolate. A Church that grasps this dimension of revelation with faith, hope and charity will always produce an abundance of vocations to this office. It is where priesthood is insufficiently honoured among the faithful that such vocations enter steep decline.[2]

If we go on to enquire what is the message that the Catholic priesthood addresses to culture, we find that the apostolic teaching office of presbyter and bishop cannot be separated from such a sacrificing priesthood. And this in turn means that the content and tenor of their preaching cannot be sundered from that of the Eucharist itself. And the Eucharist is a doxological mystery, addressed to the triune God through the Mediator Jesus Christ and celebrated in the apostolic succession in diachronic continuity with the Church of all ages, as well as synchronic continuity with the Catholic Church spread throughout the world the sign and guardian of whose unity is the Petrine office-holder, the bishop of Rome. When, further, we ask ourselves what it is priests are to teach in the apostolic office they need always to bear in mind these constitutive dimensions of the Holy Eucharist where their apostolic priesthood is focused. Evidently, their teaching, like the Mass itself, must take as its content the Glory of God, revealed as the fruitful plenitude of the Trinitarian love in the Saviour sent to make the world 'immediate to' the Father – which task he fulfilled in his sacrificial death, his resurrection and outpouring of the Spirit. Equally evidently, their teaching must also mirror the Mass in the fashion in which they express this content: it must reflect the rule of faith handed down from the apostles, the treasury of the apostolic deposit, received from the Lord as it is also handed on to us, handed on via the intervening generations that have explored its riches in Tradition and handed on, also, in so far as we maintain the bonds of the apostolic fellowship in the universal Church. As Tertullian writes, 'The Church issued from the apostles, the apostles originated in Christ, and Christ from God',[3] and this 'apostolo-centric', Christocentric and ultimately theocentric character of the Catholic priesthood is what enables it to be authority-bearing for the faith-community without becoming authoritarian or domineering, since it is, as the Structuralists say, 'decentred': in this triple fashion the priesthood's authority lies elsewhere than in itself – in the apostles, in Christ, in God.

The distinction between the 'teaching Church' and the 'learning Church' was always too simple, for the *sensus fidei* of the laity is a manifestation of Tradition, of what the Greeks call the *ekklēsiastikon phronēma*, the mind of the Church, and thus a locus of revelation from which the high priests of the apostolic ministry – the bishops – must learn. Naturally, though, identifying that *sensus fidelium* is itself an act of ministerial discernment, which has to weigh votes as well as count them. It is not always to be found (it is perhaps rarely found) by opinion polls and media surveys. Today, the teaching office of the priesthood is not so likely to be damaged by insufficient awareness of its dependence on the apostles, on Christ and on God, sinning against that fundamental humility which should lead it to seek out witnesses to God among the lay faithful to inspire its exposition of what evangelical faith, hope and charity look like in Christian lives. Such clericalism, if it ever existed in the Gargantuan proportions currently alleged of the Church's past, is unlikely to be a major problem now. The more pressing danger is of the emergence of an autonomous, totally emancipated laity, taking classical catechetical instruction to be paternalism and an interference with liberty of mind. Already in the 1950s the American poet and critic Allen Tate had identified the menace of an individualism that held itself aloof from the ordinary authority of community and tradition, considering itself 'emancipated' from the limits of external expression in fallible institutions.[4] When that rich soil for dissent from communal and traditional norms is ploughed through with the grain of 'cafeteria Catholicism' and New Age syncretism it can soon sprout and bear a harvest. Professor James Hitchcock has spoken here of a 'Gnostic' failure of imagination in some quarters of the Church: 'a growing incapacity to recognise imperfect vehicles of human and historical reality as means for revelation of divine transcendence'.[5] Naturally enough such attitudes affect the confidence of the clergy, becoming in time interiorised by them and engendering – on the worst-case scenario – a contempt for their own status as mediators between Christ the Head and his people. The final upshot of such a process can only be to have Christians without the Church.

The difficulty some lay religious educators find with the classical catechesis now represented by the new *Catechism* is a case in point, and a challenge to priests. A responsibility is laid upon them by their ordination to serve the transmission of the apostolic faith in all its integrity. Their ministry does not only have – at least in its episcopal form – at very exceptional, long separated moments, the duty of defining the apostolic kerygma. In all its forms – episcopal, presbyteral, diaconal – and at all times it has the duty to remain defined *by* that kerygma, and has the task of becoming transparent to that kerygma. It is in the nature of our ministry that we cannot rest if the apostolic faith is not being communicated to the people. We cannot surrender the educational process to often disoriented and semi-secularised professionals, just as we cannot let the formation of opinion in the Church fall into the hands of publicists who too often seem guilt-driven and anxious chiefly to be accepted and applauded by an anti-Catholic world. As the Greek theologian Metropolitan Emilianos Timiadis has put it, when clarity as to our responsibility for transmitting the faith becomes blurred, the relation between the priest and the layperson comes to lose its purity. For the pastor's task is to teach so lucidly and persuasively that the layperson becomes the equal of the saints, and only then can the shepherd rest.[6]

## Converting a nation

I write these words, then, as myself a priest, and I write them in England. In this local, particular place (and where places are concerned, there are no other kinds!) the object of our priestly apostolate can hardly be anything other than the conversion of England. We know that the phrase, whose accuracy as a mission statement was once taken wholly for granted, is now a controversial one. It raises the question of the nature of our society and the supposed consensus on pluralism to which, it is presumed, the declarations of the Second Vatican Council on respect for liberty of conscience and the values represented in both other religions as also in humanism have committed us. But if our 'mission statement' is simply one of improving the quality of our collaboration with the agencies which function in civil society or with representatives of other faith communities, and with enhancing the general neighbourliness of national co-existence – perfectly desirable at their own level as these aims are – it has to be said that, whatever else this mission statement may be, it is not a statement of mission. St Dominic, in sending out, in the first days of the Order, even novices to preach, remarked as an explanation to the discombobulated, 'Stored grain rots', and whatever the sagacity or otherwise of his formula for a noviciate (quickly abandoned by his Order), the remark identifies something that is crucial about the psychology and even the ontology of faith. Just as we rarely understand an idea so well as when we are trying to explain it to others, so we rarely feel so committed to our faith as when we are trying to communicate it to them. If there is no expectation that we shall want to share our faith with others (and I mean 'sharing our faith', not in the altogether secondary American sense of pooling autobiographical musings but in the evangelical sense of the word), then we can soon come to have the sneaking suspicion that it may not be especially worth having in the first place. If this be true, then nothing can have done greater harm to Catholic psychology in England than the effective withdrawal of commitment to the conversion of England as a desirable goal.

I mentioned above that this was not just a matter of the psychology of faith but of something deeper, of *ontology* – an ontology stemming from supernatural grace. It is a condition of the fruitfulness of the grace given us with the sacramental character of baptism and confirmation, as for that matter of Holy Order, that we ourselves must go and *bear fruit* – by witnessing to others about the Saviour who has so blessed us. Of course, such witnessing does not always need to be done after the fashion of the Catholic Evidence Guild. There is the silent testimony of a Christian life, and the hidden witness of contemplative monks and nuns in cloisters. But both of these find their apostolic meaning only within the prolongation of the mission of the Jesus Christ who, once he was lifted up, willed to draw all to the Father through himself – draw them, so we believe, by gathering them into his holy Catholic Church, which is the anticipated assembly of the heavenly Zion, the pledge of the Kingdom. To abandon the objective of the conversion of England is not only, therefore, bad psychology, leading to a seeping demoralisation and loss of conviction of the value of what we possess. It is also a formula for sterilising the power of Christian initiation and ministerial consecration by undermining the proper subjective dispositions that make for their fruitfulness. It is creating an *obex* (as the Neo-Scholastic sacramentologists say), an obstacle to the full flowering of the Gifts of the Holy Spirit which should accompany justification and sanctification in these sacraments.

What we are to be engaged upon, as the English martyrs and the confessors of the nineteenth century Catholic Revival would have agreed, is not simply the communication of the faith to others in general but in a very special way to our *nation*. The great missionary command with which the risen Lord leaves his own at the end of Matthew's Gospel bids them teach and baptise entire populations, whole aggregates of people: *ethnē*, 'the nations', though of course the act of baptismal faith must be ratified by each as well as by all. When Augustine of Canterbury baptised king Ethelbert we should not suppose that he regarded the implications of this baptism as the same as those of any English catechumen whatsoever. The baptism of the king involved in some way the people as a whole.

Ernest Renan (not someone I quote often) once gave a justly celebrated definition of what a nation is. It is, he says, a soul or spiritual principle composed of two things: the common possession of a legacy of memories, and the will of people to live together. What Renan does not tell us is where this soul comes from. The birth of a nation – and the word derives, like the word 'nature', from *nascor*, 'to be born' – is something mysterious, but something more mysterious still is for a nation to be born supernaturally, to come into existence, as the English people did with the conversion of the seven Anglo-Saxon kingdoms, by response to a divine call. A nation whose very existence is bound up with the baptismal covenant, is a nation with a vocation – which must mean at the least a community that cannot ultimately be satisfied with living anthropocentrically, but must always be haunted by a memory of how once it lived up to a fuller vocation, a call to God-centred existence. Before ending this 'epilogue', I shall say something about where I think we can still trace signs of that baptismal covenant, and so find realistic confidence for the extension of the Church in our country.

But what are we to say, then, about 'pluralism', about the idea of a multi-religious, multi-cultural society where all groups are at parity not only before the law but also in establishing the aims, values, commonly acknowledged truths, shared criteria for judgement and in general self-definition of the society in question? Put like that, we can say this is an empty notion in which no one save a thoroughgoing epistemological relativist could believe. Only in the world of *Alice in Wonderland* could it be supposed that the civil law and public opinion could simultaneously affirm all the contradictory theses and conflicting claims to be found in such a society as our own. Such an unconditional pluralism could be realised only by the withdrawal of the legislature from most aspects of life and the acceptance by public opinion of the extreme liberal view that the only social virtue which needs to be practised is toleration – and even then it would enter into self-contradiction as it found itself condemning intolerantly those citizens (such as Muslims) who would find such a society an altogether unacceptable moral vacuum. Pluralism is a concept to which politicians find it is useful at times to make appeal, in the eclectic way that the ethicist Alasdair MacIntyre described recently à propos of the Chief Rabbi's *The Politics of Hope*. MacIntyre explains how modern governments 'generally have to win the allegiance of heterogeneous, competing and changing social groups'.[7] In a modern democracy the only politicians who will be successful for long, MacIntyre writes, are those who have learned to speak with a sufficient number of different voices, and know how to exchange one set of principles for another as occasion demands. The rhetoric of pluralism is a useful one for intimidating communities considered to have potentially hegemonic aims (such as Catholicism) or a narrative account of English identity which licences the continuance of certain traditional institutions and their associated ethos (like Anglicanism), and it is the more useful when uncritically absorbed by the intellectual and bureaucratic élites of those communities themselves.

Here we must not let ourselves be intimidated. Of course we recognise plural*ity* – the right of groups of all sorts to exist and thus inevitably the possibility of their flourishing even when they are not only wrong-headed but wrong-hearted. But if we believe that England is the Dowry of Mary we can never recognise plural*ism*. For that would be tantamount to saying that we renounce unconditionally and for ever the objective of a basic spiritual and ethical unity as the public norm of life together in this land. Realising that norm would be compatible with the continued existence and flourishing of other solidarities; but in an England the great majority of whose inhabitants had freely accepted the Catholic faith those groups would not set the overall public tone. If we hold with Hans Urs von Balthasar that the Christian revelation is a revelation greater than which none can be conceived, which can integrate all that is true and valuable in other religions and ideologies while leaving to one side what is untruthful and damaging in them, we shall rejoice that one day this may be so. Given that the Catholic Church is now probably the fastest declining of the historic churches in England, the reader may think that I inhabit cloud-cuckoo land. But my point is not that this is likely to happen, but that the faith will not flourish unless the conversion of England be entertained as a desirable goal – desirable because allowing grace to abound for more and more. The following prayer, which I take from the Burns, Oates and Washbourne *Ritus Servandus* of 1937, may not be historically accurate in every particular but it gives the general idea:

> O Merciful God, let the glorious intercession of thy saints assist us; particularly the most blessed Virgin Mary, Mother of thy only-begotten Son, and thy holy apostles Peter and Paul, to whose patronage we humbly recommend this country. Be mindful of our fathers Eleutherius, Celestine and Gregory, bishops of the holy city; of Augustine, Columba and Aidan, who delivered to us inviolate the faith of the holy Roman church. Remember our holy martyrs, who shed their blood for Christ; especially our first martyr, saint Alban, and thy most glorious bishop, saint Thomas of Canterbury. Remember all those holy monks and hermits, all those holy virgins and widows who made this once an Island of Saints, illustrious by their glorious merits and virtues. Let not their memory perish from before thee, O Lord, but let their supplication enter daily into thy sight; and do thou, who didst so often spare thy sinful people for the sake of Abraham, Isaac and Jacob, now, also, moved by the prayers of our fathers reigning with thee, have mercy upon us, save thy people, and bless thine inheritance; and suffer not those souls to perish, which thy Son hath redeemed with his most Precious Blood.

One might think that prayer contains too many instances of the words 'holy' and 'glorious', but a little more holy glory would not come amiss in a Church which too readily lets itself be seen as a public corporation to be administered rather than a bridge between this spot of earth, on the one hand, and on the other, heaven with all its celestial powers.

What we should be offering our fellow countrymen and women is a classical Catholicism – what could be more classic than the patristic Christianity of Gregory the Great who sent Augustine of Canterbury for the original conversion of the *Angli*? – but a classical Catholicism expressed through the greatest possible richness of culture, symbolised in those books, vestments, vessels and relics for which Augustine in turn sent to Rome. By 'culture' here, we must think, however, not only of mentefacts and artefacts, ideas and material objects, vital as these are to such ensouled animals as ourselves but also, and above all, of the moral structure and content of a culture, the kinds of virtue it commends.

## Can Christendom awake here?

What are the chances that, if this is our divine strategy, we shall succeed? Arguments both transcendental and empirical can be offered. The transcendental argument is that man was made for the true, the good and the beautiful, and so a revelation which offers the highest possible integration of *truth*, the deepest *good* which is holiness of life, and the richest *beauty*, which is the Glory of God epiphanising in Jesus Christ and his saints and attested by their glorification in worship, devotion and art, cannot but draw people to itself. The Spirit of God is at work in all these dimensions of being – truth, goodness, beauty – for these are the points at which creation's obediential potency for God is actualised by the Spirit's supernatural leading.

There is, however, an equally transcendental caveat to enter. The caveat concerns the spirit of evil, that spirit who prefers human beings confined within the myopic, the petty and the squalid, those three enemies, respectively, of the true, the good and the beautiful. In the last forty years there has been a tendency to underestimate the activities of this spirit of evil; it is really remarkable how almost entirely absent he is from the texts of the Second Vatican Council, which on the one hand offer a conspectus of great swathes of revelation and a perspective on the general human situation before God, and on the other hand were written or approved by men whose lives had spanned the rise of Stalinism and Hitlerism, and the two world wars of this century. Only a foolish optimism would appeal to the resurrection to justify ignoring this domain. True, Christ has conquered sin and death, and the continuing power of the one Jesus called 'the prince of this world' is now only provisional. But there is a French proverb which wisely states, 'It is only the provisional that lasts'. One consequence of not recognising the durability of the provisional is the bland assumption that the arena of culture is a neutral one where the Church can simply be present by general benevolence, whereas in fact the realm of culture is a conflictual and contested one – in the words of Matthew Arnold , a 'darkling plain where ignorant armies clash by night'.

One inference we can draw from that is the need to analyse the providential strong points in our culture where leverage for successful mission may be obtained, and fortunately, these are not lacking. Here is where we come to the empirical arguments involved. And the main thing we should note is the report of sociological surveys that a majority of the people of these islands are typified by what such surveys often term 'passive Christianity'. Undeniably, people's involvement with the historic churches to which they nominally belong is rapidly declining. The value which young people, in particular, place on Christianity is depreciating while at the same time New Age practices are burgeoning as witnessed by the mythology and witchcraft shelves of high-street bookshops and the sidestreet emporia selling crystals, jewellery and books on magic to be found especially (so the pundits tell us) in seaside, market and university towns. The court of Ethelbert, where a pagan reaction set in soon after the king's baptism, would doubtless have been happier with this environment than with Augustine's monastery. A recent survey, *British Cultural Identities*, edited by two academics at the Liverpool John Moores University comments:

> In gross terms, the people who attend the churches are few, elderly and overwhelmingly female. The people in the New Age shops are young, enquiring and unbound by any sense of religious duty, motivated rather by their generation's belief in personal freedom.[8]

However, that is far from all such reporters have to tell us. They go on to say of Christianity: 'Most British people feel in some way reassured by the background presence of this religion'; 'a majority of people feel themselves to be "Christian" in terms of their general principles'; 'in moments of crisis it is to the Christian God in some form that . . . most British people . . . will turn in private prayer';[9] and they inform us that *Songs of Praise* regularly attracts greater numbers of viewers than does the weekly showcase of the national sport, *Match of the Day*. The general conclusion of these authors is, therefore, that

> While membership of all Christian churches in Britain, and church-going, are in steep long-term decline, active Christianity is not, in general, being replaced by atheism but rather by a less taxing and harder to define 'passive Christianity' (a vague belief in a God, and a vaguer belief in Christ, but a strong adherence to the idea of being Christian).[10]

That suggests a large reservoir of sympathetic expectation out there waiting to be tapped, and if the Liverpool academics are somewhat more negative about younger generations in this regard, their account of what goes on in youth culture in such respects as recreation and sex makes it clear that there are no longer any stable alternative ways of doing things in that subculture which can create – as happened in the 1960s – a secular orthopraxy inimical to the Church. This is, as they put it, in a borrowed Americanism, 'Generation X' where all is so fluid that anything is possible.

This general conclusion is echoed in Grace Davie's 1994 study, *Religion in Britain since 1945. Believing without Belonging*. There this committed Anglican sociologist writes that the contemporary scene in this island should arouse in Christians

> optimism that contemporary Britain is not as secular as they might, perhaps, have imagined (the proverbial glass is, after all, half full); pessimism in view of the immensity of the muddle that passes for religious belief in this country (in this sense the glass is not only half-empty, but draining fast).

The inference she draws from these observations is worth remarking:

> There can be no getting away from the fact that the drifting of belief away from anything that might be termed orthodoxy is a major challenge to the contemporary churches, a far greater one – in my opinion – than the supposedly secular nature of the society in which we are obliged to live.[11]

## Counting the cost

I have already written, in this epilogue, of the *truth* we can offer, and how its full dimensions are to be gauged by reference to the Holy Eucharist, the sacerdotal centre of the office of priest from which midpoint the specific modes of teaching and pastoral care must be determined. The truth we offer is plenary truth because it is eucharistic truth and therefore must be doxological and Trinitarian, Christological and Paschal – as well as ecclesial in its integration of Tradition across both time and space. I now want to say that the goodness we hold out to people is also full to overflowing for a similar eucharistic reason. The primary offering we make is not self-sacrifice but the offering of Christ in the Mass. There can be no offering of ourselves, our souls and bodies, except in union with that. But once joined to Christ's oblation we can by the grace of God take ever deeper within us the sacrifice that is really present in the sacrament. The Eucharist empowers us to die daily to self, to offer ourselves to the Father, in the words of Romans, as 'a living sacrifice, holy and acceptable to God, which is your spiritual worship' (12.1). That is true of all the faithful, but our privileged contiguity as priests to the sacrifice of Christ in the Eucharist should impose on us an awesome responsibility to lead sacrificial lives. That is what the ordaining bishop is to tell the new presbyter in the Roman Pontifical:

> The sacrifice of Christ will be offered sacramentally in an unbloody way through your hands. Understand the meaning of what you do; put into practice what you celebrate. When you recall the mystery of the death and resurrection of the Lord, strive to die to sin and to walk in the new life of Christ.

Priestly morality, priestly *mores*, are to be founded in a special way on the sacrifice of Christ. And this should not only shape the idea of goodness we hold out to people by way of missionary invitation and make that idea a supremely challenging one. It should also affect the reality of the way we ourselves live out the office of sanctifying, teaching and pastoring to which we have been called.

First, we must expect to be poured out as Christ was – not, however, exploited or manipulated, for that would be to collude with abuse by others of our human dignity but freely investing that dignity in a liberal squandering of our energies and our very selves for the sake of God and his Church. We should not imagine – as the siren voices of popular psychology might sometimes lead us to imagine – that this must be to cross the grain of the human nature in which we were made to God's image. Rather, psychological theories of the need for all-embracingly self-referring self-fulfilment are what have harmed us – not only because, in the ecclesial context, they militate against the entire ethos of sacrifice and mission, but also because, in an ordinary human context, they mistake the true nature of human fulfilment itself, as many poets for instance, themselves not Christian believers, could attest. The paradox of self-development is that it comes about not through being aimed at but as self-sacrifice's unintended by-product. Somehow, giving and receiving are intrinsically reciprocal. In his poem, *Gesang der Geister über den Wassern*, Goethe compares the human soul to a body of water which can only receive renewal by rain from the clouds if it has first yielded itself to be taken up from the depths. Self-affirmation, in other words, is inseparable from self-transcendence. Only self-surrender produces personal fruitfulness, a theme of the poetry of Hugo von Hofmannsthal which gave Balthasar his key terms of *Hingabe*, 'surrender', and its consequence, *Fruchtbarkeit*, 'fruitfulness'.

Second, such self-giving renders the priest a spiritual father and thus an icon of Christ who, as the Office hymn in the Roman Breviary puts it, is 'Father of the world to come'. Christ is generative but in an eschatological fashion.

> Today there is need for more, not less, emphasis on the paternal dignity of the bishop and priest. Our culture would make us believe that there is only one form of fatherhood, . . . the Arian, sadistic father, as typified by Old Man Karamazov in Dostoevsky's great novel. Through the grace of God, however, the ministerial priesthood of the Church shows us another way: the possibility of the staretz, the spiritual father, who guides, teaches and heals his children. Technically, the office of staretz is a charisma and not an automatic attribute of every priest. Nevertheless, each and every priest is faced with the challenge of realizing such fatherhood in his ministry, of being father precisely for the sake of the brethren. [12]

Or, as Balthasar would put it: objective charism in the form of priestly office requires and receives subjective charisms to render its exercise fully evangelical, and this (we can add with the Thomists) the ministerial priest can expect to have through co-operation with the sacramental grace of Order and the 'title' to actual graces which the 'character' of the sacrament of Order involves. Perhaps one reason why Extraordinary ministers of Holy Communion are not to be made use of *praeter necessitatem* is that lay administration can obscure the foundation of the fatherly role of the priest in giving to the people the life-giving elements of the Eucharist, from which his spiritual fatherhood has its deepest source.

Thirdly, if in the Eucharistic Liturgy the priest is the image of Jesus Christ, the head of the Church, he is also by the same token the image of the Lord who is the Church's Bridegroom, and this makes the priest's nuptial relation with the Church, expressed in the Mass, a necessary conditioning factor in his practice of morality. It seems to follow that we should never want to do anything that dishonours the Church our Bride. How many married men are kept from fornication or deviant sex or solitary sex by the thought of the dishonour they would do their wives in so acting? Would there be so many clerical scandals in this area if we thought of the Church in the same way?

After the divine *truth* we have to proclaim on the basis of the Mass, and the divine *goodness* we have to exemplify on the same basis, there remains only the divine *beauty* we have to praise, and this beauty is, as Balthasar (once again) has shown, the glory of the divine Love poured out for us in the kenosis of Christ which is sacramentally perpetuated in the sacrifice of the altar. Decline in awareness of the sacrificial nature of the Eucharist and loss of reverence for the reserved Sacrament come from the same cause: a weakened hold on the identity of the sacramental sacrifice with the action of the Lamb, permanently seized as he is in this posture of intercession for us. In the 1990s, we are, I think, in much the same position as the Anglican Tractarians of the 1830s. We need to recover a sense of awe at the magnitude of this supreme ordinance God has given to the Church. In 1838 Newman wrote to Robert Isaac Wilberforce, the finest systematic theologian among the Tractarian converts-to-be, in praise of the eucharistic theology of the Irish 'old' High Churchman, Alexander Knox. Anticipating Balthasar in his treatment of the Eucharist as a revelation of the awesome Glory, Knox wrote: 'The Eucharist is guarded by terrors strictly akin to those of Mount Sinai.' But the awe it should strike up in us is the *timor filialis*, the fear that belongs to sons in the spirit of the gospel, for Knox goes on: 'Thus apprehended it would of necessity be valued, venerated and loved; it would be [and here he trembles on the edge of the Catholic position] all but adored.' Knox drew the partical conclusion that we should

> delight in the institution to which those impressive symbols give character and meaning; and love the society, and even the place, in which this mystery is transacted – the mystery of Him, who liveth, and was dead, and is alive for evermore – revisiting his people as effectually, though invisibly, as he came to his apostles, when the doors were shut, for fear of the Jews; coming – as it becomes Emmanuel, God with us, to come – for a purpose, in which all his former acts become effectual; and coming with a glory which, were it unveiled, could be insupportable to our feeble nature.[13]

The Liturgy is a reality which began by streaming forth from the resurrection, a reality which the ascended Christ continues to celebrate in the presence of his Father, pouring it out on the world through the Spirit to create the Church. This has momentous consequences for what we are about in our 'routine' liturgical celebrations, as Père Jean Corbon, author of the final section of the *Catechism of the Catholic Church*, shows in his study *The Wellspring of Worship*.[14]

His appeal for liturgical life in the Church to go deeper is cognate with the programme which the American liturgiologist Mgr Francis Mannion has launched under the title 'Re-catholicising the reform' – by which he means, as he explains, 'renewing the spiritual, mystical and devotional dimensions of the revised rites; bringing about a renaissance of liturgical music, art, architecture and poetry, and a refinement of the practice of liturgical celebration'. He speaks of 'the necessity of a renewal of the sense of the cosmic in the liturgy that will overcome the present tendency of liturgical celebration towards narrowness and self-enclosure', and likewise of 'a recovery of the sacred and the numinous in liturgical expression that will act as a corrective to the sterility and rationalism of much modern liturgical experience', of 'a renewal of the eschatological orientation in Catholic worship wherein the connection between the heavenly and earthly liturgies is again encountered' and a renewal too, last but not least 'of the doxological, praise-filled character of worship capable of rescuing present-day liturgical practice from its excessively pragmatic, didactic and functional conceptions'.[15] It is when our prayer allows the saving mystery of worship – *au fond* the prayer in us of Jesus Christ, the slain and glorified Mediator between God and the world – its true amplitude that we become aware of the full extent and true direction of the Catholic mission, and so can gauge the quality of the sacrifice that, in union with Christ, we, ordained and lay, in our different modalities, are asked to make.

An interpreter of the inter-war 'Catholic Revival' in its American guise has written:

> What disappeared in the wake of the Vatican Council was more than a 'preconciliar' Church definable only in pejorative terms – a 'Pius epoch' . . . of negative uniformity. Rather, despite its conspicuous limitations, it was a highly imaginative world of myth, meaning and ritual based upon the classical vision of Catholicism's cultural mission . . . Concerned in its essence with the spiritual and cultural recreation of Western civilisation, the Catholic Revival was a religious revitalization movement courageously attempting the ever elusive goal of conjoining contemplation and action. . . .[16]

It is a second stab at such Catholic 'revivalism' – shorn of all trace of sociological sectarianism – that is required today.

## Envoi

If an 'Epilogue' can have an 'Envoi', I would choose for it some verses of Chesterton's Alfred poem, *The Ballad of the White Horse*, where the fugitive king, recalling an illumination in his mother's prayerbook ('very small, / Where a sapphire Mary sat in stall / With a golden Christ at play'), suddenly finds trees and flowering plants around him take on the same vividness, and in a moment 'there Our Lady was / She stood and stroked the tall live grass / As a man strokes his steed'. The Virgin's message to Alfred is of an eventual barbarian return – an invasion this time, more subtle, more intellectual. It is a message also of its *ultimate* lack of success.

I know that weeds shall grow in it
[England, the 'garden of the Mother of God']
        Faster than men can burn;
And though they scatter now and go,
In some far century, sad and slow
I have a vision, and I know,
        The heathen shall return.

They shall not come with warships
        They shall not waste with brands.
But books be all their eating,
        And ink be on their hands.

Not with the humour of hunters
        Or savage skill in war,
But ordering all things with dead words,
Strings shall they make of beasts and birds
        And wheels of wind and star.

. . .

What though they come with scroll and pen,
        And grave as a shaven clerk,
By this sign you shall know them,
        That they ruin and make dark.

. . .

By thought a crawling ruin,
        By life a leaping mire,
By a broken heart in the breast of the world,
        And the end of the world's desire;

By God and man dishonoured,
        By death and life made vain,
Know ye the old barbarian,
        The barbarian come again—

When is great talk of trend and tide,
        And wisdom and destiny,
Hail that undying heathen
        That is sadder than the sea.

In what wise men shall smite him,
        Or the Cross stand up again,
Or charity or chivalry,
My vision saith not; and I see
        No more; but now ride doubtfully
To the battle of the plain . . . [17]

The doubtful outcome, we notice, concerns the short haul. The struggle is, as the French say, *à longue haleine*: not for the short of breath at all. But the final reign of charity will not take place – any more than did the Redemption, or does at large the work of grace – without co-operative human participation, by ingenious courage.

## NOTES

1. Irenaeus, *Adversus Haereses* IV. 6, iii.

2. 'Does not the faithful's "right to the Eucharist" imply a correlative obligation on their part to provide sufficient and suitable candidates for the priesthood? In the past the laity supplied themselves with priests by offering themselves as candidates, by generosity in parenthood, by fostering the ideal of priestly vocation in their children, by inviting promising young men to be candidates for priesthood, or, in the early church, by electing married candidates on condition they promise to live after their ordination as celibates', B. Ashley, O.P., *Justice in the Church. Gender and Participation* (Washington, 1996), pp. 72–3.

3. Tertullian, *De praescriptione*, 37.

4. P. A. Huff, *Allen Tate and the Catholic Revival. Trace of the Fugitive Gods* (New York and Mahwah, N.J., 1996), pp. 89–93.

5. J. Hitchcock, *The New Enthusiasts. What they are doing to the Catholic Church* (Chicago, 1982), p. 104.

6. E. Timiadis, *The Orthodox Understanding of Ministry* (Joensu, 1990), p. 165.

7. *The Tablet*, 26 April 1997, pp. 540–1, by way of reviewing J. Sacks, *The Politics of Hope* (London, 1996).

8. M. Storry and P. Childs (eds.), *British Cultural Identities* (London and New York, 1997), p. 281.

9. Ibid., pp. 279–89, passim.

10. Ibid., p. 288.

11. G. Davie, *Religion in Britain since 1945. Believing without Belonging* (London, 1994), p. xii.

12. J. Saward, 'Priesthood, Suffering and Sacrifice', *Christian* 4.1 (1977), pp. 39–40.

13. A. Knox, *Remains* (London, 1836), II, pp. 432–3.

14. J. Corbon, *The Wellspring of Worship* (ET New York, 1988).

15. M. F. Mannion, 'Agendas for Liturgical Reform', *America*, 30 November 1996, p. 16.

16. Huff, *Allen Tate*, pp. 23–4.

17. *The Collected Poems of G. K. Chesterton* (London, 1933; 1937), pp. 311–14.

# Index of Names

*Note:* Most names appearing in notes are not indexed. However, where authors of material quoted in the text are named only in notes, there are references to the pages on which the note referents appear.

Adam of Bremen 229
Adam, Karl 26
Adamson, Patricia *see* de Menezes
Agatha, Saint 125
Andrewes, Lancelot 182
Andrews Bell, Joan *see* Bell
Anscombe, Elizabeth 53
Aquinas, Thomas 57, 62–7, 108, 109, 154
  Balthasar and 141
  on form and beauty 28
  *Lauda Sion* 134, 234
  and society/the State 2–3, 4, 79, 81, 86
Arendt, Hannah 81
Aristotle 14–15, 61, 62–3, 65, 109
Arnold, Matthew 30, 242
Ashley, Benedict 52, 126–7
Atkins, Peter 13
Augustine of Canterbury 238, 241, 242
Augustine of Hippo 121, 125, 223, 225–6, 227

Bach, Johann Sebastian 110
Bachofen, Johann Jacob 119
Bagehot, Walter 83
Balthasar, Hans Urs von 24–5, 72, 113, 240, 245, 246

Balthasar (*continued*)
  and aesthetics 24–5
  on the Bible 167
  on Péguy 153–4
  on Religious life and life in the world 135–41
  terminology 25, 72, 244
Barthes, Roland 108
Bauckham, Richard 167
Beauvoir, Simone de 117
Becker, Joseph 142
Bell, Clive 107
Bell, Joan Andrews 125
Belloc, Hilaire 5
Benedict, Saint 94, 95–6
Bergson, Henri 146
Bernanos, Georges 145, 212
Bernard of Thuringia 225
Bisignano, Simon of 81
Bloy, Léon 145
Bodin, Jean 84
Borella, Jean 43, 44, 45 (nn. 7, 9), 81
Borg, Marcus 170
Brague, Rémi 5
Brecht, Bertolt 209
Bremen, Adam of 229
Bretherton, L. 87 (n. 38)
Brown, P. 106 (n. 8)

251

Butler, Joseph  182
Bynum, Caroline Walker  122, 123

Carey, Anne  142–3
Carey, George  197
Carlson, Allan C.  91 (n. 1), 92
Carlyle, Thomas  30
Carrithers, Michael  10–11
Casson, J.  87 (n. 38)
Catherine of Genoa  122–3
Catherine of Siena  125
Chardin, Pierre Teilhard de *see*
     Teilhard de Chardin
Chayanov, Alexander
     Vasilevich  93
Chenu, Marie-Dominique  57
Chesterton, G. K.  50, 64–5, 66, 96–8,
     247–9
Childs, Brevard  166
Childs, Peter  242–3 (nn. 8–10)
Clark, Stephen  73
Claudel, Paul  112–13, 145
     *L'Annonce faite à Marie*  164–5
     and the Bible  163–4, 165, 167
     conversion  205, 210–11
     and the Liturgy  109–10, 112–13
Clitherow, Margaret  125
Clutterbuck, R.  49 (n. 16)
Congar, Yves  185
Constantine the Great  188
Corbon, Jean  246
Corbusier *see* Le Corbusier
Cottier, Georges  228
Crossan, John Dominic  168, 170
Cule, Peter  xii (n. 2)

D'Ors, Alvaro *see* Ors
da Vinci, Leonardo *see* Leonardo
Daley, Brian E.  225 (n. 8), 226
     (n. 10)
Daly, Mary  119
Daniélou, Jean  57, 150
Davey, P.  103 (n. 2)
David, King of Israel  30, 73
Davie, Grace  243

Dawkins, Richard  13
Dawson, Christopher  4
Day, Dorothy  125
de Beauvoir, Simone *see* Beauvoir
de Menezes, Patricia  154, 155–6,
     157, 158–9
Decourtray, Albert  37
Dégas, Edgar  108–9
Derrida, Jacques  59–60
Descartes, René  55, 56
Di Ianni, A.  142 (n. 16)
Dimitrios I, Patriarch  190
Dominic, Saint  237
Dostoevsky, Fyodor  213, 245
Drewermann, Eugen  27
Dru, Alick  147
Dulles, Avery  58
Duployé, Pie  146

Edwards, Adrian  126
Eilifr  230
Eliot, T. S.  4–5
Elliott, Peter  33
Engels, Friedrich  118–19
Ernst, C.  62 (n. 18)
Estevez, Jorge Medina *see* Medina
     Estevez
Ethelbert, King of Kent  238, 242
Eusebius of Caesarea  188
Evdokimov, Paul  113

Fabro, Cornelio  64
Figgis, J. N.  83, 88
Fiorenza, Elisabeth Schüssler  120,
     126
Forster, E. M.  166
Forsyth, Peter Taylor  113–14
Foucauld, Charles de  209–10
Francis of Assisi  223–4
Friedan, Betty  117
Frost, Francis  159
Funk, Robert  168–9

Gadamer, Hans-Georg  58
Geertz, Clifford  4

Gilbert, W. S. 96, 114
Gilley, Sheridan 96 (n. 8)
Gilson, Etienne 109
Goethe, J. W. von 244
Gouges, Olympia de 117
Greene, C. 87 (n. 39)
Gregory the Great 241
Gregory Palamas 187
Grisebrook, W. Jardine 21
Grisewood, Harman 13, 14
Guardini, Romano 35
Guarino, Thomas 13–14 (n. 6), 56,
    58, 59–60 (n. 14)
Guerric of Igny 158

Habermas, Jürgen 56
Haldane, John 55
Hammond, Henry 182
Harnack, Adolf von 208
Hawking, Stephen 13
Hegel, G. W. F. 63, 172, 177, 220
Heidegger, Martin 58
Hesychius of Salonae 225
Hill, William 58–9
Hillman, James 23 (n. 6)
Hitchcock, James 236
Hodges, Herbert Arthur 23–4, 25,
    113
Hofmannsthal, Hugo von 244
Hoon, Paul Whitman 28–9
Hopkins, Gerard Manley 110,
    221–2
Howe, John 183
Huff, P. A. 247 (n. 16)
Hutchens, S. M. 196–7
Huvelin, Henri 209, 210

Ianni, A. Di *see* Di Ianni
Ignatius 138, 140
Igny, Guerric of 158
Irenaeus 172, 234

James, Henry 64
Jenson, Robert W. 172–3 (n. 21)
John of the Cross 50, 215

John of Paris 81
John Paul II, Pope xi, 12, 67–8,
    156–7, 192, 227–9
    on economics and the family 93,
        99
    and the Liturgy 34
    and the millennium 227–9
    and Orthodox churches 185, 190,
        192
    on the Religious life 132, 133
Johnson, Luke Timothy 170–1
Joinville, Jean, Sire de 150
Jones, David 113, 229
Josipovici, Gabriel 60–1
Journet, C. 157 (n. 25)
Julian of Norwich 157
Jungmann, Josef 26, 35

Kant, Immanuel 55, 107, 108
Kasper, Walter 58
Kavanaugh, Aidan 21–2
Ken, Thomas 182
Kierkegaard, Søren 64
Knox, Alexander 246
Knox, Ronald 183, 207

Lamb, M. W. 18 (n. 16)
Lampert, Evgeny 220, 226 (n. 9)
Lasch, Christopher 2, 80, 123
Laud, William 182
Le Corbusier 104
Leeuw, Gerardus van der 29
Leonardo da Vinci 36
Levinas, Emmanuel 60–1
Lewis, C. S. 195
Lindbeck, George A. 178–9, 199
Lonergan, Bernard 56, 57
Loughlin, Gerard xi–xii (n. 1)
Louis IX of France (Saint Louis) 150
Lubac, Henri de 57, 210–11

McDannell, Colleen 106
McGrath, Alister 171–2
MacIntyre, Alasdair 15, 66–7, 79,
    80, 239

Mallarmé, Stéphane 42
Malraux, André 126
Mandelson, Peter xii
Mannion, Francis 15, 17 (n. 15), 94,
    95–6, 246–7
Margaret Clitherow, Saint 125
Marie Antoinette, Queen of
    France 117
Marion, Jean-Luc 60
Maritain, Jacques 79, 109
Marmion, Columba 214
Marsilius of Padua 81
Martin, Céline 206
Martin, Thérèse *see* Thérèse of
    Lisieux
Mary (mother of Jesus) 67–8, 125,
    127, 226
Maurer, A. A. 109 (n. 18)
Maximus the Confessor 27, 187
Medina Estevez, Jorge 39
Melchizedek 233
Menezes, Patricia de *see* de
    Menezes
Merton, Thomas 82–3
Metternich, Klemens 131
Meynell, Hugo 57
Migliorino Miller, Monica *see* Miller
Milbank, John xii
Miller, Monica Migliorino 125–6
Milton, John 30
Molnar, Thomas 81–2
Monica, Saint 125
Moore, Henry 107

Neuhaus, Richard John 15
Newman, John Henry 36–7, 48,
    182, 183, 209, 246
Nicholls, David 83
Niebuhr, H. Richard 17
Nietzsche, Friedrich 208
Norman, E. 214 (n. 19)

Obolensky, Dmitri 85
Ockham, William of 73, 81
Oden, Thomas 47–8

O'Donovan, Oliver 72–8, 85–6
Ors, Alvaro D' 85
Otto II, Emperor 84
Owens, Joseph 14–15

Papadopoulos, Dimitrios 190
Pascal, Blaise 209
Paul, Saint 5, 12, 126, 140
Paul VI, Pope 12, 31, 34, 159, 176
Pawley, Bernard 176
Pawley, Margaret 176
Péguy, Charles 145–54, 157
Perpetua, Saint 125
Peter, Saint 5, 197, 200
Pius V, Pope 107
Pius IX, Pope 1
Pius XII, Pope 23
Plato 62–3, 65, 109
Proclus of Constantinople,
    Saint 158

Quelquejeu, B. 111 (n. 20)

Radford Ruether, Rosemary *see*
    Ruether
Rahner, Karl 46 (n. 8), 56, 110
Raine, Kathleen 43
Ramsey, Michael 176
Ratzinger, Joseph 12, 26, 27–8, 29,
    31, 33
Régamey, Pie 132, 133, 134, 135
Renan, Ernest 238
Reyntiens, Patrick 30–1
Riestra, J. A. 118 (n. 6)
Romanides, John 191
Rorty, Richard 55
Rose, Hugh James 182
Rouault, Georges 112
Rousseau, Jean Jacques 73
Ruether, Rosemary Radford 120

Sacks, Jonathan 239
Saint-Simon, Comte de 117
Santmire, H. Paul 223
Sarment, A. du 112

Saul, King of Israel 73
Saward, J. 163, 164, 245 (n. 12)
Sayers, Dorothy L. 50
Scarisbrick, J. J. 160
Schumacher, Ernst Friedrich 98
Schüssler Fiorenza, Elisabeth *see*
    Fiorenza
Scruton, Roger 103 (n. 1), 107, 108
Simon of Bisignano 81
Skeat, T. C. 165–6
Snorri Sturluson 230
Sokolowski, Robert 57
Solzhenitsyn, Alexander 213
Spretnak, Charlene 41–2, 56 (n. 6)
Stalin, Joseph 192
Stein, Edith 211–12
Steiner, George 109
Stevens, Wallace 107–8
Storck, T. 42 (n. 3)
Storry, Mike 242–3 (nn. 8–10)
Strauss, Leo 81
Stroik, Duncan 104
Suarez, Francisco 139
Sundberg, Albert 165

Tate, Allen 236
Teilhard de Chardin, Pierre 210–11,
    214
Temple, William 99
Teresa, Mother 125
Teresa of Avila 125, 211, 215
Teresa Benedicta of the Cross
    (Edith Stein) 211–12
Tertullian 235

Thérèse of Lisieux 156, 205–8, 211,
    212
Thiering, Barbara 169–70
Thomas Aquinas *see* Aquinas
Thomas, Philip 183
Thuringia, Bernard of 225
Timiadis, Emilianos 236
Trubetskoy, Evgeny 112, 113

Valéry, Paul 109
van der Leeuw, Gerardus *see* Leeuw
Velimirovich, Nikolay 193
Vermeš, Geza 169
Vladimir I of Russia (Saint
    Vladimir) 21
Voegelin, Eric 81, 86–7
von Balthasar, Hans Urs *see*
    Balthasar
von Harnack, Adolf *see* Harnack
von Hofmannsthal, Hugo *see*
    Hofmannsthal

Walker Bynum, Caroline *see*
    Bynum
Walsh, David 80–1, 213
Weber, Max 122
Weil, Simone 79–80
West, Angela 120–1, 124
Wilberforce, Robert Isaac 246
William of Ockham *see* Ockham
Willis, G. G. 35–6 (n. 39)
Wittgenstein, Ludwig 47

Zundel, Maurice 107